Digital Reference Services

Digital Reference Services has been co-published simultaneously as *The Reference Librarian*, Numbers 79/80 2002/2003.

Digital
Reference Services

Bill Katz, PhD
Editor

Digital Reference Services has been co-published simultaneously
as *The Reference Librarian*, Numbers 79/80 2002/2003.

Routledge
Taylor & Francis Group

LONDON AND NEW YORK

Digital Reference Services has been co-published simultaneously as *The Reference Librarian*™, Numbers 79/80 2002/2003.

First published 2002 by The Haworth Press, Inc.

2 Park Square, Milton Park, Abingdon, Oxfordshire OX14 4RN
605 Third Avenue, New York, NY 10017

Routledge is an imprint of the Taylor & Francis Group, an informa business

First issued in paperback 2020

Cover design by Jennifer Gaska

Library of Congress Cataloging-in-Publication Data

Digital reference services / Bill Katz, editor.
      p. cm.
      "Co-published simultaneously as The reference librarian, numbers 79/80, 2002/2003."
      Includes bibliographical references and index.
      ISBN 0-7890-2319-9 (alk. paper) – ISBN 0-7890-2320-2 (pbk. : alk. paper)
      1. Electronic reference services (Libraries) 2. Reference services (Libraries)–Information technology. 3. Internet in library reference services. 4. Academic libraries–Reference services–United States–Case studies. 5. Electronic reference services (Libraries)–United States–Case studies. I. Katz, William A., 1924- . II. Reference librarian.
Z711.45.D546 2004
025.5'2–dc22

                                           2003017538

ISBN 978-0-7890-2320-9 (pbk)

Digital Reference Services

CONTENTS

Preface xvii

INTRODUCTION TO PART I

Digital Reference: An Overview 1
Bill Katz

POINTS OF VIEW

Virtually Yours: Thoughts on Where We Have Been and Where
We Are Going with Virtual Reference Services in Libraries 19
Diane Kresh

The Digital Reference Fallacy 35
R. David Lankes

Bad Moon Rising: A Candid Examination of Digital Reference
and What It Means to the Profession 45
Jonathan D. Lauer
Steve McKinzie

OPERATION PRINCIPLES AND AIDS

Mediated Online Searching and Digital Reference 57
Amanda Spink

Stocking the Virtual Ready Reference Collection 67
Danianne Mizzy
Elizabeth Tillapaugh Mahoney

A Checklist for Starting and Operating a Digital Reference Desk 101
Ann Marie Breznay
Leslie M. Haas

CHAT SERVICES

Hurry Up and Wait: Observations and Tips About the Practice
   of Chat Reference   113
    David S. Carter

Communication Strategies for Instant Messaging and Chat
   Reference Services   121
    Jody Condit Fagan
    Christina M. Desai

Real-Time Chat Reference and the Importance of Text-Chat   157
    Steven Ovadia

INTRODUCTION TO PART II

Opportunities for Real-Time Digital Reference Service   163
    Matthew R. Marsteller
    Jackie Schmitt-Marsteller

ACADEMIC LIBRARIES

Usage and User Analysis of a Real-Time Digital Reference
   Service   183
    Kelly M. Broughton

Going Where the Students Are: Live/Web Reference at Cal
   Poly Pomona   201
    Kathleen Dunn
    Ann Morgan

Virtual Reference at Duke: An Informal History   215
    Phil Blank

Evaluating Online Real-Time Reference in an Academic
   Library: Obstacles and Recommendations   225
    Jana Ronan
    Patrick Reakes
    Gary Cornwell

Our Experience with Two Virtual Reference Services
    at IUPUI University Library   241
      Polly D. Boruff-Jones

KANAnswer: A Collaborative Statewide Virtual Reference
    Pilot Project   257
      Marcia Stockham
      Elizabeth Turtle
      Eric Hansen

Virtual Reference Services: The LSU Libraries Experience   267
      Melanie E. Sims

Ask a Penn State Librarian, Live: Virtual Reference Service
    at Penn State   281
      Susan A. Ware
      Joseph Fennewald
      Lesley M. Moyo
      Laura K. Probst

Chat Reference: One University's Experience   297
      Kathy A. Campbell
      Marie F. Jones
      Jerry Shuttle

PUBLIC LIBRARY

Going It Alone: Can a Small/Medium-Sized Library Manage
    Live Online Reference?   311
      Joyce Ward
      Dana Mervar
      Matthew Loving
      Steve Kronen

Index   323

ABOUT THE EDITOR

Bill Katz, PhD, is internationally known as one of the leading specialists in reference work today. He is currently a professor at the School of Library and Information Science, State University of New York at Albany. He is the author of many books, including *Introduction to Reference Work; Magazines for Libraries; Reference and On-line Services: A Handbook*; and *Readers, Reading, and Librarians.* Past editor of *RQ,* the journal of the Reference and Adult Services Division of the American Library Association, Bill Katz is also the editor of *The Acquisitions Librarian* and *The Reference Librarian* (The Haworth Press, Inc.).

Preface

This publication is devoted to digital reference services.

The first part is concerned with basic principles, opinions and discussions of such services. The second part is turned over to case histories where the aforementioned principles are in operation.

This format was chosen because of the importance and range of the subject matter and the need to give it the broadest coverage possible.

Thanks to all of the contributors who made this collection possible.

Bill Katz

[Haworth indexing entry note]: "Preface." Katz, Bill. Published in *Digital Reference Services* (ed: Bill Katz) The Haworth Information Press, an imprint of The Haworth Press, Inc., 2002/2003, pp. xvii. Single or multiple copies of this article are available for a fee from The Haworth Document Delivery Service [1-800-HAWORTH, 9:00 a.m. - 5:00 p.m. (EST). E-mail address: docdelivery@haworthpress.com].

INTRODUCTION TO PART I

Digital Reference:
An Overview

Bill Katz

SUMMARY. Real time digital reference services are now a standard part of reference work in medium to large sized libraries as well as numerous smaller libraries. Aside from the basic questions of whether or not this new computer service will flourish, are the day-to-day activities which make it possible. The contributors to this gathering of opinion and pragmatic activity offer numerous reports and theory about the development and growth of the new approach to answering reference questions. There is a wide diversity of methods and ideas about how digital reference service should be offered to the public. All taking part in this discussion speak from experience and considerable thought about a revolutionary new idea. *[Article copies available for a fee from The Haworth Document Delivery Service: 1-800-HAWORTH. E-mail address: <docdelivery@haworthpress. com> Website: <http://www.HaworthPress.com> © 2002/2003 by The Haworth Press, Inc. All rights reserved.]*

Bill Katz is Editor, *The Reference Librarian* and *The Acquisitions Librarian* and Professor Emeritus of Information Science, SUNY, Albany, NY.

[Haworth co-indexing entry note]: "Digital Reference: An Overview." Katz, Bill. Co-published simultaneously in *The Reference Librarian* (The Haworth Information Press, an imprint of The Haworth Press, Inc.) No. 79/80, 2002/2003, pp. 1-17; and: *Digital Reference Services* (ed: Bill Katz) The Haworth Information Press, an imprint of The Haworth Press, Inc., 2002/2003, pp. 1-17. Single or multiple copies of this article are available for a fee from The Haworth Document Delivery Service [1-800-HAWORTH, 9:00 a.m. - 5:00 p.m. (EST). E-mail address: docdelivery@haworthpress.com].

1

KEYWORDS. Digital reference services, real time reference services, Aska services

Will it? Won't it?

These two puzzling questions shadow the development of real time digital reference services. Authors in this work make a gallant effort to answer both queries. Check back in a few years time to see who was right, who was wrong.

Meanwhile, consider what this type of reference service means. In mid 2001 Carol Tenopir asked 70 major American research librarians "to describe changes in their reference services over the past three years and how electronic resources have impacted them." All offer e-mail services as well as the traditional telephone, fax, etc. About one-third reported some form of real time digital reference. Almost all have this type of digital reference in the planning stage. Many believe that in a few years real time digital reference will be as common as telephone, e-mail and older similar services.[1]

Real time digital reference service consists of a patron asking a question online and carrying on a conversation (much as on a telephone) with the librarians. The librarian usually wants to have a bit more information about the question. The patron replies. The librarian asks for modification of the question. The patron explains. And so it goes until an answer is given by the librarian.

Digital reference service can be thought of as an online reference interview which can run to less than a minute to "as long as it takes" to reach a satisfactory response. It has numerous advantages for the librarian. The user must clearly think out a query or set of questions, which can be set down in writing. In turn, the librarian can clearly indicate the source(s) to use, often with links to those sources online or the librarian typing in the appropriate reference URL. Often the process eliminates the ubiquitous librarian complaint that the user can't explain what he or she needs.

"Live online reference services" is another descriptor of digital reference services. It is one of the best. It indicates precisely what is involved.[2]

The Cleveland Public Library has a succinct explanation for this shift in reference work. It is typical of responses from all libraries.

> Your public library has a long-standing tradition of meeting the information needs of your community. As technology advances and

life styles change, we seek out innovative and convenient ways to provide these traditional services. KnowItNow offers authoritative answers anytime to any question. Whether you need help with homework, statistics for a business presentation, or travel tips, KnowItNow is here to help you find what you are looking for.[3]

Modifications of the real time online chat, sometimes referred to as "instant messaging," tend to include: (1) The ability of the librarian to show on the patron's screen a relevant Web page. This is known as "Web push" and simply is the ability of the librarian to transfer the answer found to the user's screen with a click. (2) Carried a step further and the librarian can show the patron what he or she is doing in searching for an answer. The client can follow step by step the search itself or how to use a particular reference work online. Some systems work two ways, i.e., the librarian can see what the user is doing online as well. (3) The final, or is it traditional move is to allow a telephone voice conversation, but without the use of the actual telephone. All that is needed is compatible software with speakers and microphones. Known in the jargon as "Voice over IP."

READY REFERENCE QUESTIONS

About half the digital queries are ready reference. Another third are directional, policy or procedural. Few research level questions are asked.

Survey indicates digital reference excels for answering ready reference and directional type queries. It fails, or simply is not used by librarians or many experts, for search and research queries. "This almost visceral reaction against research questions in digital reference is often tied to the nature of the interview, or the lack thereof, . . . so librarians feel they cannot satisfactorily respond to such a request for fear of answering the wrong question or simply not being able to understand the request at all."[4]

The response does not call for another study. The need is to give librarians, off and online, the experience, education and subject competency to field research questions. Inevitably those who frequently are involved with in-depth queries develop skills and confidence not found among librarians who concentrate only on ready reference.

Most libraries offer a window on the type of daily questions (and answers). This is FAQ, i.e., frequently asked questions. (Some call it "archives," others "favorite questions and answers," etc.) A feature of almost all systems, FAQ allows a user to evaluate not only the type of question asked, but the depth of the responses. On a day-by-day operating schedule, the FAQ section serves as a quick way of finding an answer. Rather than go through steps taken by two or three to dozens of people, the user flips to the FAQ on the off chance his or her question has been asked and answered before. All systems suggest this as one of the first procedures.

Students and working librarians who may be curious about what type of questions people ask–both online and in person–in the library should turn to a few FAQ commercial sites. Questions change daily, although some seem perennial favorites, e.g., see *Yahoo*'s daily updated "Most popular questions" (http://ask.yahoo.com/ask/most) where there is a running count of how many times a question is asked. Here are a few favorites compiled over several years (as of 6 June 2002):

1. How do I request a birthday card from the President for my 91-year-old aunt? Sent: 221 times.
2. Why is the number 666 associated with the devil? Sent: 123 times.
3. Is there a web site that helps you identify a tree by its leaves? Sent: 81 times.
4. Does the Library of Congress keep a copy of every book ever printed? Sent: 38 times.
5. How do nations qualify for the World Cup? Sent: 26 times.
6. What does the "D" stand for in D-Day? Sent: 24 times.
7. What does the thread count of sheets refer to? Sent: 13 times.

SERVICE FOR 24 HOURS/7 DAYS A WEEK

Few libraries or systems have the staff or the funds to offer digital reference services 24 hours a day, seven days a week. The normal structure for 24 hours, 7 days a week service is to divide the work. Usually from around 9 a.m. to 5 p.m. the library's own staff answers queries. After around 5 to 9 or 10 p.m. other libraries in the area may assist, or the library itself will continue answering, although with a more limited staff.

Local methods of reaching the 24/7 goal are often in place. Users employ e-mail to put questions. When a librarian is on duty they are answered. Slowly, but successfully. A unique approach which does bring 24/7 service is suggested by a group of 14 public libraries in northeastern Ohio (NOLA) ask–a question service at (www.askusquestions.com). During library off hours, the librarians answer questions in their homes. Most of the questions are from students involved with homework.

Some are doubtful that all libraries need offer digital reference service 24 hours a day, seven days a week. Obviously, this differs from library to library, community to community. One answer is to put in place a national (international) 24/7 service such as sponsored by the Library of Congress and OCLC, augmented by full or partial around the clock services by local libraries.[5]

Beyond the local library, there are now in place both national and international systems of digital reference. All of these eventually will expand, and some see the day when they will dominate the service. Instead of a local query, the patron will plug into the national system, or at least when the question is more complex than simply where is the bathroom, or what is the population of New York City.

The major question about worldwide digital reference service, locally or internationally, is who pays for what. How will publishers react if a service subscribed to by individual libraries is now only taken by one which offers access to the, say index, to millions of users. What if answers online become so accurate and fast that there no longer is a need for either print or Web sites of dictionaries, encyclopedias and all other reference works? The scores of financial questions about access to digital collections and databases yet has to be resolved, but numerous proposals are under consideration.

A revolution took place in mid 2002 when *The Library of Congress QuestionPoint* went online to answer reference questions. A national-international system, it opens reference desks the world around to individuals and reference librarians at 24/7.[6]

QuestionPoint (www.questionpoint.org) is a collaborative reference service, primarily between the Library of Congress and OCLC. It includes libraries worldwide in a Global Reference Network. Essentially it permits an individual in front of a computer to ask any question imaginable and expect an accurate, current reply in a short time. The query is channeled through the local library where, if closed or cannot be answered there, the question is sent on to *QuestionPoint*, i.e., about 180 major libraries around the country. If not answered in the U.S., questions are routed from one library to another internationally.

Some see this, as they do most digital reference services, as the death knell of one-to-one library reference work. Others, more optimistic and in the opinion of this author more realistic, see *QuestionPoint* as simply another aid in fielding questions. It is not the end of traditional reference work, particularly where in-depth answers are required or the question is so complex as to be awkward to explain at a terminal.

As *QuestionPoint* is open only to libraries, the individual pays nothing. Single or group library fees range around $2,000 a year–as contrasted with from five to ten times or more the fee for commercial services, which install library virtual reference software and hardware.

Ask a Librarian (www.loc.gov/r/askalib/ask-main.html) is the Library of Congress direct online reference service which may be used directly by individuals, and not through their own library. It follows the usual pattern, but beyond putting the question, the Library asks for "reason for research," "education level" and "resources consulted–where have you looked already." A "chat service," i.e., digital reference is indicated for each broad category under which questions fit. There are, too, "frequently asked questions" with answers under each section. Average reply time, by e-mail, is "within five business days." It is *not* a 24/7 service.

Commercial 24/7

On a national scale, there are commercial systems which answer the 24/7 dilemma for the local library. The best known:

LSSI (Library System and Services) *Web Reference Center Virtual Reference Desk* (http://vrs.lssi.com) is a commercial outsourcing site for libraries with, or contemplating digital reference services who wish to offer patrons twenty-four hour, seven day a week service. Staffed by experienced librarians and trained paraprofessionals, the LSSI offers one-to-one reference. The *Virtual Reference Desk* may be used in numerous ways. Primarily it augments existing library service and comes in when the library is closed, or there are too many people asking for online help, or when the library can't answer the question. Some libraries may avoid personal service and turn all digital reference queries to the VRD site.

Questions are answered "when the client library is closed or otherwise unable to respond to questions from its patrons . . . Staff have access to the databases of our client and so use these resources."

EVALUATION

Not everyone, including this author, is convinced digital reference is the ultimate answer to rapid, reliable, easy reference services. There are numerous arguments in opposition.

From the point of view of the user, digital reference can be one more technological headache which the telephone will cure: "Almost all forms of digital reference are slow–slower than telephone discussions, slower than one-on-one, face-to-face interaction." Librarians at the University of Illinois report that the average digital reference transaction runs nearly ten minutes, more time they admit than would be the case were the interview in person or even over the phone. The reference staff at Lippincott Library of the Wharton School of the University of Pennsylvania experienced a length of service similar to that of the University of Illinois. They concede that digital reference interactions take them considerably longer than other forms of reference. Chat has what they call a different pace than telephone conversations.[7]

A consensus among both librarians and laypeople is that digital libraries may be a blessing, but like a Sorcerer's Apprentice they simply bring in too much information. "Users don't want 'data dumps,' they want things that are very summarized, analyzed and closer to what they can use for a decision point. . . . They get frustrated with the amount of information out there–Is it timely? Is it accurate? How do I find the things I really want? We still need a trained information scientist to interview the client in order to understand the decisions they are trying to make, in turn providing a very tight information package."[8]

Digital reference service fails or succeeds on level of quality, or simply whether or not the person receives the type of answer expected. How to reach this goal is of concern, and numerous ideas are available.

A consortium of experts, under the auspices of the Department of Education's *Virtual Reference Desk* (www.vrd.org/locator), developed levels of digital reference quality in some detail.[9] Primarily the group points out that any working service must include: (1) Accessibility: available on the Web to access in a foreign language. (2) Prompt turnaround: the goal is 100% answers within one to two business days. (3) Clear policies: from question-answering procedures to types of answers provided. (4) Interactive: offer real time reference interviews and response. (5) Instructive: not only offering clues to what the user may obtain online to answering a question, but provision of subject experts to provide answers. (6) Authority: have subject experts who cannot only answer questions, but tell the user how to find answers online. (7) Privacy: all communications between users and the library are held in complete privacy. (8) Review and evaluation: a periodical process to check satisfaction of both users and staff. (9) Provide related information: show basic resources on the Web as well as lists of links, frequently asked questions, etc. (10) Publicize services.

A later study developed detailed methods of evaluation the quality of digital reference services.[10]

Comparative points which measure the quality of non-library and library based digital reference services are suggested, also, by the *Virtual Reference Desk*. Researchers should ask questions about the site's functionality:

- How much time is taken to submit questions?
- How are questions submitted?
- What kinds of things are required of users in order to submit questions (e.g., e-mail address, login name, etc.)?
- Must subject areas be identified to answer?
- Are there FAQs?
- What are their policies, if any are stated?[11]

Evaluation of the answers will include the following:

- How much time is taken for a user to receive an answer?
- Was further information requested?
- How long was the answer?
- What kind of information did the answer contain (e.g., sources, referrals, factual answers, etc.)?
- Did the expert answer the question asked?
- Is the answer verifiable?

Other important nitty-gritty considerations include such problems (with various solutions) as: (a) What's to be done when several people are online at the same time? (b) If an involved question, how is the user informed of how much time it will take to answer? (c) What standard online and print resources should be easily at hand for answers and what stock online queries about library services can be answered by various in-house links? (d) Can a distance library answer questions put by users who primarily go to their local library for help? Do some people require the knowledge of the community by local librarians? The answer is the ubiquitous "yes or no." It all depends on the situation. Nevertheless, this is a question which must be answered, and will be over a given period of time.

The pressing question which rarely is addressed in all the excitement is easy enough: "Are there many people out there who want such a service?" Furthermore, are there enough to justify the expense? Related questions: Why not use fax, e-mail, or, for that matter, the telephone?

How many are in a rush to find an answer that they will use digital reference, when more familiar methods work just as well, if not better?

Pros and Cons

Pros and cons of digital reference services are summed up by Carnegie Mellon University, which has maintained a service since late 2000. A survey of librarians and graduate students found the following "pros" and "cons" dominated:

Pros

1. Provides immediate assistance for remote users.
2. Good for distance education students.
3. Since the patron is already online, s/he can implement the librarian's instructions right away.
4. Better than e-mail for conducting a reference interview.
5. Allows anonymity.
6. Raises awareness of the library among the user community.

Cons

1. Staffing the chat services without hiring additional personnel places greater demands upon already busy librarians.
2. Schedules for librarians become less flexible.
3. Librarians sometimes lack the necessary subject knowledge.
4. The librarian receives no visual or auditory cues during the reference interview.
5. Less interactive than in-person or phone reference.
6. Typing takes time.
7. Some patrons log off before librarian finishes answering a query.
8 If communications are slow, users may just log off or leave before connecting.[12]

The most serious roadblock to digital service is staff and space. The online librarian must be given time and quiet to respond in real-time to the online query. Where there are more than a few such questions each day, there has to be a method of alerting the staff to someone going on line with a query as well as providing immediate service. This is similar to separate sections in large libraries where phone calls are fielded by a special staff. And, as in that situation, the staff is relieved every one or two hours.

Given the difficulties of staff, space and budget it is little wonder that most of today's digital reference services are limited to large libraries. The exception, as with telephone and e-mail services, is where the volume of queries is small and the regular staff can handle the work at or near the reference desk. The "catch" is that as the popularity of digital reference grows, so does the volume of queries.

COMMERCIAL DIGITAL REFERENCE SERVICES

A serious challenge to library reference services on or offline is the commercial digital reference system. Several are as well or better known to people, and particularly students, than the library. For example, *AskJeeves* and *Questia* are frequent sources of information.

There is a place for such resources. Not only can the reliable, current commercial services help laypeople, but they can be a backup for librarians particularly for current, ready reference type queries. Generally they fail, for they were never organized for such purposes, at in-depth queries and research.

The challenge is to show the public that in most cases the library is a better place to turn, e.g., see the earlier discussion about library Web sites, etc.

Types of Commercial Systems

There are two basic types of aska commercial services, often with variations.

The first is a modified search engine. Here one asks a question and a search engine looks for the best Web sites. The important addition, though, is a faceless editor who checks out the sites and then selects, often with comments, the best choices.

The second, and best, is the expert system. Here a person skilled in a given field answers a question. The answer may or may not be supported with documentation.

Most commercial services are free, but one gets what one pays for, i.e., the truly superior systems charge accordingly. The for fee services tend to serve a narrow professional audience from lawyers to businesspeople.

The commercial systems are geared primarily for ready reference type questions. Typical queries are familiar. Most are "where" and "how." How can I find something on waxing floors? Where can I find the lyrics to "Old Folks at Home"? What should I call my dog? Where can I find information on AIDS? I am looking for pictures of early airplanes. And so it goes. The least likely of these questions to be answered properly is the one on AIDS because it can go quite beyond a typical ready reference response. On the other hand naming a dog or finding lyrics is the ideal question for a commercial service. Well, it's not quite that simple, and a description of a few of the commercial services will make this clear.

Search Engine Systems

Among the best, and typical of the search engine type group:

Ask Yahoo (http://ask.yahoo.com). A conversational type answer is given to the online question. This is followed by a link to a site for a detailed answer. If the person answering the question can't find an answer at a specific site, then no answer. Even when a Web page is found, it may be less than satisfactory, i.e., too brief, out-of-date, not reliable, etc.

On balance, though, *Yahoo* does well enough. For example, an answer about a Presidential birthday card comes from an online "page from the White House Greetings Office." Yes, people over 80 can secure such a card. Satisfactory reply. But when someone asked "How do you identify a book as being a first edition or first printing?" the response is based primarily on an online article "Identifying First editions for beginners." No authority given, brief, and too general. The *Yahoo* nameless editor knows this. At the end of the explanation: "It's essential to get a reference book" for a complete answer. Sometimes there is a free source online, lifted from the print edition, and this is called up to answer "How do you write a bibliography?" The online sources are standard and first rate.

AskJeeves (www.askjeeves.com) is a typical search engine service. It does have a major blessing–the first item is what anyone wants to see: "What can I help you find today?" with a box to enter the few words which will categorize the query.[13] The next page is a series of six or seven general suggestions where to find the answer (via previously asked questions or "encyclopedic resources"). If this fails, one moves on to the familiar box to type in a query and then wait for a reply. As with *Yahoo* an answer is found on the Net with links to the site as well as a brief annotation to explain how the site may answer the query. No Web page with a likely reply–no answer.

There is little human intervention, i.e., the site "processes each query syntactically (to analyze the grammar) and semantically (to determine meaning) and then *Ask Jeeves'* answer processing engine provides the question template response (the list of questions the users see after they ask a question) . . . *Ask Jeeves* helps users select a query from a pre-defined set of queries on a given topic."[14] How effective is it? Not very. In a 2000 study 12 simple questions were put to the service. All had been answered quickly in a library. There were no trick queries. *Jeeves* was not able to answer any of the questions.[15] On the other hand, the strength of the·service is that it gives access to more than 7 million answers–i.e., if mechanically one can match the right answer with the question.

Expert Systems

Expert commercial services, preferable in most cases, rely on volunteers who truly are expert in given subject areas from medicine and law to tarot cards. A question is posted and one or more experts respond with e-mail answers. Rarely, is the expert in direct communication with the person asking the question. The answers or advice is based on the experience and knowledge of the expert. He or she may support an answer, or even suggest an answer at a Web site, but this is unusual.

Most experts are anonymous. Some post brief biographies and explain why they are experts in this or that subject. [Editors at the search engine systems are not named or otherwise identified.] Where experts are available, the users are asked to rank them in order of their satisfactory or less than satisfactory reply.

The aska systems which rely on experts rather than online Web sites for answers are most satisfactory.[16] Among the best, and typical of the group:

Abuzz (www.abuzz.com) is sponsored by *The New York Times*, and as most of the sites depends on advertising for support. It relies on unpaid experts for the answers. According to the publisher these are "Knowledgeable, intelligent people like you. They're not paid experts, but people who enjoy sharing knowledge for knowledge's sake. They're the distinctly non-technical ingredient that makes *Abuzz* more interesting than a chat room, more convenient than a new group, more responsive than a message board and more human than a search engine."

Before turning to an expert, the user is advised (as in all systems) to first check the "questions and answers by category" (i.e., frequently asked questions). Failing to find an answer, the user then fills in a box with a brief query. Usually within one or two days one or more of the volunteers e-mails the user with an answer. Inevitably the replies are opinion based on experience and/or turning to someone else, or a Web site for additional information. Most replies are good to excellent.

Google Answers (http://answers.google.com) has an expert system with a twist. The user determines how much to pay for an answer. Rates range from $4 to $50.[17] Most of the payment goes to the expert. As with *Abuzz* and similar services the usual steps are followed. One is asked for an e-mail address, a password and the question. The user is urged to turn to "previously asked questions" with answers first. If this fails, then type in the question and select a category (from business to health) in which you think the query fits. Continue to payment information, decide how much to pay ($4 to $50, with $4 being the usual), give your credit card number and await the reply.

Perhaps it is the fee, but the quality of the replies often are impressive–particularly to practical questions which someone with experience is likely to know. This ranges from the best digital camera to purchase to how to approach a landlord with a problem, or where to find information on repairing a teapot.

Queries are not completely limited to easy-to-answer questions. In fact, what is impressive is the amount of information a layperson in Seattle, Atlanta or New York (and all points east-west-north-south) is likely to give to the topic.[18] Also, they normally add a Web site or two "for more on the question."

Along with *Abuzz* Google has one of the best of commercial services available, at least those which rely on expert advice.

AllExperts (www.allexperts.com) claims to be "the oldest and largest free Q&A service on the Internet." Be that as it may (it was founded in 1998) it, too, has a unique approach. Here the user may choose a specific expert rather than accept whom the expert service chooses. There is a "search for" box which allows the user to enter a few words or a phrase. The next step is a "category search" where the system lists the most likely category or categories where one can find an expert to answer the question. Given that one turns to the list of volunteer specialists. For example, enter a query on "medicare" and the user is referred to "Medicare, Medicaid, insurance, HMO problems." Under that is a listing of about a dozen experts. Each gives a brief summary (from 50 to 100 words) about his or her qualifications. One selects one or more names and sends on the question. Answers of varying length and scope appear within one to three days. They seem good.

Comparisons

The commercially sponsored digital reference services rarely measure up to library sites. Why? (1) Few have "real time" dialogs. Most rely on the user typing in a question and awaiting an e-mail response. (2) Almost all commercial sites simply search the Web for answers. Rarely do they turn to standard reference works. Therefore, if the answer is not at a Web site the question is not considered. (3) Several commercial sites have a mix of expert opinion and Web sites. The expert is their strongest bid for quality service, but usually falls short of what one may find in a library. (4) As most services do not charge, the user gets what he or she pays for.

The major drawback, though, is lack of authority. Not always, as some expert opinion is just that, but for the most part there is little indication how reliable the answer will be, particularly when not supported by current, reliable data.[19]

Librarians offer a superior service, but how many people know? For every person using the Net, only about one out of three are familiar with a reference library, more or less what a librarian can do to help them find answers. The primary thing libraries may learn from commercial sites is how to reach the public, how to establish and market expert services and here there is much help, particularly online.

Digital Help for Librarians

Numerous sites, usually operated by experienced librarians, are available to not only help the reference librarian with public relations problems, but with keeping up with the field. Among the best:

LiveRef (sm): (http://www.public.iastate.edu/~CYBERSTACKS/ LiveRef.htm). A current, frequently updated listing of digital reference services by type of library. This is maintained online by Gerry McKiernan, Science and Technology Librarian at Iowa State University Library. Includes electronic discussion lists as well as "other bibliographers," "surveys and comparisons" and related lists, all with online links.

The "academic and research" listings is by far the largest (4 pages of 11). Public libraries occupy less than a page as do, combined, school, special, government and other. The bibliographies, which are quite current, take up about another four pages. The relative emphasis and length of these areas indicates the obvious: academic libraries not only are the more involved, but articles, conferences, discussion, etc., also focus on this group.

D-Lib (www.dlib.org) concentrates on digital library research and is funded, among others, by the National Science Foundation. It issues the monthly magazine online, *D-Lib Magazine*, as well as special reports and notes on projects. Among the sections are "subject area gateways, calendar of events, and technical reports and papers." It is a first place to turn for a complete overview of current digital activities.

Of particular interest is the "Ready Reference" section (www.dlib. org/reference.html) where the focus is on links to organizations concerned with digital libraries. The "clearinghouse for digital library research" runs to several pages and includes the obvious (Library of Congress) and the lesser known (Bibliotheque Municipale de Lyon).

The Virtual Reference Desk (www.vrd.org), sponsored by the U.S. Department of Education, covers digital reference and allied areas from resources and networks to book reviews.

This is particularly useful for the annual VRD conference proceedings. It has a special section which is dedicated to "AskA+Locator" as well as "AskAConsortium."

Web-based reference services (http://www.multcolib.org/products/ digref/resources.html), subtitled "online Northwest," originates at the Multnomah County Library (thanks to Peggy Hadid and Donna Reed), but is in no way provincial. It covers print and online information about digital reference services throughout the United States and the world. Each item has a brief 20 to 50 word descriptor. Most are current. Some, but not all, may be reached online.

The Teaching Librarian (http://pages.prodigy.net/tabol) is maintained and regularly updated by Stephen Francoeur. While concerned with all aspects of reference services, e.g., "exploring the intersection of reference services, technology and instruction," it has much emphasis on digital reference. See the "index of chat reference services" grouped by consortium, country, library type and software for an excellent overview of what libraries are involved in digital reference.

An ongoing bibliography of real time digital reference services, as well as related electronic developments, is available from Vanderbilt University and Marshall Breeding, the technology analyst there. The site: (http://staffweb.library.vanderbilt.edu/breeding/bibliography.html).

ListServs

Dig_Ref (http://vrd.org/dig_ref/dig_ref.html) is a listserv where librarians exchange information, questions, opinions, etc., about digital reference services.

Digital Reference Services (www.groups.yahoo.com/group/dig_) unlike many such listservs is not solely for reference libraries. It includes commercial "ask-an-expert" services. The parallel organizations, according to the listserv, have much to learn from one another. One of the best listservs on digital real-time reference, this requires membership (free) to the Yahoo groups. According to the explanation for the site, it "seeks to bring together experts who answer questions, and is a forum for ask-an-expert services to libraries." The list discussed all aspects of providing question and answer services. In addition to the current listserv, there is an archive which goes back to 1998 with thousands of listings. Past queries move from whether libraries answer online questions from out-of-state to "How do expert Aska services handle . . . questions." As with all such services, both questions and answers are solicited.

Libref (www.library.kent.edu/libref-1). The major listserv for all reference librarians, this is required reading for anyone who wants to keep up with the reference process. While this focuses on all types of reference work, digital reference services often is a major topic.

Live Reference eGroups (www.egroups.com/group/livereference) focuses on the day-to-day operation of digital reference services in various types of libraries across the United States.

REFERENCES

1. Carol Tenopir, "The Virtual Reference Services in a Real World," *Library Journal*, July 1, 2001, p. 38.

2. Nancy Maxwell, "Establishing and maintaining live online reference services." *Library Technology Reports*, July-August, 2002. See p. 7-8 for a short dictionary of terminology used.

3. "Welcome to the KnowItNow Website" *Cleveland Public Library* (www. knowitnow24x7.net/learnmore.html), page 2 of 5.

4. Joseph Janes, "Digital reference: reference librarians' experiences and attitudes," *Journal of the American Society for Information Science and Technology*, Vol. 53, No. 7, 2002, p. 561. This conclusion is hardly new. It has been a given for decades, it is just as true for print as for digital reference service.

5. Richard Dougherty, "Reference Around the Clock: Is it in Your Future?" *American Libraries*, May, 2002, pp. 44-46.

6. Barbara Quest, "QuestionPoint marks new era in virtual reference," *NewsBreak* (www.infotoday.com/newsbreaks/nb020610-1.htm), June 10, 2002.

7. Steve McKinzie and Jonathan Lauer, "Digital Reference" *Against the Grain*, September 2002, p. 36. The authors point out other problems from cost to lack of efficiency.

8. Leslie Shaver and Nikki Enright, "The Day of the Electronic Library," *Information Outlook*, August 2002, p. 30.

9. "Facets of Quality for digital reference services," Version 4, October 2000. Virtual Reference Desk (www.vrd.org/facets-10-00.shtml).

10. "Assessing Quality in Digital Reference" Draft, January 12, 2001. (http://quartz.syr.edu/quality/Overview.htm).

11. [Online] Joseph Janes, "Ask-an expert service" Digital Reference Desk, October 16-17, 2000. (www.vrd.org/conferences/VRD2000/proceedings/rolfe-hill-intro.shtml).

12. Matt Marsteller and Paul Neuhaus, "The chat reference experience at Carnegie Mellon University," June, 2001, p. 2.

13. This simple, direct approach is fine, but the system has five pages of explanation about how to search–five pages which most people will skip because of massive details. A lesson here for libraries. People want an answer, not a manual on how to find an answer.

14. Gobinda Chowdhury, "Digital libraries and reference services: present and future," *Journal of Documentation*, No. 3, 2002, p. 265.

15. *Ibid.*

16. As the aska-expert-Web sites tend to come and go rapidly, one way to keep up is to query a search engine. For example, *Google* (which itself has such a service) lists dozens under "aska sites"; and fewer under "reference-ask an expert-for a fee." It is best, at least in the beginning, to stay with the substantial, proven sites which are mentioned in this text.

17. *InfoRocket* (www.inforocket.com) began this with another approach. Here users post questions and experts bid to answer the queries. Users pay only for satisfactory answers.

18. "Google Answers Researcher Training Manual" (http://answers.google.com/answers/researchertraining.html). This is a 10 page plus instruction manual for experts with what is required to become a Google researcher. A good deal of the information on citation style, "do's and don'ts" will be useful to librarians, and particularly to students. See, too, the section on "Answers Help and Tips."

19. Joann Wasik, "Information for sale: commercial digital reference and aska services," *Virtual Reference Desk* (www.vrd.org/AskA/commAskA.shtml). Similarities and differences between commercial and nonprofit are explained; see an annotated list of major commercial sites.

POINTS OF VIEW

Virtually Yours:
Thoughts on Where We Have Been
and Where We Are Going
with Virtual Reference Services in Libraries

Diane Kresh

SUMMARY. The world of the reference librarian is changing. As more
and more patrons go to the Internet first to meet their information needs,
libraries must be there to help them locate and obtain relevant information. Libraries have been experimenting with virtual reference tools for
some time. This paper will provide a brief overview of the development
of virtual reference services, examine the need for and provide lessons
learned from implementing virtual reference services in a major research
library. *[Article copies available for a fee from The Haworth Document Delivery Service: 1-800-HAWORTH. E-mail address: <docdelivery@haworthpress.
com> Website: <http://www.HaworthPress.com> © 2002/2003 by The Haworth
Press, Inc. All rights reserved.]*

Diane Kresh is Director, Public Service Collections, Library of Congress, 101 Inde-
pendence Avenue SE, Washington, DC 20540 (E-mail: Dkre@loc.gov).

[Haworth co-indexing entry note]: "Virtually Yours: Thoughts on Where We Have Been and Where We
Are Going with Virtual Reference Services in Libraries." Kresh, Diane. Co-published simultaneously in *The
Reference Librarian* (The Haworth Information Press, an imprint of The Haworth Press, Inc.) No. 79/80,
2002/2003, pp. 19-34; and: *Digital Reference Services* (ed: Bill Katz) The Haworth Information Press, an imprint of The Haworth Press, Inc., 2002/2003, pp. 19-34. Single or multiple copies of this article are available
for a fee from The Haworth Document Delivery Service [1-800-HAWORTH. 9:00 a.m. - 5:00 p.m. (EST).
E-mail address: docdelivery@haworthpress.com].

KEYWORDS. Virtual reference service, digital reference service, chat service evaluation, standards and best practices, library cooperation and collaboration, change management, library education

The computer is only a fast idiot, it has no imagination; it cannot originate action. It is, and will remain, only a tool to man . . .

–ALA statement on the Univac computer
exhibited at the 1964 New York World's Fair

The world of the reference librarian is changing. By now, this statement is not exactly a news flash. And the early predictions of doom and gloom for the library profession have largely proven to be unfounded as the once feared dot coms have dot bombed. It is still too early to tell what impact services like Google answers (http://answers.google.com/answers/main) may have on the library profession but suffice it to say that librarians have gotten the message and have begun moving aggressively (yes, aggressively) toward meeting patrons at their point of need. In fact, it turns out that they have been doing that for quite some time as a brief review of some notable online reference service benchmarks will demonstrate. One of the first reference services to go online was the Electronic Access to Reference Service (EARS), initiated by the University of Maryland's Health Services Library in Baltimore, in 1984 (Wasik 1999). The first "live" customer service chat service may be traced back to a company called Telebase, a fee-based reference and document delivery service (Ware, Howe, Scalese, 2000). Telebase launched the first live customer service online chat capability with Compuserve in 1985. The service, called SOS, allowed users to ask for search help or for clarification of the answers that they retrieved online. Librarians began experimenting with MUDS and MOOS, early interactive media used mainly on college campuses in the early 1990s (Eustace, 1996). Email reference services began in the early 1990s in some academic (Bristow, 1992, 1995) and public libraries. There also arose more specialized email services that dealt with specific communities of users: Joan of Art (1993) a service from the National Museum of American Art (http://www.nmaa.si.edu/); Ask Eric (1992), (http://www.askeric.org/), an internet-based service providing education information to teachers, librarians, counselors, administrators, parents, and anyone interested in education throughout the United States and the world; and the Virtual Reference Desk Network (http://www.vrd.org/network.shtml), a collaborative Internet-based question and answer service which provides support to Ask-an-Expert (or AskA) services by accepting out-of-scope and overflow questions. Think homework help ("Ask Dr. Math" or "Ask A Mad Scientist"), assistance for teachers and parents. Although technically a listserv, Stumpers (http://domin.dom.edu/depts/gslis/stumpers), which began in 1992, serves the reference library community in a variety of ways. It's a place to turn to for help when one is "stumped" by a question. But it is also a means of keeping one's reference skills up and increasing awareness of hot topics, current events and issues and trends in the field.

In the realm of live or chat reference service in a library, Bill Drew at Suny Morrisville, New York is generally credited with initiating the first chat service in the Fall of 1998. This service served as a model for Sam Stormont's TalkBack Project (http://www.library.temple.edu/ref/interactref.html), initiated at Temple University in November 1998 (Stormont 2001). Before the live service which he co-developed with Marc Meola, Stormont had established an email reference service at Temple in 1995.

In the late 1990s, librarians began building consortia around the use of chat software. One of the first significant consortial, statewide services was the Metropolitan Cooperative Library System (MCLS) (http://www.247ref.org/portal/access2.cfm?lib='Public'), a mix of public and academic libraries launched in southern California (McGlamery and Coffman 2000; Helfer, February 2003). Santa Monica Public Library was the first public library in California to offer chat when it went "live" to the public in July 1, 2000. The year 2001 brought Cleveland's Know it Now (http://www.cpl.org/vrd/learnmore.html) serving Cuyahoga County, Ohio and the communities of the CLEVNET Libraries. This service also provides health and medical information to its patrons through a partnership with The MetroHealthLine and homework help is available, as well. Many other libraries have followed suit offering live reference services. A useful resource for articles and status reports on live reference projects has been compiled by Bernie Sloan, Senior Library Information Systems Consultant for the University of Illinois (http://www.lis.uiuc.edu/~b-sloan/digicase.htm).

The Library of Congress got into the virtual reference act in 1999 with its launch of the Collaborative Digital Reference Service (CDRS), a web-based cooperative network comprised then of 16 libraries (Kresh, 2000). LC formed a partnership with OCLC in 2001 and together, they created QuestionPoint (http://www.questionpoint.org/) which now boasts a subscription base of more than 300 libraries worldwide. QuestionPoint makes available a range of reference tools–including chat and email–

and includes an automated routing capability, based on fielded metadata, for the library that wishes to send questions out to QuestionPoint's Global Reference Network (GRN). In January 2003, The National Library of Canada, a founding member of CDRS/QuestionPoint, launched Virtual Reference Canada (http://www.nlc-bnc.ca/vrc-rvc/index.html), a bilingual web-based reference service undertaken by the National Library of Canada and the community of Canadian libraries and research institutions. There are also some collaborative live services–services offered by two or more libraries–being planned or are already underway (Sloan 2003) (http://www.lis.uiuc.edu/~b-sloan/collab.htm).

The groundbreaking Internet Public Library (IPL) (http://www.ipl.org/) deserves its own spot on the online reference pantheon. Begun in 1995 as a graduate student project at the University of Michigan's School of Information (Janes 1998), the IPL was the first public library on the Internet that offered everything from email based assistance to online collections, reference help, exhibits and a children's story hour. Talk about learning by doing . . .

And North American libraries are not the only ones experimenting with new forms of reference service. The National Library of Australia launched "Ask Us" in January of 2003 (http://www.nla.gov.au/infoserv/askus.html); and the Brisbane City Council Library Service, Queensland Australia and Richland County Public Library in South Carolina have joined forces to form the first inter-continental 24/7 live service, "Answers Now" (http://www.richland.lib.sc.us/answersnow.html) which went online in November 2002.

Professional conferences are jammed with sessions on "how we did it here." The Virtual Reference Desk (VRD) Project, operating out of the Information Institute of Syracuse University in New York, sponsors a conference (http://www.vrd2003.org/index.cfm) which provides an annual gathering for practitioners of virtual reference. Job advertisements for librarians hope to attract dynamic collaborators who will move reference and information services into the 21st century. And articles about library web-based services regularly appear in the popular press (e.g., *The New York Times, Wall Street Journal, Chronicle of Higher Education, Christian Science Monitor*) as virtual services have become more commonplace.

WHAT IS VIRTUAL REFERENCE, ANYWAY?

Reference librarianship, indeed all of librarianship is about making resources accessible to people when they need them. Technology has become an integral part of reference service as we explore smarter, better, faster, ways of making information available. Whether we call it "virtual," "digital," "live" (which begs the obvious, if it's not live reference is it dead?), "interactive," "real time," "web-based," or my personal favorites, "synchronous" and "asynchronous," it's still reference. The tools have changed, the mission of reference librarianship has not. Given all of the technology that is available, what we must guard against is using technology for technology's sake.

Email, in-person, telephone, chat, written correspondence, even faxes, are all viable means of communicating with a library. Those libraries fortunate enough to be able to support a range of service options provide the best chances for patrons to receive meaningful service. A library's success in this environment is dependent upon using the traditional strengths of librarians–identifying, organizing, indexing, evaluating, disseminating information–to create new services. And in the process, rethink what and how to provide service so that the imported technology is not just an overlay on a workflow that did not work that well to begin with (Seeman, 2002). Such rethinking will ensure that the software will be used in the most productive ways possible.

WHERE HAVE WE BEEN?

From the early days of MUDS, MOOS, and the short-lived video-conferencing, through email services and now chat, there is a plethora of tools to choose from with new ones entering the marketplace all of the time. Many articles have appeared in the professional literature describing the relative merits of types of services (Kasowitz, 2001) and providing tables comparing features and pricing of software products (Hirko, 2002). A website created and maintained by Stephen Francoeur, a librarian in the Information Services Division of the William and Anita Newman Library at Baruch College, part of the City University of New York, offers comparative information on software, definitions and links to other sources (http://pages.prodigy.net/tabo1/digref.htm). In short, there is now enough collective experience that librarians can begin to demand more of what they really want and need from, for example, a chat product (Coffman, 2001). Many chat products already offer a range of basic services. At the low tech end, there is instant messaging (IM), which is not proprietary and a library can get started with "real" time reference right away without a huge investment in software or staff training (Foley 2001) (http://www.vrd.org/conferences/VRD2001/

proceedings/foley.shtml). Call center software, first popularized by Lands End and other catalog sales operations, is also popular with libraries. Call center software (e.g., eGAIN, used by both LSSI and 24/7) allows page pushing, and co-browsing (where the librarian and the patron are looking at the same "pushed" page). It works with most platforms and usually does not require a patron download. Because call center software is used in catalog sales, it was designed to answer questions so other useful features include: question queuing and routing, scripts, and an archive of questions and answers (knowledge base). A transcript of each session is available to both the librarian and the patron. On the downside, such software is expensive and requires significant staff training.

What is the early feedback on virtual reference? In a survey conducted by Joseph Janes, Assistant Professor and Chair of Library and Information Science at the Information School of the University of Washington and Founding Director of the Internet Public Library, most librarians created virtual reference services in response to patron needs (Janes, Hill 2002). As early fears of being overwhelmed by volume have abated, librarians have begun to think more critically about what niche digital reference fills in the range of reference services a library provides. There is passion for the subject matter and there is excitement about this new era of reference librarianship as statements made in the literature and at conferences can attest to.

With chat software, specific pluses have been noted. The biggest plus; we are reaching patrons we never would have reached. One advantage over email is that chat can help clarify a reference question which would take longer to do in email. Chat can also be an effective tool in bibliographic instruction as the librarian assists the patron in learning more effective ways to search the Internet, through co-browsing and escorting. Chat can also be used in more formal library instruction (Jaworowski 2001). The availability of the complete transcript of the reference transaction facilitates followup and provides managers and supervisors with a potential training tool and perhaps disprove the McClure/Hernon 55% rule (reference librarians are right only 55% of the time: McClure, Hernon, 1985). And there is patron comfort level and satisfaction; the patron is already on the Internet and can get live reference help from a librarian without leaving the desktop. On the down side, some transactions never get off the ground; the system crashes or the patron's browser crashes; and co-browsing proprietary databases is difficult (Boyer, 2001). And finally, most librarians have experienced the "disappearing patron" phenomenon. The patron logged on, submitted the question and then just . . . went . . . away. In such situations it is often hard to tell whether the problem was technical or a lack of awareness on the patron's part of the process. Other problems . . . chat is time-consuming, everything has to be typed out. Some librarians worry that they are taking too long with a question. A few librarians I informally surveyed at the Library of Congress, expressed difficulty in handling more than two patrons at once (multi-tasking) and found the chat experience to be both exhilarating and mentally exhausting. The next generation of librarians will probably not have the same difficulties with multi-tasking if my 14 year old son, who sits at the computer instant messaging with friends while playing a computer game, with the television in the next room blaring and the homework book open on his lap, is any example. The chat reference experience also seems superficial to some librarians and there are the usual worries about quality, the challenge of conducting the reference interview, limiting the searches to the fast and easy (web content) and ignoring the research oriented and comprehensive (all the analog stuff). Of course, one can always give the patron a choice and allow for the librarian to transfer the question from live chat into an email question to be handled more fully later. Features to watch include Voice Over Internet Prototcol (VoIP) and testing different virtual reference software packages so we can reach out to other communities, for example, tools that work with screen readers for serving the visually impaired.

Not all librarians are enthusiastic about live references services (McKinzie and Lauer 2002) (http://www.charlestonco.com/features.cfm?id=112&type=ed), however, and argue that virtual tools (email, chat) will never take the place of in-person and telephone reference. Again, the point is not either or. Offer a range of communications options and let the patron decide.

IF WE BUILD IT, THEY WILL COME

Well, yes and no. Informal surveys that appear periodically on the Dig-Ref Listserv (http://www.vrd.org/Dig_Ref/dig_ref.shtml) have shown that the numbers for email and chat reference are still not overwhelming, but they are growing. To increase growth, libraries have to do a better job of letting their patrons know what services are available to them. To that end, there is hardly a library out there that has not redesigned its Home Page to advertise its reference and information services more effectively. When the Library of Congress debuted its redesigned

Home Page in the spring of 2002 with an "Ask A Librarian" option prominently featured in the services column, we witnessed a significant rise in use. For example, in all of 2001, there were only 36,555 online reference inquires. From late April through December of 2002, however, there were more than 35,000 online inquiries for a new average of close to 6,000 questions per month. Although marketing their services has not been a traditional strength of librarians historically, many librarians have taken steps to publicize their new virtual services, by adding "Ask a Librarian" buttons to their home pages, sending out mailers and getting coverage from the local press.

Librarians have also been using their evaluation skills to create virtual reference shelves and FAQs to allow for some self-help on the part of the patron (http://lii.org/; http://www.ipl.org/; http://www.loc.gov/ rr/askalib/virtualref.html). Such tools serve many purposes: in the real time environment, they help buy time while the librarian thinks through a reference strategy. They can also build patron awareness of what resources libraries have available online and what resources on the web librarians feel confident pointing patrons to. They help keep librarians actively engaged in evaluating and assessing web content and creating new tools for answering questions and locating information. Related to this subject is a virtual customer service agent program being piloted at the National Library of Medicine (NLM) (http://wwwns.nlm.nih.gov/). Neither a search engine nor chat, the automated agent software uses natural language processing and pattern matching to answer basic questions. Answers are scripted by reference librarians, based on common questions they have answered many times. NLM selected an automated customer service agent because it is available 24/7; gives consistent answers; and does not get bored with repetitive questions. Such tools present interesting possibilities for libraries and could become part of a tiered service strategy. For example, the patron might begin with an automated agent and move on to other elements of the online service depending on whether or not the initial need was met.

The use of a knowledge base is another tool librarians have been experimenting with to create content and reuse it. A knowledge base is an online archive of edited (to protect the privacy of the individual and sustain the currency of the information) questions and answers that may be separately searched, by subject or keyword. Why create a knowledge base? While there may indeed be few exact repeat questions, our patrons are not exactly sure what they are asking for or what they need so why not let them have access to vetted Q&A related to their subject and let them decide if the information is useful? Such a resource might even cause them to reshape their thinking or see their topic in a new light. Leaving aside the obvious concerns about creating metadata for each record and the time and staff resources it would take to do so, there is still a fair number of libraries interested in converting their old email files and new chat transcripts into a searchable database. This is an area to watch.

IT TAKES A VILLAGE

One of the best by-products to come out of the reference evolution is the building of community. The Dig_ Ref listserv, moderated by VRD, is an excellent source for thinking out loud and problem solving, information seeking and sharing. Members routinely discuss best practices, share or request information about software, draw attention to articles and conferences, announce job opportunities, and evaluate service growth. A sense of "we're all in this together, so why not share," pervades. With the growth of the Internet and the continued growth of print and other library media, the consensus is that no library can do it all alone. Through working together, either in informal consortia or collaborative networks, more patrons can be reached and much more can be accomplished. Cooperation and collaboration have always played important roles in building library systems and services (Bunge and Ferguson, 1997). Can anyone imagine the library profession today without cooperative cataloging, interlibrary loan, or the U.S. Newspaper Project (USNP)? The NACO program for cooperative cataloging (http://www. loc.gov/catdir/pcc/naco.html) passed its 2 millionth record mark in October 2002, further testament to the power of sharing resources and expertise.

TAKING DIGITAL REFERENCE TO THE NEXT LEVEL

The traditional concept of a library is being redefined from a [physical] place to access paper records or books, to one which also houses the most advanced [media], including CD-ROM, the Internet, virtual libraries, and remote access to a wide range of resources. Consequently, librarians increasingly are combining traditional duties with tasks involving quickly changing technology.

–U.S. Dept. of Labor Occupational Outlook Handbook

Virtual reference services strikes at the heart of what the profession needs to address if librarians are to be effective in meeting the patrons where they are. New skill sets are required of librarians and I am not just talking about keyboarding. Today's librarian must work in a world witness to the acceleration of the pace of change; the ubiquity of technological innovation; rapid globalization; volatile economic issues; expanding educational formats and opportunities; demographic shifts; population diversity; changing workplace structures; new demands and expectations from workers; and changes in customer expectations and lifestyles (ALA 2001 http://www.ala.org/congress/2nd_congress/finalreport.html# soc). How do we equip new librarians to work in the global workplace? To help them work as a member of a team that may extend beyond the bricks and mortar of their home institution to an online consortium or collaborative network? Today's librarians need skills in: technology and information systems, project management, copyright and licensing, contract administration, and evaluating web resources. They need to be advocates and collaborators, they need to be entrepreneurial so that they are willing to test new solutions. They need to be able to multi-task, be skilled in negotiation and conflict management. And finally, library education needs to move beyond a focus on the container to a focus on information and knowledge and how it is used by people (Myburgh, 2003). Understanding the impact information has on the quality of life and the relationship between society and technology is central to a professional and international perspective.

FROM THE TRENCHES: LESSONS LEARNED

To borrow from the US Army recruiters, change is not just a word . . . it's an adventure. The Library of Congress embarked on a path toward online reference in 1990 when its first internet connection was established and it has not looked back since. If your library still has not jumped into the online reference world or if you have a need to reassess where you are with your virtual services, here are some things to think about.

1. Start with a Vision. Know where you are going so that you will know where you are when you get there. The importance of vision can not be underestimated. Defining a vision means knowing your patrons, looking at your service, finding out where the gaps are and figuring out how best to fill them. Decide what kind of service or services to provide and at what level based on patron needs and take concrete steps to

achieve that. For example, if your goal is to respond to patron inquiries with a certain time frame (e.g., five days), what steps is your library going to take to ensure the goal is met? Not every library can or should be 24/7, providing all services all the time for everyone. The library that needs 24/7 only occasionally can work with other institutions or commercial services (Koch, 2003) to ensure that coverage. Service begins and ends with the library patron; and if you don't know what they want, ask them. Think of creative uses for the live reference tools. Consider sponsoring focused chat sessions with a library expert or subject specialist to accompany a library exhibit opening, to provide a discussion forum for a hot news topic. Invite authors of newly published books or artists opening new exhibits to participate in focused chat sessions. Use live reference tools to package and deliver information in new and innovative ways; discover new information sources and create new content.

2. Obtain staff buy in. Even the best ideas will not fly without staff buy in. Present the possible service and change options and let staff be part of the solutions. Staff forums for general briefings on new directions and tasks groups for figuring out the details are effective ways to involve staff and play to their strengths. Do not expect everyone to get on board all at once. Start small with a group of enthusiastic supporters ("early adopters") and build from there. A critical mass of supporters will eventually develop. If you force adoption of a new service model before staff are ready, you will be defeated in the long run. Involving staff may take longer but you will have a better and better supported service in the end. Do not underestimate or undervalue the ways in which staff view themselves as professionals. They may feel that they went into the profession for a set of reasons that are no longer valid. Stress that the work is the same, only the tools are different. The same service values that brought us into the profession in the first place still apply.

3. Rethink reference–which means a number of things, not the least of which is how reference can be supported by other jobs in the library. Know your users and re-examine your workflow (Penka 2003). Build-in more feedback mechanisms, how will we know patrons are served if we do not ask them? Reexamine your organization and look at strengths and weaknesses. Increasingly, we see new models of librarianship emerging in which the skills and expertise of reference librarians, catalogers, and programmers combine to create new services and products to enhance public service. This trend can be seen in the Bibliographic Enrichment Advisory Team (BEAT) at the Library of Congress. Formed in the mid-1990s, this research and development group includes members from cataloging, reference, and network development offices at the

Library, and focuses on projects which enrich the content of Library of Congress bibliographic records to improve access to the resources described by the records. Through such projects as the linking of bibliographic records to born digital materials, digitized public domain texts, tables of contents, summaries, or reviews, new synergies among library professionals can spring to life. Reference librarians, with their real-world knowledge of users' information seeking behavior, catalogers, with their appreciation of authority control and description, working with IT programmers, who can automate much of the work, can bring about results that not only lead to improved access to resources for users, but gives team members new perspectives, skills, and appreciation for the expertise of their colleagues.

4. Increase professional development. Invite luminaries in the field to come to your library for workshops or lectures. Encourage staff to attend conferences, consider staff exchanges, or partner with a library school and offer credit for projects so that the time of staff professionals can be freed up to do other things. The students get real life experience in their profession, the professional gets time to be refreshed and re-energized (Yontz, 2003). If budgets are low and funds scarce, collaborate with another institution . . . get the message out that the world is changing and the staff has to change with it. Experiment with telework or expanded work weeks so that staff can be equipped to work at home and take classes or attend workshops during the day to increase professional development.

5. Get beyond the bricks and mortar of the library building. Who do we serve? If a patron comes to us from outside of our geographic area or tax base, should we turn him or her away? New services require new funding and business models. There are many public libraries that already agree to answer questions from outside of their tax bases. Others are more restrictive. Set up informal networks; determine if a collaborative network is right for you. Help build the brand of libraries and make sure that no question goes unanswered. Raise the profile of librarians as trusted advisors and information mediators.

6. Establish standards and best practices. This is definitely not an area to go it alone. The National Institutes of Standards Organization (NISO) is well along on issues of interoperability and metadata for library profiling and knowledge base tools (http://www.niso.org/news/reports/netref-report.html). The International Federation of Libraries Association's (IFLA) Standing Committee on Reference has tasked a group with drafting best practices for virtual reference. Important work by Charles McClure and R. David Lankes has been published on defin-

ing measures and standards for assessing the quality of digital reference service (McClure, Lankes, Gross, Choltco-Devlin, 2002). These are important elements to be built upon as virtual reference matures. The Dig_Ref listserv offers lots of practical advice about how to administer digital reference services including offering suggestions and sharing experiences on staffing, the kinds of questions that should be handled in the virtual environment, time frames for answering, and patron privacy (e.g., how long to keep a transcript). Begin codifying benchmarks so that they can be shared with the community and so that you know when you have reached your goal. Start with some basics: decide what questions would best be answered by a virtual reference service and decide how long it should take to answer a question. Set up protocols for answering the questions . . . be brief, be clear, give the user time to respond, check in frequently, and stay away from library jargon (Williamson, 2002). There is not a one size fits all virtual reference set up . . . experiment, seek advice from others and decide what works best for you based on your vision (mission) staffing needs and patron needs.

7. Build trust. Ever hear of the GLS? It is the "Greedy Library Syndrome," coined by Buff Hirko of the Washington State Library and it means that "no one can handle my patrons as well as I can." I have also heard, "what will my faculty think if I refer a question to another library for answering?" What will that same faculty member think if you are not availing yourself of all relevant resources that could be tapped from another library? Consortia, collaborations, library cooperatives will not work without trust. It is just that simple. Build on one another's services and share expertise and access to collections held by other libraries. Why not increase our knowledge of the world's collections and engage in problem solving across time zones? Collaborate on searching for an answer with a librarian at another library. Build new information onto previously asked questions. Consider forming "affinity groups" (e.g., a band of local history and genealogy libraries) or other flexible networks to allow librarians to work together in many different configurations. Such networks could be based on language groups, subject specialists, regional libraries, the possibilities are endless.

8. Dream big; tackle the hard issues. And take risks. Virtual reference has not all been figured out yet. There is still plenty of room for innovation. For example, in developing QuestionPoint, the vision has been to create a "one-stop-shop" service. This service would include a discovery element with broadcast searching of a variety of databases and a fulfillment option with document delivery options such as ILL. Our most recent research is also pointing in the direction of portals and open URL

technology that will support multi-protocol searching based on Z39.50, HTTP, telnet, and proprietary protocols. Consider using intelligent software agents to free the valuable time of the professional (Zick, 2000). Libraries also need to work together to find a solution regarding access to licensed databases for the customer who is beyond the defined service area (e.g., a college campus). This is a really big issue involving publishers, copyright owners, vendors and software developers. Librarians must be at the table voicing their needs and being a part of the solution.

9. Think globally, act globally. Internationalization, presenting reference information in context, language skills, these are all important issues. Not every country is wired. Not every country is free and open with information. Countries have different copyright laws and trade agreements that govern the free flow of information. Relationships among nations change and are at times better or worse which also affects the free flow of information. Connecting people around the world is hard but necessary. With virtual reference, librarians have a chance to do something big and significant, beyond bricks and mortar, beyond our geographic borders and time zones. Success will not come easily but it will come if we think openly and broadly about solutions.

10. Just do it. Librarians, as trusted advisors and mediators of information, are necessary (Carlson, 2002) (http://chronicle.com/free/2002/10/2002100301t.htm). But with library budget cuts, fewer library education programs and the availability of commercial web-based information services, the future of libraries is not altogether clear. In a recent lecture at the Library of Congress, Joe Janes rightly observed that the fight is on for the future of libraries. We have an opportunity to demonstrate the vitality of our services; that we are still alive in the digital world. If there are no libraries and librarians, there are no doctors, lawyers, teachers, architects, artists. "Digital reference matters but it will not if we: do it badly, do it alone; do it only one way; do it in secret; do it too slowly; or from a position of fear."

In short, be brave, be bold, be thoughtful and if you build it, they will come.

REFERENCES AND BIBLIOGRAPHY

Boyer, Joshua. "Virtual Reference at the NCSU Libraries: The First One Hundred Days." *Information Technology and Libraries*, v.20, no.3 September 2001 pp. 122-128. URL: http://www.lita.org/ital/2003_boyer.html/.

Bristow, Ann. "Academic Reference Service over Electronic Mail." College and Research Libraries News. No. 10 (Nov. 1992) pp. 631-2.

Bristow, Ann and Buechley, Mary. "Academic Reference Service over E-mail: an Update." College and Research Libraries News. No. 7 (July/Aug. 1995) pp. 459-62.

Bureau of Labor Statistics, U.S. Department of Labor, *Occupational Outlook Handbook, 2002-03 Edition*, Librarians. URL: http://stats.bls.gov/oco/ocos068.htm.

Coffman, Steven. "We'll Take It from Here: Further Developments We'd Like to See in Virtual Reference Software." *Information Technology and Libraries*. Volume 20, Number 3, September 2001 pp. 149-153. URL: http://www.lita.org/ital/2003_coffman. html/.

Curtis, Susna and Barbara Mann. "Cooperative Reference: Is there a Consortium Model." *Reference & User Services Quarterly*, volume 41, issue 4, Summer 2002.

Eustace, Ken. "Going my way? Beyond the WEB and the MOO in the Library." *Australian Library Review*. Vol. 13 Number 1, February, 1996 pp. 44-53.

Ferguson, Chris D. and Bunge, Charles A. "The Shape of Services to Come: Values-Based Reference Service for the Largely Digital Library" *College & Research Libraries* Vol. 58, No. 3, May 1997.

Foley, Marianne. Instant Messaging Reference in an Academic Library: A Case Study. *College and Research Libraries*, 63(1), 36-45. January 2002.

Fritch, John W. and Scott B. Mandernack. "The Emerging Reference Paradigm: A Vision of Reference Services in a Complex Information Environment." *Library Trends*, v.50, i.2 (Fall 2001) p. 286.

Helfer, Doris. *Searcher*, volume 11, issue 2, February 2003, p. 63.

Hernon, P. and McClure, C. (1986). "Unobtrusive Reference Testing: The Fifty-Five Percent Rule." *Library Journal* 111 (Apr. 15), pp. 37-41.

Hirko, Buff. "Live, Digital Reference Marketplace." *Library Journal netConnect* 10/15/2002. URL: http://libraryjournal.reviewsnews.com/index.asp?layout=article& articleid=CA251679.

Janes, Joseph. "The Internet Public Library: An Intellectual History." *Library Hi Tech*. 16(2) 1998 pp. 55-68.

Janes, Joseph and Chrystie Hill. "Finger on the Pulse: Librarians Describe Evolving Reference Practice in an Increasingly Digital World." *Reference & Users Quarterly*, volume 42, issue 1, Fall 2002, pp. 54-65.

Jaworowski, Carlene. "There's More to Chat then Chit-Chat: Using Chat Software for Library Instruction." Information Strategies 2001, Holiday Inn Select, Fort Myers, Florida November 14-16, 2001. URL: http://library.fgcu.edu/Conferences/infostrategies/ presentations/2001/jaworo.

Koch, Neal. "Ready with answers around the clock." *The New York Times*. August 29, 2002.

Kresh, Diane. Offering high quality reference services on the Web: The Collaborative Digital Reference Service (CDRS). *D-Lib Magazine* (6) 2000. Available online at: http://www.dlib.org/dlib/june00/kresh/06kresh.html.

McClure, Charles, R. David Lankes, Melissa Gross, Beverly Choltco-Devlin. Statistics, Measures, and Quality Standards for Assessing Digital Reference Library Services: Guidelines and Procedures. 2002 URL: http://quartz.syr.edu/quality/.

McGlamery, Susan and Steve Coffman. "Moving Reference to the Web." *Reference & Users Quarterly*, 39(4), Summer 2000.

McKinzie, Steve and Jonathan Lauer. "Virtual reference: overrated, inflated and not even real." *The Charleston Advisor*. Volume 4, number 2, October 2002. URL: (http://www.charlestonco.com/features.cfm?id=112&type=ed).

Penka, Jeffrey. "The technological challenges of digital reference." *D-Lib Magazine*, volume 9, Number 2 February 2003. URL: http://www.dlib.org/dlib/february03/penka/02penka.html.

Seemon, Corey. "Invisible Fences: A Shocking Theory for Re-Examining Workflow." *Computers in Libraries*. July August 2002.

Stormont, Sam. "Interactive reference project: Assessment after two years." Paper presented at Facets of Digital Reference Service: The Virtual Reference Desk Second Annual Digital Reference Conference, October 16-17, 2000. URL: http://www.vrd.org/conferences/VRD2000/proceedings/stormont.shtml.

Unites States Department of Labor. *U.S. Dept. of Labor Occupational Outlook Handbook* URL: http://stats.bls.gov/oco/oco1002.htm.

Ware, S. A., P. S. Howe, R. G. Scalese. "Interactive Reference at a Distance: A Corporate Model for Academic Libraries." *The Reference Librarian*, no. 69/70: 171-179 (2000).

Wasik, Joann. Building and Maintaining Digital Reference Services. EDO-IR-99-04 March 1999. URL: http://www.ericfacility.net/ericdigests/ed427794.html.

Williamson, Janet. "The Reality of Virtual Reference: A View from the Edge." *Feliciter*, Issue 3, 2002.

Yontz, Elaine. "On My Mind: How You Can Help Save Library Education." *American Libraries*. Vol. 34, No. 1 (January 2003) p. 42.

Zick, Laura. "The Work of the Information Mediators: A Comparison of Librarians and Intelligent Software Agents." *First Monday*, 5 (5) May 1, 2000 URL: http://www.firstmonday.dk/issues/issue5_5/zick/index.html.

The Digital Reference Fallacy

R. David Lankes

SUMMARY. This article discusses the fallacy that real-time and asynchronous digital reference software are fundamentally different. Instead the author argues that the only real difference is lag time, and that this difference does not support the separation of digital reference functions. An attempt is made to create a unified model for digital reference and digital reference functions. Lastly, the author presents some practical considerations for libraries seeking to purchase digital reference software. *[Article copies available for a fee from The Haworth Document Delivery Service: 1-800-HAWORTH. E-mail address: <docdelivery@haworthpress.com> Website: <http://www.HaworthPress.com> © 2002/2003 by The Haworth Press, Inc. All rights reserved.]*

KEYWORDS. Digital reference, digital reference software

INTRODUCTION

Digital reference is a rapidly evolving domain, with new issues being identified on nearly a monthly basis. As with all active and growing fields, certain issues tend to polarize discussion, or create camps. These camps are often shifting, and created for expediency, to seek partnerships, and/or to create a dialectic for discussion and exploration (much

R. David Lankes is Director, Information Institute of Syracuse University, Syracuse, NY 13244.

[Haworth co-indexing entry note]: "The Digital Reference Fallacy." Lankes, R. David. Co-published simultaneously in *The Reference Librarian* (The Haworth Information Press, an imprint of The Haworth Press, Inc.) No. 79/80, 2002/2003, pp. 35-44; and: *Digital Reference Services* (ed: Bill Katz) The Haworth Information Press, an imprint of The Haworth Press, Inc., 2002/2003, pp. 35-44. Single or multiple copies of this article are available for a fee from The Haworth Document Delivery Service [1-800-HAWORTH, 9:00 a.m. - 5:00 p.m. (EST). E-mail address: docdelivery@haworthpress.com].

like playing the devil's advocate in a conversation). However, these dialectic groups can also inhibit cross-group discussion, and are often proved fallacious as more information is gained within a field.

The author argues such a polarization is occurring in digital reference, and further that this polarization is based on a fallacy; namely that synchronous and asynchronous digital reference are in some way two distinct approaches to digital reference. This belief in the fallacy of synchronous versus asynchronous systems comes out of the Digital Reference Research Symposium (http://quartz.syr.edu/symposium) held at Harvard in 2002 to develop a research agenda in digital reference.

This article is also meant to further refine thoughts and data put forth in Lankes and Shostack (2002) that argue for the continued relevance of asynchronous systems. In that article the authors state, "in the authors' opinion, real-time systems and asynchronous systems will need to co-exist (or rather digital reference systems will need to support both forms of interactions)" (Lankes and Shostack, p. 354). In light of work in the research symposium, and subsequent thinking, the author believes that there is only one significant difference between synchronous and asynchronous systems, lag time, and that this difference should not lead to completely incompatible systems, planning or even staffing. The author will highlight practical consequences of such a new conceptualization of digital reference system.

THE NEED TO RECONCILE SYNCHRONOUS AND ASYNCHRONOUS SYSTEMS

The continued division between real-time and asynchronous systems has very real consequences for the library profession. It often creates a division between proponents of existing asynchronous (e.g., e-mail based) systems and staff that wish to go to real-time systems. This divide often masks the most important question, "what do our users want?" This lack of user involvement was cited in Gross et al.'s (2001) analysis of the literature. Unfortunately, without this user information digital reference committees and libraries are often left basing decisions on stereotypes (e.g., "the younger audience we want to reach always use chat and instant messaging, therefore we must use the same technologies"–ignoring this same population is a heavy user of e-mail), peer pressure (e.g., "every other library is using real-time systems, therefore we must use real-time"), or vendor marketing materials (e.g., "the only digital reference systems available on the market are real-time systems"–of course web and e-mail systems do not market themselves as digital reference products, though they work well for digital reference applications).

What many libraries have discovered is that both real-time and asynchronous features are needed. Longtime asynchronous systems such as AskERIC, even before they adopted real-time software, would use phone calls to get real-time data from patrons. It was simply faster and more efficient with certain types of users and questions. Many real-time services will follow-up with e-mail for additional information, or use the real-time software only to provide a reference interview.

The point is, that by artificially dividing these two communication modes into system requirements, we have no systems that serve the complete range of digital reference needs. Even so-called "real-time features" such as co-browsing have a place in asynchronous interactions.

While at first this may seem counter-intuitive, consider the problem of proprietary database access. This has been a persistent problem in current real-time systems, and has been overcome by the use of proxy servers. Librarians can "push" information from proprietary databases to a patron's browser, keeping all licensing intact (because it is done by a librarian in the normal course of their jobs). The asynchronous solution has been to violate license and send a copy of a licensed resource to a patron.[1] What is needed is a single solution that can queue on-demand licensed resources requested by a librarian into a "safe-haven" where a patron can gain access to the resource within a licensing agreement, for a pre-determined purpose, and/or a pre-determined time. That way, a patron can access that resource either with a librarian, or at a later time (in an asynchronous setting).

Other features that are currently handled differently, but are in fact needed by both approaches include: queuing of patrons, and routing of patrons to a qualified expert or librarian. Table 1 lists some key digital reference functions, how they are currently implemented in both real-time systems and asynchronous systems, and an example of how they might work in a unified approach.

This list is based on the assumption that real-time and asynchronous approaches can be unified–that they are, in fact, the same thing. This assumption comes from a detailed examination of the General Digital Reference Model (Pommerantz et al.).

TABLE 1

Feature and Need	Real-time Approach	Asynchronous Solution	Advantage of Unified Approach	Examples
Co-Browsing: To share licensed resources to identified patrons remotely	Proxy Servers	Item Forwarding	Maintain license agreements and serve patrons legally	Much like electronic reserves, a librarian places a licensed article or resource in an electronic "holding tank" with an expiring password. This holding tank can either be accessed by escorting the patron into the holding tank or by sending the password to the user through e-mail (or the web).
Queuing: To queue patrons in line for an available resource based on some priority measure	Queues or "Waiting Rooms"	Inbox Management	Be able to shift users to their mode of choice, or eliminate patron wait-time for real-time librarians when a question can be asked asynchronously	A patron clicks on an "Ask a Question" button. They are alerted to an estimated wait time, and given the option to leave a question, and possibly a time to interact in real-time.
Screen Sharing: To manipulate user resources at the desktop level	Applet Installation	Providing detailed set of step-by-step instructions	Allow a librarian to manage a patron's computer at the desktop level	The user downloads an applet allowing a limited time (and limited access) to a patron's machine. This access can either be initiated immediately, or at some later time.
Expert Routing: To send a question to the right expert based on some criteria	Creating different queues	Forwarding, or creating differentiated list of subjects	Experts create a single profile and establish a single mechanism for receiving questions	A librarian enters a system profile that identifies what type of questions s/he is willing to answer, and when. If a user's question matches at a given time, chat is initiated, if not, a question is put in a queue to be picked up later.
User Evaporation: To identify when a session was ended by patron choice rather than wondering if there was a technical problem, or if the user is simply taking a long time to respond	Having the patron affirmatively close a session (normally by hitting a button)	Receiving a thank you message	Creating a unified session management system for improved statistics and resource management	Using the web, cookies can be dropped for each digital reference question (versus per user).

THE GENERAL DIGITAL REFERENCE MODEL

The digital reference model pictured in Figure 1 is a general process model developed through an empirical study of high-capacity digital reference services, primarily in the math/science area (Lankes, 1998). The model consists of 5 steps:

1. *Question Acquisition* is a means of taking a user's questions from e-mail, web forms, chat, or embedded applications. This area of the model concerns best practice in "online reference interviews" and user interface issues.
2. *Triage* is the assignment of a question to a process or topic expert. This step may be automated or conducted via human decision support. Triage also includes the filtering of repeat questions or out of scope questions.
3. *Experts Answer Formulation* details factors for creating "good" answers such as age and cultural appropriateness. Answers are also sent to the user at this point.
4. *Tracking* is the quantitative and qualitative monitoring of repeat questions for trends. Tracking allows the creation of "hot topics," and may indicate where gaps exist in the collection(s).
5. *Resource Creation* concerns the use of tracking data to build or expand collections and better meet users' information needs within and outside of the digital reference process.

This model was developed originally to capture the workings of asynchronous digital reference services. However, it seems to capture the workings of synchronous systems as well. In systems such as 24/7 Reference, online librarians choose users from a list of waiting patrons in a queue. This is exactly the same process (at this level of abstraction) as an expert (the online librarian) choosing a question in a list of waiting questions. Both are examples of triage. Analogies can be made at every step of the processes. In real-time systems answer formulation happens in real-time interactions with patrons through chat and co-browsing. In web and e-mail systems this takes place either in the form of a constructed response normally e-mailed to the user, or through a serial exchange of messages (also, normally over e-mail). Tracking is nearly identical in all digital reference systems and involves looking at the transcripts of exchanges (almost always a semi-structured text file). Resource creation is the last step, and nearly as unexplored in any mode of interaction to date.

FIGURE 1. General Digital Reference Model

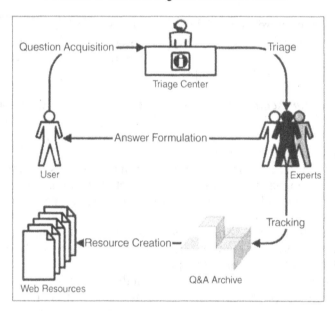

INTRODUCING THE CONCEPT OF LAG TIME
INTO THE GENERAL MODEL

The author argues, once again, that there are more than simple analogies between real-time and asynchronous services: they are the same activities. Question acquisition seeks to get a user to identify a question as much as possible before the involvement of an intermediary. This is often done through web forms regardless of what system lies behind the form. What is important is that this model represents a real-time system. All digital reference services can be seen as real-time systems. When a user inputs a question, s/he receives feedback. This is often a web form followed by a web page stating the question was received, and what will happen next ("we'll get back to you within two days," or "wait, a librarian will be with you shortly"). The point is that at different times in interacting with a digital reference system, the user must wait for a system resource. That may be a web page loading, a librarian coming into a chat environment, or a proprietary database returning a result set. This waiting on system resource, the author will refer to as "lag time."

Lag time is a well-known concept in the information retrieval world. It is assumed that there is a balance between what a system provides to a user, and how long the user must wait to get that response. When you type a query into Google, you expect good results, and you expect not to wait "too long" to get those results. However, it is also assumed a user will wait longer for better results. So metasearch engines (web sites that simply run a query on several existing search engines then combine the results), often take longer to get a result set, and will often "time out" a given search engine if it takes too long. However, it is assumed the user will wait longer to get a more complete set of results.

There are two factors identified in this subtle (and often experimental) equation between a user's willingness to wait, and a system's ability to produce good results. The first is an interface issue; the second is a performance issue. In the interface, if an information system makes clear what it is capable of (and what is required of the user . . . like waiting a specified amount of time) the user feels informed and can make an informed choice ("I am willing to wait for that result"). Switching back to a digital reference context, if a system says that it will take up to two days to respond, the user is informed and can choose whether to wait or not. They are more likely to be satisfied if you meet or exceed expectations, than if you let the user determine their expectations alone. This is clearly seen in the AskERIC customer service survey data (Lankes and Shostack, 2002) where users were informed of a two-day turn-around time and they were highly satisfied. Imagine if a user was put into a queue for a real-time system and had to wait three hours for a librarian to come online. The user would hardly be happy if they were expecting a minute or two wait time.

The second part of this equation (balancing wait and results) is the performance of the system. If the user's expectation of the result are met or exceeded, the user will be highly satisfied. So even if the user had to wait, but they received as much, if not more, relevant information than they needed, they will be satisfied. So if a librarian feels rushed to get information in a real-time setting and sends just adequate information to a patron they will be less satisfied than if the librarian took a day to reply, but sent excellent information to the patron. Once again, the point is that lag time is only one factor in meeting user expectation, and, the author would argue, less important than (or at least ameliorated by) the performance of the system (i.e., was the user's question answered well).

So, the author has postulated that the only significant different between current real-time and asynchronous systems is lag time, and that lag time exists in all digital reference systems, and has the same positive or negative effect regardless of the means of librarian/patron interaction. In other words, you must set and meet user expectations for waiting for answers. Further these expectations can be set to any time or any mode within digital reference systems.

The means of setting users' expectations are two fold: clearly delineating the lag time in a digital reference system in the interface to the user, and clearly meeting users' expectations in the answers the system provides.

CONSEQUENCES FOR SYSTEM DEVELOPERS AND PRACTITIONERS

This may all seem like a rather academic discussion, but it has very real and current application to system designers. Digital reference systems must stop trying to develop separate real-time and asynchronous systems. Rather they should build unified solutions that can account for varying lag times and interactions. In order to build such unified systems, a unified feature set needs to be constructed. Certainly this feature set includes the items listed in Table 1 with routing, queuing and co-browsing.

For practitioners this means demanding more from vendors and software developers. Until these two modes are married, tools will be grafted together (often with varying licensing schemes), and will favor one approach over another. While interoperability standards, such as those being developed by NISO, may provide some relief in integrating systems, nothing can replace bottom-up system construction of a unified digital reference system.

Of course, this unified approach leads inevitably to one more level of integration, system integration across all reference modes (i.e., desk, phone, correspondence, digital). Seeing digital reference as a core service, and part of reference, it makes sense that integrated reference management software will emerge. In fact, it would seem to follow that such integrated systems may well become part of integrated library solutions. While the architecture for such an integration of reference into the complete technical infrastructure of libraries is well beyond the scope of this paper, it is well worth thinking about. Certainly, one step in the absence of such a reference-wide and library-wide architecture is adherence to common software development and acquisition practice.

A library considering the purchase (or construction) of a digital reference package should look for:

- Adherence to known and widely accepted technical standards: The most obvious of these standards is the NSIO standards for networked reference. The problem is, as of this writing, it is not yet even released, so it holds future promise. Instead, look for more general compliance with Internet standards such as XML, SOAP and web services that are seeking to make applications interoperable by sharing database information and functions over the web.
- Willingness of vendors to place source code in an escrow account in case of later discontinuation of the product or vendor: If the .com boom of the late '90s taught libraries anything it is that promising software might disappear if the company providing the software does not have a sound business practice. Already we have seen digital reference software packages arrive and disappear. To mitigate the negative effects of this, libraries should seek some assurance such as direct access to source code, or the holding of source code by a trusted third party in the event a product goes out of support.
- Ability of software to interoperate in an open method: This is related to the first bullet, but speaks to a broader willingness of the vendor to make their products work with in-place systems such as OPACs. Will the vendor allow connections directly to an underlying database? Will the vendor share high-level architectures? The point is to assess how open the software provider is to working with you and your local implementation.
- Willingness on the part of the vendor (and ability) to negotiate pricing: Many digital reference packages are rapidly evolving. They are fixing problems in the field. That means that some of what is promised is not yet available, or not available at time of installation. Vendors and software producers should take this into account, and understand that libraries are often underwriting ongoing development of market share. Vendors should be willing to absorb some of the costs of this development process and be flexible in licensing. The less flexible a vendor is in licensing, the more stable their product should be.

This is a small list, and very much incomplete, but it is a starting point. Libraries must act as responsible and learned consumers in this market. They must also take the lessons they have learned from licensing other software and information products (e.g., databases, integrated library systems, etc.) and apply it to the domain of digital reference. If digital reference is to become a core service, we must approach it with maturity, and not as a "cool new" tool with heightened expectations for usage, and lowered expectations on the part of software producers.

NOTE

1. The author acknowledges this is far from a legal opinion, and fair-use does factor into this discussion.

REFERENCES

Gross, M. & McClure, C. & Lankes, R. (2001). Assessing Quality in Digital Reference Services: Overview of Key Literature on Digital Reference. Available http://quartz.syr.edu/quality/VRDphaseIILitReviw.pdf.

Lankes, R. D. & Shostack, P. (2002). "The Necessity of Real-Time: Fact and Fiction in Digital Reference Systems." *Reference and User Services Quarterly* 41(4).

Lankes, R. David (1998). *Building & Maintaining Internet Information Services: K-12 Digital Reference Services*. ERIC Clearinghouse on Information & Technology; Syracuse, NY.

Pomerantz, J., Nicholson, S., Belanger, Y., & Lankes, R. D. (Forthcoming). "The Current State of Digital Reference: Validation of a General Digital Reference Model through a Survey of Digital Reference Services." *Information Processing & Management*.

Bad Moon Rising:
A Candid Examination of Digital Reference
and What It Means to the Profession

Jonathan D. Lauer
Steve McKinzie

SUMMARY. The profound impact of digital reference claimed by its proponents is overstated. Librarians tend to overvalue technology, assume its intrinsic value in improving library operations and services, and undervalue the human factor of librarian expertise and professional competence. Overstating the impact of trends within librarianship is a cyclically recurring phenomenon and the hype surrounding digital reference is a current example. In most libraries, the adoption of digital reference is not likely to be cost effective nor its utility an improvement on structures already in place and functioning well. Librarians have difficult decisions to make regarding the allocation of resources. The superiority of traditional reference approaches should not be gainsaid by misdirected emphasis on digital reference. *[Article copies available for a fee from The Haworth Document Delivery Service: 1-800-HAWORTH. E-mail address: <docdelivery@haworthpress.com> Website: <http://www.HaworthPress.com> © 2002/2003 by The Haworth Press, Inc. All rights reserved.]*

Jonathan D. Lauer is Library Director, Murray Library, Messiah College, One College Avenue, Box 3002, Grantham, PA 17027 (E-mail: jlauer@messiah.edu). Steve McKinzie is Social Science Librarian, Waidner-Spahr Library, Dickinson College, Carlisle, PA 17013 (E-mail: mckinzie@dickinson.edu).

[Haworth co-indexing entry note]: "Bad Moon Rising: A Candid Examination of Digital Reference and What It Means to the Profession." Lauer, Jonathan D., and Steve McKinzie. Co-published simultaneously in *The Reference Librarian* (The Haworth Information Press, an imprint of The Haworth Press, Inc.) No. 79/80, 2002/2003, pp. 45-56; and: *Digital Reference Services* (ed: Bill Katz) The Haworth Information Press, an imprint of The Haworth Press, Inc., 2002/2003, pp. 45-56. Single or multiple copies of this article are available for a fee from The Haworth Document Delivery Service [1-800-HAWORTH, 9:00 a.m. - 5:00 p.m. (EST). E-mail address: docdelivery@haworthpress.com].

10.1300/J120v38n79_04

KEYWORDS. Digital reference, traditional reference services, professionalism

Some in the library world hail digital reference with such enthusiasm that they imply it may be more revolutionary than the MARC format and more useful than the creation of the online index. We disagree. Indeed, we are generally skeptical about digital reference's overall usefulness and value, and by the profession's tendency to be uncritically enthusiastic about the advantages of every form of new technology. The library world has been far too gullible, far too willing to regard any technical advance as a service advance, too eager to insist that whatever the new technology may be, it will inevitably provide better, more convenient, more effective service for our patrons. Half the time we have been wrong about the supposed value of these various technologies and the rest of the time only half right.

In this article, we dispute the more enthusiastic proponents of digital reference, some who even appear in the pages of this publication. In doing so, it is important to note what we are *not* claiming. We are far from saying that digital reference does not work, or that it is of no value. On the contrary, in certain places and in certain contexts, digital reference can be highly useful and effective. Neither are we asserting that technology itself is at fault nor that it merits immediate distrust. Technology has much to offer, and librarians should explore thoroughly its potential and promises. It is only when our colleagues champion the superiority of digital reference over traditional forms of reference that we grow alarmed. In other places, we have argued that digital reference could affect collection development adversely and that it may be overrated.[1] Here we argue more comprehensively. We contend that digital reference, placed in the immediate context of reference and library pedagogy and the broad context of professional librarianship and human culture, has three major problems. These realities should force librarians (practicing reference librarians and administrators alike) to take a hard and critical look at the entire phenomenon. We elaborate below.

First, librarians tend to overvalue technology, and the largely uncritical enthusiasm about digital reference is a case in point. We have skipped down the primrose path of supposed radical paradigm shifts before. It may profit us to be cautious, even skeptical, about the radical changes that technology has wrought or that librarians claim it has effected.

Second, the value of digital reference has been overstated. We charge that the new service is not cost effective and that, from the perspective of efficiency and practicality, is often not worth the investment. Quite frankly, it fails to measure up to the advantages of more traditional and less expensive approaches to reference.

Third, and perhaps most disturbing of all, the hype surrounding digital reference reveals the profession's fascination with dispensability, a pernicious tendency to undervalue librarian expertise and professional competence. It is almost as if librarians are trying to work themselves out of a job, a perspective that is as unrealistic as it is damaging to the profession. Digital reference, if it is to be effective, ought to complement traditional reference, but only where a need for it is clearly evident, its advantages clear, and its cost effectiveness thoroughly demonstrated. Too often, however, it either undermines or downplays more effective service alternatives.

All three of these concerns force us to look askance at digital reference. Although we applaud those who are ready to explore new options and to push the envelope, we believe caution, even skepticism, may be for most libraries the best response to digital reference, a service whose time has not yet come and may, indeed, never come for most libraries.

TECHNOLOGY, PARADIGMS,
AND UNFETTERED ENTHUSIASM

Anyone who takes the time to view librarianship outside of its immediate context has to concede that the profession tends to overstate the effects of technology. Every so often the profession fairly loses its head over some peripheral issue and goes bonkers. If you have been following the profession's fascination with digital reference service, you will no doubt conclude it is like that now. The term "digital reference service" is not easy to define, but it can best be understood as reference service in "which people submit their questions and have them answered by a library staff member through some electronic means (E-mail, chat, web forms, etc.), not in person or over the phone."[2]

Champions of this latest form of reference are not shy about their new-fangled alternative, nor do they downplay the magnitude of the changes they fancy are upon us. The more rhetorical among them argue that reference, as we know it, is about to change forever. They insist that the user culture has altered drastically. Fiber optics, the Internet, and patron expectations have overturned everything. In fact, they contend, the new way of approaching things is so fundamentally different from the old, that reference librarians will have to transform their role radically. The new revolution will mean altered codes of conduct and altered modes of operation. And they deem librarians who support reference service will need "new sets of values and beliefs."[3] Now, before we embrace this new paradigm, all of us in the profession would do well to remind ourselves that this is déjà vu all over again. These less-than-balanced calls for an overhaul of the profession and incautious clamors for a total reinvention of library services seem to occur in cycles.

In the 1960s, librarians argued that microforms (film, fiche and cards) would render library building expansion unnecessary. Libraries would need no more shelf space. In the 1980s, library administrators contended that the debilitating properties of acidic paper would soon destroy vast percentages of our bound holdings. The "slow fires" of acidic paper were expected to devastate much of what our libraries contained by the new millennium. Some even called for the deacidification of vast numbers of books and the development of the technology necessary to undertake this urgent project. In the 1990s, iconoclastic technocrats argued that digitization would render print collections obsolete. Print was dead or soon would be. Not only that, libraries themselves would be replaced by the World Wide Web.

Right now, advocates of digital reference are telling us that we must create a new paradigm, evolve into a higher species of reference animal (with an accompanying approach to collecting reference resources), or lose our place in the information food chain. Like their esteemed colleagues of the past, the no-expansion librarians, the acidic paper alarmists, and the proponents of an all-digitized future, the new revolutionists are victims of their own hyperbole. The current moment in library history is not as revolutionary as they purport. The changes abroad are not as great as they allege. Proponents of the supposed "new paradigm" of reference are overstating their case. It is time to regain our bearings and recover our sanity. Or, to put it more succinctly, we need to rediscover and reassert the strengths and dynamism of traditional reference.

EFFECTIVENESS, COST-EFFICIENCY AND LIMITED RESOURCES

Please do not misunderstand us. Librarians ought to be exploring E-mail Reference, Instant Messenger chat, and the host of other interactive technologies that promise to help us disseminate information to our users and knowledge into the minds of our readers. Digital chat and Instant Messenger reference, especially such interactive products as LSSI, 24/7, certainly have their place in the reference librarian's tool kit. But giving a tool or, more specifically, a practice, a place in the toolbox, is altogether different from adopting a new paradigm. In order to appreciate the place and purpose of this new reference tool, however, we need to consider some of its disadvantages. We suggest there are three key service issues that should be kept in mind to understand digital reference, issues which lead us to assert that traditional reference is still the best way to serve our users.

First of all, most forms of digital reference are slow—slower than telephone discussions, slower than one-on-one, face-to-face interaction. Librarians at the University of Illinois report that the average digital reference transaction runs nearly ten minutes—more time, they admit, than would be required in person or even over the phone.[4] The reference staff at Lippincott Library of the Wharton School of the University of Pennsylvania experienced a digital reference transaction time lapse similar to the University of Illinois. They also admit that digital reference interactions take them considerably longer than other forms of reference. Chat has a "different pace" than telephone conversations.[5]

In addition to the extra time needed for such transactions, one has to face the added administrative challenges the alternative service entails. Even a casual exploration of the literature regarding digital reference service reveals librarians' candor about the extra burdens it presents. They note a profusion of new demands: additional software to master, new procedures to adopt, extra protocols to establish, significant new costs to explain, and new ways to deal with their regular users—ways that are often neither effective nor helpful. As one author conceded, "When engaged in chat, it can be awkward explaining to a patron walking up to the desk that the librarian is in fact helping another patron, not just checking e-mail or ignoring them."[6] All of these drawbacks—enormously significant in the difficult world of scarce resources and growing librarian responsibility—dovetail with what we consider to be the biggest restrictions of digital reference. In the final analysis, digital reference is only limitedly effective. For all of the hoopla about reaching out in extraordinary ways and in unusual times, digital reference ultimately fails our users. It neither meets their information needs efficiently nor deepens their research capabilities.

We can connect with them at their convenience and on their terms to a point, but the seeming advantages fail to outweigh the service's genuine shortcomings. Digital reference does not give us, as public service librarians, the kind of in-depth contacts with our users that will enable us to build relationships or develop their searching capabilities.

In traditional reference service, librarians offer assistance that is face-to-face, locally based, and decidedly human. We believe that in-person, genuine real-time reference involves moral and emotional elements that are impossible to tap through disembodied online interaction. Consider, for example, the well-recognized educative functions of reference service. Whether we are practitioners at a small liberal arts college or librarians at a large public library, our role is the same. We are cultivators as much as disseminators of knowledge. We model habits of information trolling, gathering, selection, and dissemination—practices that are extremely difficult to develop over fiber optics.[7]

Moreover, any reference librarian can attest to the relationships that develop over time with students or readers who repeatedly seek out the librarian/mentor who first provided the service and inspiration to tough out a difficult research assignment. These relationships require contact face-to-face, in real time, in a given place.

This is why digital reference as a complete service has serious limitations. The Internet (for all of its advantages and wonders) is only minimally interactive. Anyone who has been part of a chat room, a listserv discussion, or an Instant Messenger conversation knows the limitations of these media relative even to a telephone conversation.

Online interaction can be dehumanizing and disembodying in ways that the telephone is not. It may be too much to say that digital reference service is always decontextualizing, dehumanizing, or necessarily fleeting, but certainly this is often the case.

THE HUMAN FACTOR IN INFORMATION TROLLING AND WHY IT WORKS BETTER

Two personal experiences illustrate the restrictions of digital reference. Although the illustrations are drawn from non-librarian contexts, they demonstrate how truly limiting a solely automated information source can be and how effective a more traditional approach can become.

Steve's Experience

Occasionally I purchase clothing from L. L. Bean of Camden, Maine, a company that clearly integrates cutting-edge technology and human creativity. L. L. Bean offers an online, graphic-friendly catalog, the kind that anyone who has searched online finds welcome and efficient. But often the catalog is insufficient. I cannot always be sure what products are still available, or if an item looks exactly as it appears. After selecting merchandise, I usually call a sales representative to confirm the availability of my choice, and to discuss nuances of the product not completely discernible on computer graphics. After all my questions are answered, I complete the transaction without the uncertainty of having ordered in the absence of a human intermediary.

I am thankful the marketing strategists at L. L. Bean understand the importance of this human dimension. Had they been thinking as some technophoric librarians, they might have reasoned that a purely digital approach would be more technically sophisticated, less expensive to operate, and undoubtedly the wave of the future. A solely technology-driven approach might earn the immediate admiration and envy of their competitors, as well as the lasting praise of their in-house information technologists. Fortunately, L. L. Bean understands that a completely automated approach would, in fact, result in diminished customer satisfaction and, therefore, reduced sales. Instead, they insist that a cadre of intelligent, articulate, well-trained people staff the phones. They recognize that connectivity and human interaction are absolutely necessary for effective marketing.

Jonathan's Experience

Allow me to recount recent planning before attending a major professional conference. Hoping for lodging outside the conference hotel syndicate, my wife and I decide to explore Bed & Breakfast options. A trusty Google search yields numerous possibilities, some of which, on investigation, are already booked. A clearinghouse service, however, lists 13 downtown and Toronto Island Bed & Breakfast establishments and proves to be the treasure trove we need. I survey the choices online, comparing features and location to our desiderata.

Online registration could complete my investigation, provided I can determine our first and second choices, but I have many questions that the website in question simply cannot answer, regardless of how many links it includes. Are our first and second choices still available? Should we wish to stay on the Islands, where would we park our car? What is the daily fee? What is the ferry schedule? How late in the evening does it run? What is the fare? I need answers to these questions before booking makes sense, so I call the toll-free number listed as an alternative to booking online.

The result of that call is a pointed reminder that I am still human and that the quickest route to an answer is another human. The booking agent is cordial, knowledgeable, patient, and informative as only an educator can be. All my questions are answered in five minutes through voice-to-voice, interactive conversation, professional to professional. Any online alternative, including a chat or instant messaging system, would have been decidedly inferior on all scores–efficiency, effectiveness, accuracy of information, but most important, completeness to the point of satisfied closure. I book and receive E-mail confirmation within 12 hours.

These two examples illustrate what is felt, perhaps even by a silent majority, but articulated only with caution by most, for fear of inviting ridicule as Neo-Luddites. We freely admit that we want more, not less, human interaction in the satisfaction of our information needs. We do not want more inscrutable, inefficient, ineffective phonetrees that rarely give exactly the option we need, nor do we want one more carefully crafted but, again, invariably inadequate and unsatisfactory FAQ link on a website, no matter how deep we can drill. And why type an Instant Message and wait for the alienating technological sound prompt of the reply when talking voice-to-voice is so superior? What we maintain here is that technological connectivity is also a barrier to communication and, as such, a sometimes unnecessary impediment, and an inferior substitute to what is already in place. In short, digital reference is a poor substitute for the telephone.

Stephen Talbott offers a cross-cultural illustration of this very point in his review at Wade Davis's *One River: Explorations and Discoveries in the Amazon Rain Forest*.[8] Talbott recounts in detail Davis's experiences observing the marvelous skill of a young Ecuadorian Waorani warrior named Tomo as he hunts with a centuries old technology, the blowgun. Using poison-tipped darts, Tomo can "drive a dart through a squirrel at forty feet, knock a hummingbird out of the air, and hit a monkey in the canopy 120 feet above the forest floor."[9] Yet Tomo and others prefer to use shotguns! What is the appeal of this far inferior, obviously ill-suited-to-the-task weapon? "It is the intrinsic attraction of the object itself, the clicking mechanisms, the polished stock, the power of explosion."[10] So it seems to be for many in librarianship as they investigate digital reference. Digital reference is to real-time, real-place, or even telephone reference what the shotgun is to the blowgun for the Waorani. Why not get back to superior basics and invest our time and energies in increasing the number of well-educated librarians rather than in inferior gadgetry?

PLANNED DISPENSABILITY:
DIGITAL REFERENCE AS PART OF THE PROBLEM

Our third concern with digital reference is more philosophical or, to some degree, more psychological. Aside from digital reference being part of a technical rhetoric that has become all too typical of librarians and its failure to compete with the more dynamic and more human dimensions of traditional reference, the enthusiasm for digital reference mirrors a significant problem with librarianship as an enterprise. Librarians have never satisfactorily answered the question of whether or not librarianship is a profession. The present authors certainly believe it is, but we contend that, in terms of the prevailing behavior of our colleagues, ours is a minority view.

The majority viewpoint, which by its actions argues for a non-professional view of librarianship, manifests itself in a most peculiar corporate behavior, one that is driven, we suspect, by insecurity and low self-esteem. We call the behavior "planned dispensability," something we will discuss in more detail below.

First, allow a word about librarianship's self-image malaise. You know the historic arguments summoned to explain our *angst*: a low-status occupation becomes female-dominated in the early years of the 20th century; social injustice in an economy-crazed culture keeps salaries low; a service occupation that develops a highly technical craft then becomes denigrated for lack of a rigorous body of knowledge driving its practice; a cadre of introverted personalities populate the field–all these coalesce to help perpetuate a cycle of ignorance in the general populace of the intrinsic value of our work.[11] So in response, we promote, unwittingly in some cases, consciously and blatantly in others, the concept of planned dispensability. This psychoanalysis may appear far-fetched, but it is hard to explain the seemingly inexplicable corporate behavior by any other means.

Ironically, such behavior parades itself as a virtue. It has become ensconced, at least in the unwritten folklore of our enterprise, as a moral value of our profession. More evident in the so-called public services, this dysfunction is also present in technical services and is championed by many a library administrator. To be sure, empowerment of our readers is a good thing. But success at teaching the process of locating relevant resources falls far short of rendering the purveyor of that knowledge dispensable. Nevertheless, what we project and even articulate is that we will know we have been successful when we are no longer necessary. Our job and our goal is to educate and train our readers so that they no longer need our mediation.

This training, it must be pointed out, is not a mentoring of persons who will replace us as librarians. Rather, it is educating our clientele to become entirely independent of our intervention. This is an information literacy enterprise that proves the sages and the library-use educators passé and dispensable, and we present this as a goal of our work! When pondered dispassionately and carefully, this corporate behavior is not only counterproductive, but also tells a self-destructive lie that will lead to the demise of our profession.

Those who worry about our profession surviving until their retirement are not getting any younger. The cruel irony is that many of our young Turks, aided and abetted by mid-career librarians who should know better, are hastening the end of librarianship. Our lemming-like distraction with digital reference is a perfect case in point of a misguided profession grasping at the wrong straws.

The discussion brings us to our long-held conviction that the shortest distance between a reader's information need and fulfillment of that need always has been and always will be a human resource, dare we say it, a librarian. Dr. Johnson rightly describes two types of knowledge, that which we know and the knowledge of where to find what we do not know immediately. We will die as a profession if we continue to denigrate and deny the vast body of knowledge residing between the ears of our MLS-degreed practitioners and perpetuate the deleterious myth that our success lies in our planned dispensability, often aided by the latest razzle-dazzle to come out of the Silicon Valley. Digital reference is particularly pernicious because if offers the verisimilitude of real-time human interaction, but by its very nature and cost-time to investigate, purchase, learn, incorporate into workflows, and maintain—it dissipates attention and resources from more fundamental, valuable, and effective library services. This is too high a price to pay for the supposed bolstering of relevance its proponents claim it garners, especially in light of its complicity in the self-defeating doctrine of planned dispensability.

Some of you familiar with the Chicago area will know Morton Arboretum in Lisle. Fewer will know the late Floyd Swick, self-educated polymath and longtime botanist there. Floyd was wont to quip that there are two kinds of botanists. The first type goes into the field, gathers specimens, peers at dead plant fragments under a microscope, and eventually ventures an identification. The other type simply knows the plants.

We librarians know the sources and our mediation is indispensable to our clientele and to the healthy future of our profession. Information, knowledge and, sometimes even wisdom, is best imparted face-to-face in real time and in real proximity to another human being. To lose sight of this truth is to dissipate our energies and to hasten the demise of librarianship. Hence, our prophetic caution about the overly enthusiastic attention many are giving digital reference services.

CONCLUSION

Our threefold caveat about digital reference is not intended to discredit the potentials of the service. Librarians should be open to anything that enhances user services and enables us to serve our readers better. Digital reference should be part of the librarian tool kit at some libraries.

Nevertheless, we must keep our heads and shun the high-flown rhetoric to which our profession is so prone. Digital reference has not fundamentally altered the way we do reference nor should it. Our readers need human connectivity and human expertise. Technologies that enhance that human dimension–for example, the telephone–should not be gainsaid simply because they are older communications technology. We should see digital reference as a viable, but as yet unproven vehicle of service. Moreover, the seeming advantages of digital reference as a full-service approach to reference fail to counterweigh its deficiencies. The energy and cost of putting such a service into operation could undermine more traditional and, let us admit, much more effective forms of service.

Librarians, we assert, have difficult choices to make about where we channel our time and energies. We already have a substantive, effective, non-digital tool kit of powerful reference apparatuses. There is surely no need to revamp our approach to collection development or to weed print resources which have been proven workhorses in a face-to-face reference environment. Despite the revolutionary rhetoric that seems to emerge in decade-like cycles in library circles, digital reference can only serve as a complement to the regular modes of library public service. Digital online service modules and electronic resources can never equal the potency and effectiveness of on-site, in-house, in-place, and wholly interactive traditional reference practice and time-honored paradigms of reference collection development.

NOTES

1. Steve McKinzie and Jonathan D. Lauer, "Digital Reference: A New Library Paradigm or the Emperor's New Clothes," *Against the Grain* 14, no. 4 (September 2002): 34, 36, 38, and "Virtual Reference: Overrated, Inflated, and Not Even Real," *The Charleston Advisor* 4, no. 2 (October 2002): 56-57.

2. Joseph Janes, David S. Carter, and Patricia Memmott, "Digital Reference Services in Academic Libraries," *Reference and User Services Quarterly* 39, no. 2 (Winter 1999): 145. Note: Although such interactive librarian services as OCLC's Question Point may constitute a form of digital service, our immediate concern in this article is with the more interactive modes–a practice we exclusively refer to throughout the article as "digital reference."

3. R. David Lankes, John W. Collins III, and Abby S. Kasowitz, *Digital Reference Service in the New Millennium.* New York: Neal-Schuman, 2001, p. 11. See further Carol Goodson, *Providing Library Services for Distance Education Students,* New York: Neal-Schuman, 2001: 3-6.

4. Jo Kibbee, David Ward, and Wei Ma, "Digital Service, Real Data: Results of a Pilot Study," *Reference Services Review* 30, no. 1 (2002): 35.

5. Linda Eichler and Michael Halperin, "LivePerson: Keeping Reference Alive and Clicking: Chat Technology for Reference Services at Lippincott Library," *Econtent* 23, no. 3 (June/July 2000): 63-6.

6. Jo Kibbee, David Ward, and Wei Ma, "Digital Service, Real Data: Results of a Pilot Study," *Reference Services Review* 30, no. 1 (2002): 35.

7. We acknowledge our indebtedness in this section to the trenchant case made by Diekema and Caddell in their recent article regarding the limitations of digital education. See David Diekema and David Caddell, "The Significance of Place: Sociological Reflections on Distance Learning and Christian Higher Education," *Christian Scholar's Review* XXXI, 2 (Winter 2001): 169-84.

8. Stephen Talbott, *NetFuture* #141 (www.netfuture.org): 1-11.

9. Talbott: 2.

10. Talbott: 3.

11. This brief encapsulation of the last 125 years of library history in no way disparages the groups it describes. It rather seeks to suggest broad swaths of reality that have contributed to what we argue are unnecessary and counterproductive thinking and behavior within our profession.

Mediated Online Searching
and Digital Reference

Amanda Spink

SUMMARY. Digital reference is an important research area with the potential to enhance information delivery to library patrons. The process of digital reference involves the challenges and problems of an interactive computer-mediated reference interview. Related studies of mediated online searching have identified the major tasks during a mediated online search. The search intermediary's tasks included gathering information on the information need, previous searches on the topic by the information seeker, search terms and strategies, database selection, search procedures, system's outputs and relevance of retrieved items, and the number of topics to be searched. The information seeker's tasks include providing information to the search intermediary on their topic, discussing their previous information seeking and evaluating the online search

Amanda Spink is affiliated with the School of Information Sciences and Technology, The Pennsylvania State University, 004C Thomas Building, University Park, PA 16802 (E-mail: spink@ist.psu.edu).

[Haworth co-indexing entry note]: "Mediated Online Searching and Digital Reference." Spink, Amanda. Co-published simultaneously in *The Reference Librarian* (The Haworth Information Press, an imprint of The Haworth Press, Inc.) No. 79/80, 2002/2003, pp. 57-65; and: *Digital Reference Services* (ed: Bill Katz) The Haworth Information Press, an imprint of The Haworth Press, Inc., 2002/2003, pp. 57-65. Single or multiple copies of this article are available for a fee from The Haworth Document Delivery Service [1-800-HAWORTH, 9:00 a.m. - 5:00 p.m. (EST). E-mail address: docdelivery@haworthpress.com].

10.1300/J120v38n79_05

output. Models of digital reference interviews need to include more complex information seeking behaviors, such as successive searching and multitasking. Further research is needed to extend our understanding of digital reference processes. *[Article copies available for a fee from The Haworth Document Delivery Service: 1-800-HAWORTH. E-mail address: <docdelivery@haworthpress.com> Website: <http://www.HaworthPress.com> © 2002/2003 by The Haworth Press, Inc. All rights reserved.]*

KEYWORDS. Digital reference, tasks, online searching, information seeking, search intermediaries

INTRODUCTION

Many libraries are beginning to offer different forms of digital reference services to patrons. Digital reference services may be offered via email, instant messaging or Web-based reference forms. These services allow the patron or user to access the assistance of the librarians and library services without being physically present in the library. The growth of interactive reference services is creating the "virtual reference desk." How the "virtual reference desk" is similar to or differs from traditional "in library" reference services is a growing area of study (Trump & Tuttle, 2001). Digital reference may be simple to complex, depending upon the nature of the information seeker's problem. How is the complex digital reference interaction different from the mediated online search interactions conducted by search intermediaries? Digital reference is also emerging as an important area of librarian education and library services.

This paper first reviews the related and growing literature on digital reference. The paper then discusses findings from recent related studies modeling the tasks during mediated online searching with implications for the development of digital reference models and practice.

RELATED STUDIES

Researchers in library and information science and librarians are increasingly writing and conducting significant studies in the important area of digital reference services. A search of the Information Science Abstracts database, using the phrase "digital reference," retrieved 55 documents. This growing body of literature includes studies and papers examining different aspects of digital reference, including overview issues, reference questions, surveys and empirical studies, technology issues, case studies, standards and evaluation approaches, and model development.

Trump and Tuttle (2001) discuss the motivations for the development of digital reference services by librarians. The Internet has been a key technology that has enabled the development of digital reference services (Foster, 1999; Janes, 2001; Janes, Hill & Rolfe, 2001; Mon, 2000) and collaborative digital reference services (Kasowitz, 2001). Using the Internet and other database technologies, librarians are moving towards live, online and real-time reference services (Schneider, 2000; Tenopir & Ennis, 1998). The development of digital reference services has implications to change the relationship between librarian and patron (Wilson, 2000).

Many case studies of digital reference services have been conducted (Foley, 2002; Gray, 2000; Koyama, 1998; Oder, 2001; Stemper & Butler, 2001; Stormont, 2001). Hattery (1999) and Kresh (2000, 2001) describe the Library of Congress Collaborative Digital Reference Service (CDR). Lankes (1998) discusses the Virtual Reference Desk Project to improve K-12 digital reference services. Trump and Tuttle (2001) describe the development of a chat reference service.

Digital reference services have common issues and problems. The role of technology in digital reference services is described by Rockman (2001); including the problems of "de-personalization" of the reference service (Dilevko, 2001). Standards for digital reference services are evolving (Ellis & Francoeur, 2001; Lankes, McClure & Gross, 2001) as new tools are developed (Marvin, 2002). The effective evaluation of digital reference services and the development of best practices are being examined (Gross & McClure, 2001; Janes, Hill & Rolfe, 2001; Tenopir & Ennis, 1998; White, 2001a,b).

Some studies have analyzed reference questions submitted to various digital reference services (Carter & Janes, 2000). Diamond and Pease (2001) found that broad and complex questions were difficult to answer in a digital reference environment. Straw (2000) compared traditional face-to-face reference interviews with electronic interviews.

Further research is needed that models the digital reference interview for the development of best practices and training materials. Digital reference interviews may share similar characteristics with mediated online search interviews. During mediated online searching, an information seeker discusses their information problem with a trained search intermediary, who then conducts an online search of a database system. So far, the mediated online searching and the digital reference literatures and studies have not intersected. Examining the nature of mediated online search interviews can provide insight into more complex digital reference interviews.

MEDIATED ONLINE SEARCHING TASKS

Recent studies of mediated online searching revealed more complex information seeking behaviors that go beyond the single topic single search paradigm. Studies by Spink et al. (1998; forthcoming) have identified six major tasks during mediated online searching, including: (1) social task, (2) successive searching task, (3) multitasking search task, (4) information problem modeling task, (5) search system task, and (6) interaction task. Each task is briefly described below.

Social Task

During mediated online interviews, information seekers and search intermediaries are often engaged in a social dialogue on personal matters not directly related to the conduct of the online search (Ellis et al., 2002). These discussions are related to the social or human tasks, norms and practices of human existence.

Successive Searching Task

Successive searching occurs when information seekers often engage in more than one search interaction when seeking information on a particular topic. Spink, Wilson, Ford, Foster, and Ellis (2002) also observed information seekers requesting a second search on the same topic from a search intermediary. Successive searching is a task common to online database system and Web users. In cases of successive searching, the search intermediary elicited information from the information seeker about previous searches conducted on the same topic.

Information seeking research is attempting to understand the relevance of what causes shifts or changes in the user's information seeking process over successive searches. How can we measure a shift or move in their information seeking process and thus better understand this process and the characteristics of the longitudinal information seeking process?

Multitasking Search Task

Multitasking online searching occurs when information seekers are seeking information on more than one topic at the same time. Most multitasking searches include two topics (Spink, Ozmutlu & Ozmutlu, 2002). During mediated multitasking searches, the search intermediary coordinates searching on more than one topic during a single search.

An information seeker *coordinates* their cognitive state, level of domain knowledge, and their understanding of their information problem, into a coherent series of activities that may include seeking, searching, interactive browsing and retrieving and constructing information. We still know little about how humans coordinate the various elements of their information seeking and searching into a coherent set of multitasking processes.

Information Problem Modeling Task

The task of modeling the information problem involves the translation of the information seeker's information problem into appropriate search terminology by the search intermediary (Saracevic, Spink & Wu, 1997). This task occupies search intermediaries during both the pre-search stage–as part of the initial search strategy development–and the online stage of the search–as part of query reformulation. This involves modeling tasks related to the information seeker's domain knowledge, knowledge of database searching, previous information-seeking, and search terms and strategy, formatting input, search strategy development and progress checking.

Search System Task

Information seekers and search intermediaries discuss issues related to information required to technically conduct the online interaction, including elicitations regarding databases and search commands selected, logging on and off, and printing. The search system task occurs primarily during the online search stage, requesting information from search intermediaries in an effort to understand the technical requirements and capabilities of online searching.

Interaction Task

During the online search stage, the interactive task requires the information seeker and search intermediary to assess the search system's output. Search intermediaries were primarily concerned with prompting user evaluations of the search systems output and prompt the information seeker to interpret and evaluate the output of the search system–either for relevance, magnitude, potential search terms or format.

DISCUSSION

Mediated online searching may take place when the information seeker is present or absent for the actual search interaction. A digital reference interaction takes place when the information seeker and the librarian are remotely located from each other. However, there are some commonalities to explore between the two modes of reference interview and interaction.

The librarian in both cases must work with the information seeker to determine their information problem during a conversation or form of reference interview either in person or remotely. This form of conversation may involve a social task that varies with the individual characteristics of the interaction. The librarian needs to determine the domain knowledge and level of information seeking by the requester before proceeding further with the reference interview. This involves the librarian being aware that successive searching or multiple reference interactions may be necessary to help the information seeker work through and resolve their information problem.

The current paradigm for considering information seeking and reference interviews is based on a model of the information seeker as having one topic and conducting one search on that one topic. The librarian should also cater to the information seeker who is multitasking during the search task. People have complex and often multiple information problems to deal with during a digital reference interview. How the librarian co-ordinates this multitasking searching will evolve with the assistance of the information seeker. Our models of information seeking and human information behavior are being enhanced to include more complex and longitudinal information related human behaviors and processes.

Our models of reference interviews and digital reference interviews need to take account of more complex information seeker behaviors. Academic library patrons are often working on more than one topic or multitasking (Spink, Ozmutlu & Ozmutlu, 2002), and engaged in a more longitudinal information seeking process that involves more than one interaction with a search system and/or a librarian (Spink, Wilson, Ford, Foster & Ellis, 2002).

CONCLUSION AND FURTHER RESEARCH

The growth in digital reference services is accompanied by a need to model the tasks within this form of reference interview. Further intersection between the research into mediated online searching and digital reference is desirable. Further modeling the digital reference process can benefit the training of librarians, the provision of digital reference services and new technologies to enhance the digital reference process.

REFERENCES

Carter, D. S., & Janes, J. (2000). Unobtrusive data analysis of digital reference questions and service at the Internet public library: An exploratory study. *Library Trends, 49*(2), 251-265.

Diamond, W., & Pease, B. (2001). Digital reference: A case study of question types in an academic library. *Reference Services Review, 29*(3), 210-218.

Dilevko, J. (2001). An ideological analysis of digital reference service models. *Library Trends, 50*(2), 218-244.

Ellis, L., & Francoeur, S. (2001). Applying information competency to digital reference. *Proceedings of Libraries and Librarians: Making a Difference in the Knowledge Age, August 16-25, Boston, MA.*

Ellis, D., Wilson, T. D., Ford, N., Foster, A., Lam, H. M., Burton, R., & Spink, A. (2002). Information seeking and mediated searching. Part 5. User-intermediary interaction. *Journal of the American Society for Information Science and Technology, 53*(11), 879-882.

Foley, M. (2002). Instant messaging reference in an academic library: A case study. *College and Research Libraries, 63*(1), 36-45.

Foster, J. (1999). Web reference: A virtual reality. *Public Libraries, 38*(2), 94-95.

Gray, S. M. (2000). Virtual reference services: Directions and agendas. *Reference and User Services Quarterly, 39*(4), 365-375.

Gross, M., & McClure, C. (2001). *Assessing quality in digital reference services site visit reports: State Library of Florida, Bureau of Library and Network Services and Tampa-Hillsborough County Public Library System.* Research Report. ED457863.

Hattery, M. (1999). Reference service in the digital age: Three projects. *Information Retrieval and Library Automation, 34*(9), 1-2.

Janes, J. (2001). Digital reference services in public and academic libraries. In: C. McClure and J. Bertot (Eds.), *Evaluating Networked Information Services: Techniques, Policy, Issues.* Information Today, Inc (pp. 175-195).

Janes, J., Hill, C., & Rolfe, A. (2001). Ask-an-expert services analysis. *Journal of the American Society for Information Science and Technology, 52*(13), 1106-1121.

Kasowitz, A. S. (2001). *Trends and issues in digital reference services*. ERIC Report (EDO-IR-2001-07).

Koyama, J. T. (1998). http://digiref.scenarios.issues. *Reference and User Services Quarterly, 38*(1), 51-53.

Kresh, D. N. (2000). Offering high quality reference service on the Web: The collaborative digital reference service. *D-Lib Magazine, 6*(6).

Kresh, D. N. (2001). From ssh to search engine: Reference.net on the web. *Information Technology and Libraries, 20*(3), 139-142.

Lankes, D. (1998). AskA's: Lesson learned from k-12 digital reference services. *Reference and User Services Quarterly, 38*(1), 63-71.

Lankes, R. D., McClure, C., & Gross, M. (2001). Assessing quality in digital reference services. *Proceedings of the Annual Meeting of the American Society for Information Science and Technology, November 3-8, Washington, DC* (323-329).

Marvin, S. (2002). Process for developing e-services. *Proceedings of the Information Today conference, May 14-16, New York* (pp. 255-258).

Mon, L. (2000). Digital reference service. *Government Information Quarterly, 17*(3), 309-318.

Oder, N. (2001). The shape of e-reference. *Library Journal, 126*(2), 46-50.

Rockman, I. F. (2001). Visionary pragmatism in an e-library environment. *Reference Services Review, 29*(3), 169-170.

Saracevic, T., Spink, A., & Wu, M. (1997). Users and intermediaries in information retrieval: What are they talking about? *Proceedings of the 6th International Conference on User Modeling, Chia Laguna, Sardinia-Italy, June 2-5, 1997* (pp. 44-54).

Schneider, K. G. (2000). The distributed librarian: Live, online, real-time reference. *American Libraries, 31*(10), 64.

Spink, A., Goodrum, A., & Robins, D. (1998). Elicitations behavior during mediated information retrieval. *Information Processing and Management, 34*(2/3), 257-274.

Spink, A., Ozmutlu, H. C., & Ozmutlu, S. (2002). Multitasking information seeking and searching processes. *Journal of the American Society for Information Science and Technology, 53*(8), 639-652.

Spink, A., & Sollenberger, M. (forthcoming). *Elicitation purposes and tasks during mediated information search.*

Spink, A., Wilson, T. D., Ford, N. A., Foster, A., & Ellis, D. (2002). Information seeking and mediated searching. Part III. Successive searching. *Journal of the American Society for Information Science and Technology, 53*(9), 716-727.

Stemper, J. A., & Butler, J. T. (2001). Developing a model to provide digital reference services. *Reference Services Review, 29*(3), 172-188.

Straw, J. E. (2000). A virtual understanding: The reference interview and question negotiation in the digital age. *Reference and User Services Quarterly, 39*(4), 376-379.

Stromont, S. (2001). Going where the users are: Live digital reference. *Information Technology and Libraries, 20*(3), 129-134.

Tenopir, C., & Ennis, L. (1998). The digital reference world of academic libraries. *Online, 22*(4), 22-28.

Trump, J. F., & Tuttle, I. P. (2001). Here, there and everywhere: Reference at the point-of-need. *Journal of Academic Librarianship, 27*(6), 464-466.

White, M. (2001a). Diffusion of an innovation: Digital reference service in Carnegie Foundations Master's (comprehensive) academic institution libraries. *Journal of Academic Librarianship, 27*(3), 173-187.

White, M. (2001b). Digital reference services: Framework for analysis and evaluation. *Library and Information Science Research, 23*(3), 211-231.

Wilson, M. C. (2000). Evolution or entropy: Changing reference user culture and the future of reference librarians. *Reference and Library Services Quarterly, 39*(4), 387-390.

Stocking
the Virtual Ready Reference Collection

Danianne Mizzy
Elizabeth Tillapaugh Mahoney

SUMMARY. Libraries have begun to add chat reference as a method to deliver reference service to remote user populations. To deliver quality service in a timely fashion, libraries need to construct a Virtual Ready Reference Collection (VRRC) of elite ready reference Web sites most often used during the chat reference interaction. This article explores the collection development steps needed to create a VRRC that is most beneficial on the local level. The value in creating this collection lies not just in the end product, but also in the process, which serves as a valuable training exercise. Selecting and maintaining the virtual ready reference collection will enhance the chat reference librarians' ability to deliver service in the chat reference environment. *[Article copies available for a fee from The Haworth Document Delivery Service: 1-800-HAWORTH. E-mail address: <docdelivery@haworthpress.com> Website: <http://www.HaworthPress. com> © 2002/2003 by The Haworth Press, Inc. All rights reserved.]*

Danianne Mizzy (E-mail: danianne@seas.upenn.edu) is Assistant Head, Engineering Library, University of Pennsylvania. Elizabeth Tillapaugh Mahoney (E-mail: etm@ pitt.edu) is Head, Information Sciences Library, University of Pittsburgh. At the time this article was written, both authors were acting as Coordinators of the Digital Reference Service for the University Library System, 304 Information Sciences Library, 135 North Bellefield Avenue, University of Pittsburgh, Pittsburgh, PA 15260.

The authors acknowledge the contributions of Susan McGlamery, Jana Ronan, Karen Rossi, Larry Schankman, and Jeff Wisniewski.

[Haworth co-indexing entry note]: "Stocking the Virtual Ready Reference Collection." Mizzy, Danianne, and Elizabeth Tillapaugh Mahoney. Co-published simultaneously in *The Reference Librarian* (The Haworth Information Press, an imprint of The Haworth Press, Inc.) No. 79/80, 2002/2003, pp. 67-99; and: *Digital Reference Services* (ed: Bill Katz) The Haworth Information Press, an imprint of The Haworth Press, Inc., 2002/ 2003, pp. 67-99. Single or multiple copies of this article are available for a fee from The Haworth Document Delivery Service [1-800-HAWORTH, 9:00 a.m. - 5:00 p.m. (EST). E-mail address: docdelivery@haworthpress. com].

KEYWORDS. Electronic reference services, chat reference, digital reference, virtual reference, ready reference collections, training, collection development

INTRODUCTION

What do you consider to be your "Top Ten" reference tools? Those elite, never-fail ready reference tools that you turn to first when beginning to stalk the answer to a reference query. Seasoned reference librarians can supply the print titles to answer this question in rapid-fire sequence, generally finding that the list easily grows from ten to twenty to fifty that could be considered their "most frequently used" titles. The sources that spring to mind are particular to each individual reference desk, have been selected over time, and most often meet user needs. These sources have demonstrated to each reference librarian a consistent level of accuracy, reliability, and ease of use. Because they are used so often, librarians tend to keep them close at hand in a unique shelving group referred to as the "Ready Reference Collection." The ALA Glossary defines this type of collection as the

> standard reference tools, set aside from the general reference collection for the purpose of providing rapid access to information of a factual nature. Examples of reference sources typically located in ready reference are almanacs, dictionaries, and directories.[1]

Of course, the "Top Fifty" reference tools will differ by type of library, the varying needs of the user population and the personal preferences of each librarian. However, it is clear that some of the same tools will be on each list and that almost every reference librarian's "Top Ten" list will be similar. This statement is borne out by research reported by Katz which indicates that at least three standard sources are found in most print ready reference collections, *The Statistical Abstract of the United States*, *The World Almanac* and *The World Book Encyclopedia*.[2]

It is clear that print Ready Reference Collections play a crucial role in the provision of telephone and face-to-face reference. It seems to follow that library Web reference pages are equally as important in the provision of virtual reference services. To reflect briefly on their development, one looks to the 1990s when the World Wide Web was first becoming available on library service desks. At that point, the range of possibilities was just the glimmer of an idea, but librarians seized on the reference and referral potential. The breadth of newly accessible information made librarians giddy at the vastness of the Web when applied to the reference process. Most reference librarians adopted a "smash and grab" approach to the collection of Web sites which were "book marked" with a "just in case" collecting mentality. It quickly became obvious that there were difficulties in sharing these *personal* desktop bookmark files with users because of limited portability. However, the construction of library Web reference pages soon moved the book-marked sites out of the reference librarian's *personal* space and into the *public* areas of the library Web site. The next logical step taken by many librarians was to mine the collected Web sites and links to develop a collection of ready reference sites for use with and by the public.

These library Web ready reference pages (WRRP) have a multiplicity of resources and organizational schemes, and are placed in highly visible locations within the library Web site. They are designed to be useful in a variety of ways, either in an independent fashion by the users beginning work on a research question, or in partnership with the reference librarian as reference questions are posed. They are also used for all types of reference transactions received over the telephone and email, as well as face-to-face transactions.

The newest development in virtual reference is chat or real-time reference. According to Anne Lipow in her new book *The Virtual Reference Librarian's Handbook,*

> The term virtual reference librarian, then, refers to a librarian who provides point-of-need live, interactive question-handling using chat and voice software that enable synchronous communication with a distant client.[3]

Even though chat is simply another mechanism for delivering reference to users, the nature of the chat environment presents different challenges to the librarian than face-to-face exchanges. When the librarian is engaged in a chat, or real-time, reference interview, there is often a heightened sense of pressure to respond quickly to the user's query. If the best source to answer a question is obvious or easily retrieved, the outcome of the chat reference interaction is likely to be improved. So is it necessary to create a separate Virtual Ready Reference Collection (VRRC) to meet the needs of those staffing the chat service? Since the nature of the library Web reference pages is to meet all purposes and to be useful in all settings, one might think it logical to conclude that it is not the most suitable tool. Its collection of Web sites and resources is too comprehensive and its organization too complex to navigate nimbly in the chat environment. Thus, one might expect that a first step taken by libraries developing chat reference services would include the compilation of a Virtual Ready Reference Collection.

Nonetheless, here seems to be a degree of disagreement about the need to invest time and resources to create a VRRC when the reference department could utilize resources that already exist on their own library's Web site (e.g., electronic subscriptions, pertinent resources, local information). Another question is why a library would bother to create a VRRC when there are many good examples of virtual reference collections found on the Web sites of other libraries. For that matter, why create a VRRC when resources are readily found via search engines and other mechanisms? Is there a benefit in the *work* leading up to the creation of a Virtual Ready Reference Collection that would make the time spent worth the effort?

It has become clear to the authors that the long-term benefits associated with the construction of such a collection far outweigh the work involved in finding the best resources. From the beginning of the process, the chat reference librarians developing the VRRC are forced to view the utility of a Web site as it relates to the chat reference environment. The process of selecting items for the VRRC forces the chat reference librarians to become familiar with the Web sites and enhances performance in future chat sessions. In addition, the process of culling the VRRC sources from the existing reference Web pages forces the chat reference librarians to make case-by-case decisions about the sites' effectiveness in the chat environment. By looking at the sites through this very specific lens, the creation of the "Top Fifty" list of elite, never-fail ready reference tools for the chat reference desk is successful. Once created, the VRRC resides in a *shared personal* space of the chat librarians where it can be readily accessed and easily updated. What the completed VRRC accomplishes is different from what a library Web reference page provides. Just as the conveniently located print collection of ready reference tools found behind a service desk can save time and serve as a training tool for newly arrived employees, so too the collection and use of a VRRC can save keystrokes and enhance reference performance in the chat reference transaction.

This article is suggesting a model or process, incorporating strategies suggested by Kovacs and Pitschmann,[4] to follow in the production of your own customized VRRC. It will discuss issues related to the selection, creation, organization, evaluation and maintenance of such a collection. It suggests some benchmarks for virtual reference resources that can best meet the needs of a library's chat reference service. In addition, it will outline some of the benefits of using the construction of the VRRC as a training tool for librarians on the chat reference team. At the close of the article, four appendices contain collections of resources offered for those who want to examine the tools the authors have found to be useful. The first consists of questions logs and data, the second lists exemplary virtual ready reference guide sites, the third lists quality selection aids, and the fourth, current awareness services to assist in the ongoing collection development of the VRRC.

COLLECTION DEFINITION

Scope, Audience, and Purpose

Whether you are creating your virtual ready reference collection from scratch, or adapting it from an existing resource, the process should begin with a definition of the scope of the collection. Two primary considerations are the audience and the purpose. Library Web sites and public virtual ready reference collections are in the uneasy position of trying to serve two audiences with differing needs, the end user and the professional staff. Both the organization and selection of sites must strike a balance between the needs of users using this for self-service and the needs of professional searchers delivering intermediated reference service. The VRRC needs to serve only one audience, the librarians offering the chat reference service. Its purpose is to allow the librarian to quickly access sites known to be useful in answering factual questions. The Library of Congress' BeOnline Plus Selection Criteria for Internet Resources expresses this well: priority will be given to "resources which provide substantial information on topics for which reference librarians receive frequent questions and/or which provide comprehensive referrals to sources of such information."[5] The VRRC should therefore be mounted "behind the scenes." However, it is important that the user have the option to return to the resource once the reference transaction is over, if needed. Therefore, the VRRC should still be accessible from the link or URL embedded in the transcript of the reference interaction. It will also be helpful if all the resources in the VRRC also appear in the library Web ready reference pages.

A digital reference service policy will set boundaries that will also help define the collection. The type of questions permitted and the range of clientele allowed to pose them are determining factors. Public libraries, as a rule, will accept a much broader range of questions than academic libraries who typically restrict service to questions relating to educational and research needs. Public libraries also serve a broader population. For example, a public library with a virtual homework help service will need material appropriate to different reading levels. Some libraries will allow anyone to pose a question; some have residency or affiliation requirements. Each library will develop a unique policy based on the needs of its user population, which will in turn help define the scope of the collection. While a formal collection development plan is not necessary, writing a scope statement that defines subjects and types of resources to be included is essential.

Collection Development as Training Tool

It is essential that the personnel staffing the virtual desk be as familiar with ready reference sources available on the Web as those sources housed in the print collection. When presented with a ready reference question, the goal is to *know* where to find that type of information. For virtual reference, a search engine like Google should be the last resort. But particularly with regard to the WWW, many librarians suffer from what Anne Lipow refers to in *The Virtual Reference Librarian's Handbook* as the Einstellung Effect. It is "the common human tendency to stop wanting to learn more the moment you have the best results so far."[6] The resources on the Web are vast and ever changing and the attempt to stay current can be daunting. How could one ever "know" where to find things with the same ease as in the print collection? Sauers makes the point that practice and experience are what led to this familiarity with print tools and the same process can be applied to learning a Web-based collection. He terms it "shelf reading the Internet."[7] The authors believe that in the course of selecting, evaluating, and organizing their service's virtual ready reference collection, librarians will extend their knowledge of Web-based reference resources and improve their skills in retrieving them. They will discover new resources, and new facets of familiar resources. At the end, they will know the Virtual Ready Reference Collection inside and out because they created it.

COLLECTION DEVELOPMENT PROCESS

Question Review

The VRRC development team will ideally involve as many of the librarians who will be staffing the chat service as is practical. After writing a collection scope statement, the next step is to seek out information about what questions are likely to be asked and to utilize the librarians' current knowledge of Web-based reference resources. If the library has a log of email or chat questions, examining these can provide invaluable information about types of questions asked as well as sources that have proved useful in answering them. Another data collection method could be to survey librarians staffing face-to-face and telephone reference about commonly asked types and categories of questions. For additional insight, it is possible to examine several collections of chat and email questions that have been mounted on the Web or discussed in articles. (See Appendix A.) To broadly summarize many different findings, the percentages of directional, ready reference, and research questions seem to roughly mirror the percentages in face-to-face reference. Within the non-research question category the following are common:

- Problems with remote access
- OPAC searching
- Database searching
- Holdings question–books and journals are the most frequently sought known items
- Policy and procedural questions–ILL/Document Delivery is the most frequent service inquiry

The goal of the analysis of local questions (or a sample from a comparable setting) is to make sure you have a suitable virtual resource to answer every question. If an individual librarian doesn't know of an appropriate virtual resource, then the question can be sent out to the collection development team. If no source comes to the light, this becomes a test question during the resource collection and review stage. The question review stage will end with the production of two lists. The first will be of useful virtual ready reference sites already known to the librarians, and the second will be of stumpers for which sources need to be located. This bit of reverse engineering will not only help focus the collection development on actual or likely questions but also begin to prepare the chat reference librarians for the kinds of questions they can expect to receive on the virtual desk.

Print Ready Reference Review

The next step is to review the print ready reference collection to determine which are the most heavily used sources. Looking at existing print collection development plans may be helpful in determining what subject areas are supported and to what level. A public library may collect consumer level medical resources whereas a medical school library might need both consumer and professional level resources. Another method is to survey all the librarians who use the print ready reference collection (not just those on the team) to see which sources they use the most. At the very least, the reference collection bibliographer(s) should be consulted. If statistics are kept (or available from the library management system), seeing which items are loaned out or used most frequently would be helpful. The team should then compile a list of the most heavily used print resources and subject areas of importance. Once again, this procedure has a side benefit. In reviewing the print collection, the librarians may discover print resources they had overlooked, or become reacquainted with forgotten gems, thereby improving knowledge of sources useful for traditional reference.

At this juncture, the team will see which of the most useful print tools have online counterparts in the sites already added to the VRRC. What remains will be added to the desired resources list along with subject specific resources defined in the scope statement. (Tools of local importance will be discussed later.) The "stumpers" should be discussed, and sources that answer these difficult questions should be considered for addition if they fill gaps in the Virtual Ready Reference Collection. Before the actual selection of resources can proceed, criteria for evaluation need to be developed.

EVALUATION

Reference currently straddles a hybrid world of print and electronic resources. For digital reference, it is clear that it is easiest and quickest to deliver material that already appears in digital format. As Ronan observes, "Electronic resources are obviously the preferred method for answering questions in the virtual reference environment."[8] Therefore, it is important to have explicit criteria for the team to use in evaluating potential additions to the VRRC. There are numerous sources that address selection criteria for Web resources.[9] These usually include factors such as:

- Authority
- Scope/Coverage
- Accuracy/Objectivity

- Currency
- Organization/Ease of use
- Uniqueness
- Reliability
- Special features

Rather than rehashing what is by now familiar territory, the authors are going to endorse these general criteria and focus on utility. Unlike email reference, where promised response periods commonly extend to 48 hours or longer, time is of the essence in the chat reference environment. For this setting, utility is therefore defined as any factor that will expedite access to a resource likely to contain the desired information. Preference will be given to sites that in addition to meeting the above criteria:

- Are organized logically
- Have clear navigational tools
- Have descriptive link text
- Have clear labels
- Allow simultaneous searching across multiple resources
- Are comprehensive within their scope
- Have well organized entries or search results

Another useful criteria articulated by Sowards is to show preference to "the smallest site that is likely to lead to the information."[10] For example, GPO Access provides links to a core set of U.S. government resources all from one page including the U.S. Code, the U.S. Government Manual, the Code of Federal Regulations, and cornerstone documents like the U.S. Constitution. The reference tab at Bartleby provides access to encyclopedias, dictionaries, thesauri, bibles, quotations, and the Columbia Gazetteer with federated searching. A third example is AddALL, a used/out of print book metasearch site that allows you to search across the collections of 15 online vendors.[11] GPO Access saves having individual links to all the different resources, while Bartelby and AddALL, by searching across multiple resources, maximize the chance of finding the desired information or item. In the same vein, each subject category should include at least one comprehensive guide site to serve as a gateway, or portal, to resources for questions of a more detailed or obscure nature. Utility, combined with the standard criteria, will help the team to select the resources which will best serve the chat practitioners.

Selection Aids

With the evaluation criteria in place, it is time for the team to start reviewing sources. The initial resources sought will be for the areas defined in the collection scope statement, online counterparts to the most valuable print tools, desired subject specific tools, and sites which contain answers to the stumpers. Since the team has already looked through the sites identified in the question review process, a revisit to those sites will be unnecessary. The next place should be the library's Web reference pages. After selecting resources from in-house sources, an excellent way to discover suitable sites is by examining other virtual ready reference collections. This is no different than using WorldCat or Eureka to see what a peer institution has been adding to their print collection. Appendix B has a list of a number of exemplary virtual ready reference collections to consult. Appendix C lists a number of selection aids to consult. The list includes notable subject directories, both popular and academic, online collections of reviews from library science journals, and companion sites to Internet resource monographs, among other tools. This is similar to collection development methods for print reference resources in which a librarian scans the new acquisition lists from comparable libraries, reads reference review columns in journals such as *Choice*, and monitors professional publication catalogs for newly published reference titles. A third good source is to look through the archives of the current awareness services listed in Appendix D. These current awareness services typically deliver periodic alerts of new and notable Web sites via email. Many of them archive these alerts, which are therefore a rich source of reviewed sites. One final source can be books on Internet searching which contain lists of sites. A good selection of these can be found in the annual *Choice Web Supplement*, which lists current and forthcoming titles.[12] Because of the time delay involved in the publishing cycle, online sources tend to be the most up to date. It is imperative that any site discovered in print be checked online to make sure that both the URL and the content are still accurate. (On a practical note, it is much easier to follow links to resources than it is to type in lengthy URLs.)

The team will have to organize the collection process, divvying up areas of responsibility according to subject expertise and inclination. A template should be devised to record the information to be captured about each resource as it is reviewed. At a minimum, this should include the category, title of the site, the URL as a hotlink, a brief annotation about scope, the identity of the reviewer and the date accessed. The annotations might also contain information about special or unique features. For later training exercises, a sample question or questions which the site can answer should be recorded. Sites that do not fit into an established category, but which seem to the reviewer so useful they should be included, can be submitted as miscellaneous. Sites that do not fit the profile for the VRRC, but which might be useful for the broader library Web reference pages should be compiled separately.

The reviews can be complied and distributed in several different fashions, depending on the resources and expertise available. The easiest is to employ an email distribution list. If the library's computing environment allows file sharing, the sites could be entered into a database. If the team includes someone with sufficient HTML skills, the reviews could be posted to an internal Web page. When the collection phase is complete, everyone on the team should review all the sites. The final decision making process is best left to each team to decide.

Local Needs and Local Expertise

The local section is actually the heart of the collection. Ultimately, any good Web-based ready reference collection, from IPL to Refdesk. com, will help you find standard tools like almanacs, dictionaries, or encyclopedias.[13] If you only have time to create or revise one section of your VRRC, this should be it. This is where the team can bring together links to the resources most highly used on a day-to-day basis. For any library, the number one local tool to link to is the OPAC. (Links to licensed databases will be discussed separately.) Some useful starting points include a review of the library Web site for locally oriented content such as maps, directions, hours, departments/branches, policies, services, etc. Bringing this together in one place in the VRRC, rather than having to drill down two or three levels through different categories on the main library Web site, will save a great deal of time. Another important source to scan for local content is the Web site of the larger organization to which the library belongs (school, company, city, county, etc.) and Web sites of relevant community organizations. You may extend the reach of "local resources" as far as the state level, depending on your population.

This section is the place to link directly to individual resources rather than collections or guide sites. To give a simple example, a link directly to the Web site of the local newspaper and the local weather is far better than linking to a comprehensive guide site. Links to special and archival collections should also be put here. Another important category is referrals. If you will be referring to other librarians, branches, or departments, it is worthwhile to create one page with all the pertinent information and link to it from the VRRC. If there are a set of other local libraries to which you commonly refer users, link to a page that has all their OPACs and home pages in one place. If you are going to accept questions from users outside your area with whom you cannot share licensed content, consider linking to a national library directory like Libweb so that you can refer them to their local library, and have information on document delivery services, and links to free content sites like MagPortal and FindArticles.[14] Similarly, you might consider linking to expert Ask-A services, such as AskERIC, using the AskA+ Locator from VRD, if you would normally refer questions beyond your scope or which require specialized resources.[15] You may also want to place seasonal and hot topics links here such as tax information, Black History month, important current events, and the like. One final category would be resources related to the operation of the chat reference service itself. Contact information for the librarians staffing the service, the virtual desk schedule, trouble shooting guides, etc., definitely belong here.

There are also some homegrown resources and strategies that bear replicating in the local section of the VRRC. Unique print finding aids like "tickler files" should be digitized, mounted on a Web page, and linked from the VRRC. One technique is to use the knowledgebase feature available within some chat software programs, which allows you to create entries in a Web-based searchable database. These knowledgebases are usually public so the entries created by librarians are commonly FAQs and answers to FARQs. For the purposes the authors have outlined, the knowledgebase software would need to allow some content to be restricted. Rutgers University Library's "Common Knowledge Database" is a publicly available example of this kind of tool created to support general reference.[16] Another interesting example of this type of resource is Hennepin County's Fugitive Fact File, a searchable treasure trove for trivia and miscellany.[17]

Local expertise can be a valuable source of content for all categories and is no farther away in some cases than staff members of the library who don't happen to be on the VRRC development team. Regardless of job type, individuals may have research interests, passions, or life experiences that have led them to develop knowledge of specialized Web resources. There may be a Web guru in your organization that you don't even know about. Putting out a general call for initial and ongoing suggestions will allow you to tap into the reservoir of knowledge residing within your colleagues.

As far as strategies, it may be helpful for librarians to bear in mind that on well-constructed Web sites, the site map may function like the index at the back of a reference book. Another helpful strategy may be to use the domain limit feature available in Google's Advanced Search (and on some other search engines) to limit a search to a specific Web site. Google often does a better job of returning relevant hits than a site's own "search" feature. Finally, the Edit, Find (on this page) feature within both the Netscape and Internet Explorer browsers is very useful for locating keywords on lengthy pages, similar to the "keyword in context" feature from some commercial databases. The combination of local resources, expertise, and Web-savvy tips can make the local section of the VRRC a powerful tool in delivering quality service on the virtual desk.

CORE LICENSED RESOURCES

Your Mileage May Vary

It is hard to prescribe a core set of licensed databases because most will have to be selected from resources already available to the institutions, which will vary. If you are in a collaborative where all members share all databases, or a single library serving only authenticated users, selection may be straightforward. If licensing requires differing access for different sets of users, selection may be complicated. This is why the authors have focused up until this point on freely available resources. The discussion here will mainly be of categories of resources, and mention specific products only as examples.

If available, database usage statistics will let you know which resources are currently in the highest demand overall and should be included. However, a good reference tool may have low stats because it is not familiar to end users, but should still be included if librarians often use it or if the collection team selects it. The obvious place to start is with the standard tools: almanacs and fact books, biographical sources, dictionaries, directories, encyclopedias, geographical sources, handbooks, statistics, etc. Licensed databases provide more content and more options than their free counterparts. For example, Britannica's free version contains only brief entries. Some sites, like the Thomas Register and CorpTech, provide full access but require registration. Another category will consist of essential tools for which no free Web counterpart exists, or what is available is not nearly as comprehensive. A perfect example of this is directories of associations. The free Web listings are not nearly as all-inclusive as the standard print tools, *Encyclopedia of Associations, International Encyclopedia of Associations*, and *National Trade and Professional Associations*. If this is a question that comes up frequently, it may become clear that access to a licensed equivalent, such as *Associations Unlimited* is necessary. There has been an interesting development in the last few years, wherein commercial vendors have begun offering a single search interface to a suite of reference tools. These include Gale's *ReadyReference Shelf* (14 sources), xrefer.com (+130 sources), *Oxford Reference Online* (+100 sources) and Facts.com (5 interlinked databases). If you have access to one of these federated search tools, it definitely belongs in the VRRC. If not, you can still use the *xrefer Showcase*,[18] which provides free access to 30 of the titles in its collection.

Some data is available on licensed databases which librarians hold in high regard. Kovacs collected data on core ready reference tools in 1999.[19] She repeated this listserv survey and reported the results from nearly 100 responses in November 2002 in postings to LIBREF-L. A "Top Ten" list of resources emerged in response to this question: "What are the top 3-5 CD-ROM, Tape or Online databases that you can't work without?"

1. EbscoHost
2. Gale Databases Group (Literature Resource Center, Gale Ready Reference, Gale General Periodicals, Gale General Reference Center Gold)
3. Reference USA
4. InfoTrac
5. Proquest Databases
6. Lexis-Nexis
7. WorldCat
8. Electric Library and Books in Print
9. Google, First Search Databases and Wilson Select (All three of these databases tied for ninth place.)
10. Amazon.com

Kovacs also reported that the following received at least two votes: Academic Universe, Masterplots, ERIC, MLA International Bibliography Online, Novelist and PsycInfo.[20] Whenever available, licensed reference resources should be incorporated into the VRRC. However, it may be useful to have some sort of indicator or symbol to distinguish the licensed from free resources, particularly if there will be any users with whom the librarian will not be able to share the former.

ORGANIZATION

Function Over Form

With print ready reference collections, whether for better or worse, a classified scheme of organization is almost universal. With the VRRC, the options are limited only by what is possible in HTML. Sowards gives an excellent analysis of the different organizational schemes commonly employed in library ready reference Web sites. In the course of the analysis he remarks on the tension between two opposing Web design objectives, "immediate access to 'hot links' for all URLs [meaning on the top page] and extensive resource content."[21] Many librarians will recall pages from the early days of the Web that contained excruciatingly long undifferentiated lists of links. At the other extreme are sites with link hierarchies that require clicking down five or six levels before reaching any actual content.

Unlike the library's public Web pages, which have to "look good" visually, the behind the scenes page can be designed with maximum utility as the overriding principle. The design of the VRRC should be purely functional. It should be built for speed of access because its purpose is to allow staff to quickly navigate to frequently used resources. The authors believe that utility dictates the following structure, which employs a two level hierarchy housed on a single page.

- The VRRC page should start with an index of no more than ten topics, organized by the alphabetical ordering of the category labels. (This follows the rule of thumb developed by one of the founders of the IPL Reference Center that "browsing hierarchies work best when there are no more than ten topics.")[22]
- The index section should fit within a single screen (above the fold). No vertical or horizontal scrolling should be necessary.
- The index text should link to identically labeled section headings on the same page. Each section should provide a link back to the top.

- The links for every individual resource should be listed under the appropriate category heading on the same page. This will eliminate the time involved in waiting for another page to load. This will also result in no more than two clicks being necessary to access a resource. Each category should list an absolute maximum of ten items but two or three are the recommended number. Each individual resource link should cause the resource to open in a separate window. (Use the HTML TARGET attribute with the BASE tag in the Head section.) This will help prevent accidental closure or loss of the VRRC.
- The text of links and category section headings should be clearly descriptive of the nature of the resource. If the official title of the resource Web page is unclear, an original description should be created to serve as the link text.
- Links should not need annotation. Familiarity with the resources should be developed during training.
- Links should connect to the most useful page of the resource, regardless of its level within the target site's hierarchy, whenever possible. Links to databases should connect directly to the search screen whenever possible.
- The VRRC should include a feedback mechanism. This can be as simple as an email link or a form.
- The VRRC page should display the date it was last updated.

The organizational scheme of the index is yet another decision that will have to be made on an individual basis. Depending on your setting, organization by format (almanac, dictionary, encyclopedia), organization by subject, or a combination may be most useful. What is important is to be consistent and logical. Whether you take the format approach or the subject approach, it is crucial to organize the links within each category in the same fashion. For example, for all formats, put general works first, then subjects organized alphabetically. As the collection of sites proceeds, sites should be assigned to the established categories, but the team may decide to adjust, redefine or add categories in response to what is found.

THE CHALLENGE OF COLLABORATIVES

Collaborative digital reference, where a single digital reference "desk" serves the users of multiple institutions, presents a challenge in designing an effective VRRC. For collaboratives that include different types of libraries, libraries in different locations, or the subject specialized departments of a larger entity, it may be beneficial to agree to share a core collection and develop unique pages from that base point. Naturally, the scope of "local" information that needs to be available to effectively serve users is greatly multiplied.

To see this in action, the authors requested access to the Web pages for two multi-institution collaboratives.[23] The first collaborative was 24/7 Reference, a round-the-clock virtual reference service staffed by over 50 multi-type libraries. 24/7 Reference has organized numerous resources from a behind-the-scenes page called the Reference Manual. The Ready Reference Collection, and the 24/7 Library Policies are the two the authors chose to focus on.

The 24/7 Ready Reference collection consists of a top page with 18 category links organized alphabetically. Categories may include more than one topic, for instance the People category has 7 sub-categories. Each category link spawns a separate page that consists of annotated links to individual resources grouped by sub-category. The individual resources open in the same window. The categories include tools by format (Almanacs, Encyclopedias and Fact Files), by subject (Genealogy, People), other VRRCs (Reference Links) and other digital reference services (Experts/Research Guides). Given the large number of public libraries in 24/7, it is not surprising to find categories like Homework Help and Genealogy.

The Library Policy Manual page has the following statement at the top, which clearly explains its purpose:

> As more libraries add 24/7 service, their basic policies will be listed here so that you will have fast access to basic questions about location, telephone, placing holds, interlibrary loan, and any other policy issues you may need when you are monitoring these libraries. Please feel free to make suggestions or request specific information, or to let us know if you come across a policy issue that may impact us all.

There are two pull down menus for each collaborative. The first provides access to each member library's policy profile page and the second takes you directly to each member's OPAC. The profile contains information organized into the following categories and linked where appropriate:

- Home page
- Web Catalog
- Reference Email Contact
- Databases (proxy server)
- Phone
- Location
- Hours
- Library Cards (includes all borrowing privileges and ILL)
- Loan Limits
- Renewals
- Holds
- Late Fees
- Interlibrary Loan
- Course Reserves
- Obituaries/Local History
- Other Policies

Using the Policy Manual and the Ready Reference collection, 24/7 librarians are able to quickly navigate to the information and resources necessary to answer questions for users from any library in the collaborative service. This is similar to the features found on the Librarian Resources page of our other example, the Virtual Information Desk (VID). The VID serves the users in fourteen Pennsylvania State System of Higher Education Libraries that make up the Keystone Library Network as well as the state employees registered with the State Library of Pennsylvania on evenings and weekends. All fifteen libraries in the network use the same Patron Authentication System (PASs) to verify user access and status. The screens developed for use by the VID reflect the collaboration tools needed to answer questions when the chat reference librarian is not from the same school that the user attends. Since the questions posted come from a pool of more than 100,000 people, a matrix makes it possible for the chat reference librarians to navigate available sources by school.

The Partner Resources page organizes the links in table form. The top row consists of links called School Lib Portal, Citation Styles, Librarians' Index, Access PA and SSHE Barcodes. The School Lib Portal actually links to the home page for Mansfield's School Library Program, and from there through the Mansfield Library home page to a Reference Resources page that will be covered later. Citation Styles is self-explanatory, Librarians' Index links to the subject directory Librarians' Index to the Internet, and the Access PA and Barcode links allow access to shared electronic resources. The rest of the table consists of an alphabetical list of Universities in the first column, and links to the home page, database page, catalog, reference page and Interlibrary loan page for each school.

It is interesting that the VID uses an external source, the Librarians' Index to the Internet, as its shared VRRC. It is possible to access a local resource, the Mansfield Reference Resources, but this is four clicks away from the Partner Resources page. The Reference Resources page consists of 23 top-level categories arranged alphabetically. Each category link causes a page containing annotated links to individual resources, organized alphabetically, to open in the same window. There are some links to local resources within certain categories. For example, the weather page displays a local weather report for Mansfield from the Weather Channel and a search box where you can enter city or U.S. zip code to get a different forecast. The News page has a Local Online News section with links to three local newspapers, while the Jobs & Employment page has a Pennsylvania section. The format categories (encyclopedia, dictionary, etc.) mix links to free and licensed content. Each collaborative will have to decide what works best based on its members and their user populations, but hopefully, this look at the practices of 24/7 and the VID will help others in choosing what to include and how to organize it.

TRAINING

Familiarity Breeds Success

Building the VRRC is not enough. By involving the chat reference librarians in developing the VRRC, important groundwork has been laid. Since everyone on the team will have contributed some unique content, all librarians will not be equally familiar with all sites, especially subject specific sites. Even on familiar sites there may be sections or advanced features that have not been noticed in the process of answering questions on the fly, or changes since the last visit. As staff is being trained on the virtual reference software, there is an opportunity to build familiarity with the VRRC.

Once the VRRC site is "up" and available for use, all chat librarians should be given time to familiarize themselves with the resources. When visiting the individual resources, just as with print tools, it is important to read any scope notes, often contained in the "About" section.

It is also important to take the time to examine the organizational scheme of the links from the top or home page of each resource, which function as the table of contents, examine the site map or index, which may function as an index, and note if the site has an internal search feature. What will increase familiarity even further is a set of guided searching exercises. Sauers presents sample question sets[24] that cover the standard tools (encyclopedia, dictionaries, etc.) as well as subject specific sites. An even better approach is the use of training questions each librarian on the team was directed to develop as they were selecting sites. After working through the questions individually, the team should come together to share their experiences and strategies. "Search Strategy" sessions should be held on an ongoing basis. Ronan suggests, "Plan to organize periodic in-service sessions to review resources useful for answering commonly asked questions within each discipline."[25] New resources can be introduced and changes to existing ones can be discussed to the benefit of all. These sessions will be even more beneficial if they cover topics like effective reference interview techniques for chat, software issues, and any ongoing concerns.

MAINTENANCE AND EVALUATION

Maintenance

Maintenance and evaluation are the remaining factors to consider once the Web sites have been selected to support the chat reference service. Not only do the Web sites need to be monitored for currency, but it is also important that the chat reference librarians be made aware of any changes in content or usefulness. While the reference librarian only needs to view a shelf to determine if a print ready reference tool is available to answer a question, this is not the case when the VRRC site is scanned. The desired chat reference tool will appear as it has been locally listed and annotated for the VRRC until it is changed locally; this even though the referring site has altered in content or location. Although maintenance might seem like something that can be performed as time allows, it is not. Unless ongoing attention is paid to the maintenance of the VRRC, link rot or broken links will destroy the usefulness of the work done to create the site and the confidence the chat librarians have of its value.

Monitoring for Currency

Broken links are caused by a variety of reasons and are anticipated by anyone creating a Web site. A more colloquial term for this is "link rot," which is defined by *The Jargon Dictionary*, as "the natural decay of Web links as the sites they're connected to change or die."[26] To quote Fichter on link rot "As Web sites evolve, documents, images, and objects move causing their hyperlinks to break. A click on one of these broken links results in the dreaded '404 not found' message."[27] Since it can be expected that broken links will occur, it is obvious that a plan should be in place to counteract the situation before it becomes a problem during the provision of chat reference service. This is especially important given the results of a study done by Markwell and Brooks. The study reports that 16.5% of the 515 Web sites monitored between August 2000 and September 2001 changed over that period of time.[28] The ".edu" domain contained the greatest number of links Markwell and Brooks reported had disappeared or significantly changed over the course of the study.[29]

Thus, given the nature of the Web, the review of sites for the Virtual Ready Reference Collection cannot end at the point of selection. Consistent evaluation is the best way to ensure usefulness of the VRRC over time. There are any number of free Web site maintenance tools that include automatic link checking, however, these can't tell if the content of the site has changed or has been reorganized. The chat librarians are the best "link checkers." This effort need not be the responsibility of one person, but should instead be the shared responsibility of all those involved in providing chat reference service. Current awareness of the changing Web environment should be included in the job description for all reference librarians. Therefore, it is clear that a more focused expectation is made of those on the chat reference team. A good method to accomplish an ongoing review of the direct reference sites is to divide the VRRC into subject areas. Once divided, the chat reference team members are able to choose subject areas by interest, integrating the maintenance of the site into other aspects of their job duties.

The task of monitoring changes in selected Web sites becomes much less daunting as a planned and shared activity designed to reinforce the skills needed in the chat reference interview. In this manner, the chat reference librarians and the VRRC remain robust and maintain vitality as the chat reference service moves from a fledgling operation to one of seasoned age. Responsibilities for the maintenance activity extend beyond monitoring broken links on direct reference sites to include:

- Checking the Web sites for additions in or loss of coverage
- Documenting unique features
- Evaluating the existing site against newly discovered sites of similar content
- Communicating changes to other members of the chat reference team
- Editing the VRRC to incorporate revisions as soon as problems are discovered.

Immediate communication is the most critical component of these steps for several reasons. If the first person to encounter a problem shares that information, it saves time and confusion for all the other chat librarians who might need to use that resource.

There are several methods that could be employed to communicate this information. The solution selected for each individual library will be best determined by the skills possessed by the chat reference team or by the library technical support staff. One example, a relatively new Web tool, the weblog or blog, is quite suitable for this purpose.

> A weblog . . . is a Web site of personal or non-commercial origin that uses a dated log format that is updated on a daily or very frequent basis with new information about a particular subject or range of subjects. The information can be written by the site owner, gleaned from other Web sites or other sources, or contributed by users.[30]

There are several sites that will host weblogs for free but allow you to restrict access by requiring a user name and password. "Blog sites make it possible for users without much experience to create, format, and post entries with ease."[31] The reason to use a weblog rather than an email distribution list is because content from a weblog can be archived for future use. The content won't be lost if inadvertently deleted and is accessible from any computer that connects to the Web. The weblog can serve multiple functions. System announcements, trouble reports, schedule changes, and class assignment with recommended sources for answers, are just a few examples. It can also be used as a virtual new resource shelf. Librarians can post new resources with comments for review.

Using an informal method to indicate a problem exists allows the chat reference librarian to send off a message "on the fly" without worry that the information will be criticized for content. (It is always possible to go back and investigate the situation more thoroughly at a later date.) Whether you use a weblog, listserv, or email distribution list, it is essential to bring all members of the chat reference team "into the loop" as quickly as possible. This communication forum should include those who provide technical support for the service, those managers who need to be aware of problems in library public service as well as all chat reference practitioners.

Evaluation

For the purpose of evaluation, it would be helpful to know how much use is being made of each resource linked from the VRRC. At first glance, it might seem impossible since the links to the resources will be on a single page and Web traffic analysis software like *WebTrends* only counts page views, not links within pages, and only page views of sites within your domain. However, there is a way to register usage that can be analyzed by such software. It involves creating an "invisible redirect screen." When the individual resource link is clicked, a blank redirect page will display for one second, which then automatically links to the resource's URL. This happens so quickly the user won't even be aware of it. You can then get reports of how many page views there were for the redirect page, and by extension, of its associated resource. A sample of the code for an invisible redirect page for Encyclopedia Britannica appears below:

```
<HTML>
<HEAD><head><META HTTP-EQUIV="Refresh" CONTENT="1;
URL=http://www.eb.com:180/">
<TITLE>Britannica Online Connect Page</TITLE>
</HEAD>
<BODY></BODY>
</HTML>
```

Another method to track usage is by checking the transcripts of chat interactions. Many chat reference software packages produce a record of the text of the reference interaction as well as the URL of any sites visited in the course of the session. By reviewing these transcripts, it is possible to compile statistics on how often individual VRRC sites are being utilized. Whether you have access to a commercial or a free Web site analysis product, or will be reviewing transcripts, usage evaluation is an important collection review mechanism and should be conducted on a regular basis.

CONCLUSION

This article has discussed the need for a distinct Virtual Ready Reference Collection to use in the provision of chat reference services. It has been maintained that the VRRC is more specific to the particular needs of chat reference and, as such, increases the ability of the chat reference librarian to provide a higher level of service in an expedient fashion. The nature of the chat reference encounter requires direct access to a group of elite, never-fail read reference tools that have been identified through previous success with the library's user population. The existing collections of general reference Web sites such as the Internet Public Library are useful starting points in creating a VRRC but they do not address specific, local needs.

The authors believe that there is as much value in the process of creating a VRRC as there is in the use of the final product. The process of choosing the *best* Web sites for a VRRC will enhance the chat reference librarian's knowledge of selected sites as well as increase their ease in using these sites to respond to chat reference questions. This effort seems logical and enhances each librarian's professional development. The effect is continued if the chat reference librarians share the responsibility for maintenance of the VRRC.

Obviously the VRRC will be available for use by librarians who provide reference service in other settings such as face-to-face, telephone, etc. It will therefore also help to ensure a consistent level of service in a modern, distributed, geographically dispersed reference environment. A polished, easy to use Virtual Ready Reference Collection can be achieved if the chat reference librarians follow the steps suggested in this article, take time to analyze the suggested information, and review the known user needs.

NOTES

NB. All Web sites accessed October 28, 2003. Appendices B, C, and D are available online at http://www.seas.upenn.edu/~danianne/appendices.htm.

1. Heartsill Young, *The ALA Glossary of Library and Information Science* (Chicago: ALA, 1983), 186.

2. William A. Katz, *Introduction to Reference Work: Basic Information Services, Vol. 1*. Eighth ed. (Boston: McGraw-Hill, 2002), 278.

3. Anne Lipow, *The Virtual Reference Librarian's Handbook* (N.Y.: Neal-Schuman, 2003), xx.

4. Diane K. Kovacs, "Building a Core Internet Reference Collection," *RUSQ* 39, no. 3 (Spring 2000): 234-5; Louis A. Pitschmann, *Building Sustainable Collections of Free Third-Party Web Resources* (Washington, D.C.: Digital Library Federation, 2001), 10-12.

5. Library of Congress, *BEOnline+ Selection Criteria.* Available: <http://lcweb. loc.gov/rr/business/beonline/beonsel.html>.

6. Lipow, 53.

7. Michael Sauers, *Using the Internet as a Reference Tool: a How To-Do-It Manual for Librarians* (N.Y.: Neal-Schuman, 2001), 52.

8. Jana Ronan and Carol Turner, *SPEC Kit 273, Chat Reference* (Washington, D.C: ARL, 2002), 12.

9. Pitschmann, 7-22; Linda C. Smith and Sarai Lastra, "Ready Reference on the Internet," in *Proceedings of the 21st National Online Meeting* (Medford, N.J.: Information Today, 2000), 400; Alison Cooke, *A Guide to Finding Quality Information on the Internet* (London: Library Association, 1999), 52-84, 93-98, 128-134; Sauers, 11-27.

10. Steven W. Sowards, "A Typology for Ready Reference Web Sites in Libraries," *first monday.* Available: <http://firstmonday.org/issues/issue3_5/sowards/index.html>.

11. GPO Access, *Core Documents of U.S. Democracy* Available: < http://www.access. gpo.gov/su_docs/locators/coredocs/index.html>; Bartleby.com, *Reference.* Available: <http://www.bartleby.com/reference/>; AddALL, *Used and Out of Print Search.* Available: <http://used.addall.com/>.

12. "Internet Books," *Choice Web VI* 39 Special Issue (2002): 19-25.

13. Internet Public Library, *Internet Public Library.* Available: <http://www.ipl. org/>; Bob Drudge, *Refdesk.com.* Available: <http://www.refdesk.com/>.

14. Thomas Dowling, *Libweb.* Available: <http://sunsite.berkeley.edu/Libweb/>; Instant Information Systems, *DocDel.net.* Available: <http://www.docdel.net/index. html>; Hot Neuron LLC, *MagPortal.* Available: <http://www.magportal.com/>; LookSmart and Gale Group, *FindArticles.* Available: <http://www.findarticles.com/ PI/index.jhtml>.

15. Virtual Reference Desk, *AskA+ Locator.* Available: <http://www.vrd.org/ locator/>.

16. New Brunswick Information Services Group, *Common Knowledge Database.* Available: <http://ckdb.rutgers.edu/>.

17. Hennepin County Library, *Fugitive Fact File.* Available: <http://www.hclib. org/pub/search/fff_public.cfm>.

18. xrefer, *xrefer Showcase.* Available: <http://www.xrefer.com/search.jsp>.

19. Diane Kovacs, *Building Electronic Library Collections* (N.Y.: Neal-Schuman, 2000): 39.

20. Diane Kovacs, "Results: 'Core' or 'Critical' Online or CD Database for Ready Reference," 10 Nov. 2002, <LIBREF-L@LISTSERV.KENT.EDU>; Diane Kovacs, "Addition to Results: 'Core' or 'Critical' Online or CD Databases for Ready Reference," 10 Nov 2002, <LIBREF-L@LISTSERV.KENT.EDU>.

21. Sowards.

22. David S. Carter et al., *The Internet Public Library Handbook*, (N.Y.: Neal-Schuman, 1999): 46-7.

23. Because these sites are password protected, the authors have not supplied citations for this section.

24. Sauers, Chapters 3 and 5 passim.

25. Ronan, 28.

26. *Jargon Dictionary*, Available: <http://info.astrian.net/jargon/terms/l/link_rot.html>.

27. Darlene Fichter, "Do I Look Like a Maid? Strategies for Preventing Link Rot," *Online* 23, no.5 (September/October 1999): 77.

28. John Markwell and David W. Brooks, "Broken Links: The Ephemeral Nature of Educational WWW Hyperlinks," *Journal of Science Education and Technology*, 11, no. 2 (June 2002): 106.

29. Markwell, 107.

30. *searchWebServices.com Definitions*. Available: <http://searchwebservices.techtarget.com/sDefinition/0,,sid26_gci213547,00.html>.

31. *Wikipedia*, Available: <http://www.wikipedia.org/wiki/Web_log>.

APPENDIX A

Email and Chat Question Logs & Question Set Analyses

Print

Diamond, Wendy and Barbara Pease, "Digital Reference: A Case Study of Question Types in an Academic Library," *Reference Services Review* 29, no. 3 (2001): 213-215.

Ford, Charlotte, "Questions Asked in Face-to-Face, Chat, & E-mail Reference Interactions" (paper presented at the ALA Annual Conference, Atlanta, June 2002). Available: <http://www.ala.org/Content/NavigationMenu/RUSA/Our_Association2/RUSA_Sections/MOUSS/Our_Section4/Committees10/Research_and_Statistics2/userQs.ppt>.

Garnsey, Beth A. and Ronald R. Powell, "Electronic Mail Reference Services in the Public Library," *RUSQ* 39, no. 3 (Spring 2000): 250.

Hodges, Ruth, "Assessing Digital Reference," *Libri* 52, no. 3 (Sept. 2002): 163-66.

Kibbee, Jo, David Ward, and Wei Ma, "Virtual Service, Real Data: Results of a Pilot Study," *Reference Services Review* 30, no. 1 (2002): 33.

Marsteller, Matthew and Paul Neuhaus, "The Chat Reference Service Experience at Carnegie Mellon University" (poster session presented at the ALA Annual Conference, San Francisco, June 2001). Available: <http://www.contrib.andrew.cmu.edu/~matthewm/ALA_2001_chat.html>.

Powell, Carol A. and Pamela S. Bradigan, "E-Mail Reference Services," *RUSQ* 41, no. 2 (Winter 2001): 173-175.

Sears, JoAnn, "Chat Reference Service: An Analysis of One Semester's Data," *Issues in Science and Technology Librarianship* 32 (Fall 2001). Available: <http://www.istl.org/istl/01-fall/article2.html>.

Sloan, Bernie, "Reference Service in the Digital Library," *Library Hi Tech News* 18, no.10 (December 2001): 15-19.

Electronic–All sites available as of March 23, 2003.

Sloan, Bernie, *Digital Reference Question Logs* [Web site]. Available: <http://www.lis.uiuc.edu/~b-sloan/log.htm>.

Washington State Library Statewide Virtual Reference Project, Focus Group Results. Available: <http://wlo.statelib.wa.gov/services/vrs/textdocs/VRSFocusGroup.htm>.

APPENDIX B

EXEMPLARY VIRTUAL READY REFERENCE GUIDE SITES
A list of the top VRRC available to the public.

Chicago Public Library Reference Shelf
<http://cpl.lib.uic.edu/008subject/005genref/readyref.html>

DeskRef 500: Best Sources for Quick Answers
<http://ansernet.rcls.org/deskref>

Internet Public Library Ready Reference
<http://www.ipl.org/div/subject/browse/ref00.00.00>

iTools (formerly ResearchIt!)
<http://www.itools.com/>

Librarians' Index to the Internet
<http://lii.org>

Library of Congress Virtual Reference Shelf
<http://www.loc.gov/rr/askalib/virtualref.html>

MEDLINEplus
<http://medlineplus.gov/>

MIT Virtual Reference Collection
<http://libraries.mit.edu/research/virtualref.html>

New York Public Library Reference
<http://www2.nypl.org/home/branch/links/index.cfm?Trg=1&d1=12&d3=
Reference>

Nolo Law Center
<http://www.nolo.com/lawcenter/>

Purdue University Virtual Reference Desk
<http://www.lib.purdue.edu/eresources/readyref/>

Refdesk.com
<http://www.refdesk.com/>

UIUC Digital Reference Collection
<http://www.library.uiuc.edu/rex/erefs>

University at Albany Reference Collection
<http://library.albany.edu/reference/>

UT Library Online Quick Reference
<http://www.lib.utexas.edu/Libs/PCL/Reference.html>

APPENDIX C

SELECTION AIDS

About.com
<http://www.about.com>
Each topic area has an assigned "Guide."

Academic Info
<http://www.academicinfo.net/index.html>
"A Gateway to Quality Educational Resources browsable by subject or searchable by keyword."

Best Information on the Net
<http://library.sau.edu/bestinfo/>
Resources by major hot topics. See compilation of tools listed under Resources for librarians.

Booklist Archive
<http://www.ala.org/booklist/archive.html>
Each volume has a Reference Materials section that contains a subsection entitled "Reference on the Web."

BUBL LINK/5:15
<http://bubl.ac.uk/link/five/>
"Selected Internet resources covering all academic subject areas."

Britannica Websites
<http://www.britannica.com/>
Select Websites from the Search pull-down menu.

C&RL News Internet Resources
<http://www.ala.org/acrl/resrces.html>
An archive of reviews published since February 1994. Browse or keyword search.

C&RL News Internet Reviews Archive
<http://www.bowdoin.edu/~samato/IRA/>
An archive of reviews published since February 1994. Browse or keyword search.

Choice Annual Web Review Supplement
<http://www.ala.org/acrl/choice/other.html>
"A compilation of critical evaluations of research-related web sites selected from previous issues."

Complete Planet
<http://www.completeplanet.com>

Desk Set: Ready Reference on the Web
<http://archive.ala.org/acrl/choice/sampess.html>
Companion site to essay by Beth Juhl published in Choice's annual web supplement.

Digital Librarian
<http://www.digital-librarian.com/>
"Maintained by Margaret Vail Anderson. Digital Librarian: a librarian's choice of the best of the Web."

Forbes Best of the Web Directory
<http://www.forbes.com/bow/b2c/main.jhtml>
Reviews from 1999 of "useful sites for everything from asset allocation to job hunting to pursuing a passion like woodworking. Over 3,500 sites reviewed here from 1999 to date."

Invisible Web Directory
<http://www.invisible-web.net/>
Companion site to *The Invisible Web*: by Chris Sherman and Gary Price. Searchable directory of resources that are not visible to general-purpose search engines.

Library Journal WebWatch
<http://libraryjournal.reviewsnews.com>
Use link to WebWatch under "Sections" to access this review column.

MARS Best Free Reference Web Sites
<http://www.ala.org/MARSTemplate.cfm?Section=Publications13>
"Annual series initiated under the auspices of the Machine-Assisted Reference Section (MARS) of the Reference and User Services Association (RUSA) of ALA to recognize outstanding reference sites on the World Wide Web."

MERLOT (Multimedia Educational Resource for Learning and On-Line Teaching)
<http://www.merlot.org/>
"A free and open resource designed primarily for faculty and students of higher education. Links to online learning materials are collected here along with annotations such as peer reviews and assignments."

PC Magazine Top 200 Web Sites
<http://www.pcmag.com/article2/0,4149,912123,00.asp>
From the March 25, 2003 publication of PC Magazine, this includes their "perennial favorites, the Top 100 Classics with the addition of 100 sites you might not have heard of . . . "

Pinakes
<http://www.hw.ac.uk/libWWW/irn/pinakes/pinakes.html>
Pinakes links to major subject gateways.

Resource Discovery Network (RDN)
<http://www.rdn.ac.uk/>
"RDN gathers resources which are carefully selected, indexed and described by specialists in our [60+] partner institutions."

The ResourceShelf
<http://resourceshelf.blogspot.com/>
"Resources and News for Information Professionals."

The Scout Report Archives
<http://scout.wisc.edu/archives/>
"Archives over seven years of critical annotations of carefully selected Internet sites and mailing lists."

Search Engine Showdown
<http://www.searchengineshowdown.com/>
Compares and reviews performance of the major Internet search engines.

Search Engine Watch
<http://searchenginewatch.com/>
Sponsored by Overture, this site also offers access to two newsletters, SearchDay and Search Engine Report.

Toolkit for the Expert Web Searcher (LITA)
<http://www.lita.org/committe/toptech/toolkit.htm>
"Maintained by Pat Ensor, this list is a reflection of what she uses to work in an academic library."

Using the Internet as a Reference Tool
<http://www.neal-schuman.com/sauers/>
Companion site to the book.

WWW Virtual Library
<http://vlib.org/>
"The oldest catalog of the web, started by Tim Berners-Lee, now run by a loose confederation of volunteers, who compile pages of key links for particular areas in which they are expert."

APPENDIX D

CURRENT AWARENESS

Academic Info–What's New
<http://www.academicinfo.net/new.html>
Receive a monthly announcement list.

BUBL Link Updates
<http://bubl.ac.uk/link/updates/index.html>
Documents recent additions to the Catalogue of Internet Resources.

Free Pint
<http://www.freepint.com/>
"Free Pint is an email newsletter published twice a month with tips on using the Internet for serious research."

INFOMINE: Scholarly Internet Resource Collections
<http://infomine.ucr.edu/cgi-bin/alert_service_editor>
"Sends email notifications as new resources are added to INFOMINE."

The Internet Resources Newsletter
<http://www.hw.ac.uk/libWWW/irn/irn.html>
"A free, monthly newsletter for academics, students, engineers, scientists and social scientists."

Internet Tourbus
<http://www.tourbus.com/tickets.htm>
"TOURBUS is a free email newsletter published twice a week, and read by about 100,000 people in 130 countries around the globe."

Librarians Index to the Internet: lii.org New This Week Mailing List
<http://lii.org/search/file/mailinglist>
A current awareness service of "up to thirty selections added each week."

Neat New Stuff I Found This Week
<http://marylaine.com/neatnew.html>
" . . . contains free sites of substantial reference value, authoritative, browsable, searchable, and packed with information, whether educational or aimed at answering everyday questions."

On the Net
<http://www.notess.com/write/onthenet.shtml>
A monthly column by Greg Notess appearing in *Online* which "features information resources and tools available on the Internet and the World Wide Web, specifically ones of interest to information professionals."

The Pandia Search World Newsletter and The Pandia Post
<http://www.pandia.com/post/index.html>
The first is a weekly search engine news service and the second is a bi-monthly newsletter. Both free newsletters discuss Internet searching, search engines and directories.

Refdesk.com
<http://www.refdesk.com/subscrib.html>
Subscribe to REFDESK for Dailies Link of the Day.

ResearchBuzz
<http://www.researchbuzz.com/>
"Designed to cover the world of Internet research. To that end this site provides almost daily updates on search engines, new data managing software, browser technology, large compendiums of information, Web directories."

The ResourceShelf
<http://resourceshelf.freepint.com/>
"Resources and News for Information Professionals."

The Scout Report
<http://scout.wisc.edu/>
A weekly publication designed to provide "a fast, convenient way to stay informed of valuable resources on the Internet."

SearchDay

<http://searchenginewatch.com/searchday/index.html>
This is a "free newsletter from Search Engine Watch that features Web search news, reviews, tools, tips, and search engine headlines from across the Web."

Search Engine Report

<http://searchenginewatch.com/sereport/index.html>
The Search Engine Report is a free, monthly newsletter about search engines.

Steven Bell's Keeping Up Web Page

<http://staff.philau.edu/bells/keepup/>
"Designed to help library and information science professionals develop and maintain a program of self-guided professional development."

Today's Paper Slate Daily

<http://slate.msn.com/id/76816/>
"A summary of the lead stories in the country's top five newspapers."

This Week's Useful URLs

<http://www.bccls.org/reference/useful-urls.shtml>
Also look at the Internet Reference Sources listing and use the searchable "Useful URLs" database found at <http://www.bccls.org/reference/useful-urls.shtml>.

Yahoo! What's New

<http://dir.yahoo.com/new/>
A list that enumerates newly available Web sites by subject.

A Checklist for Starting and Operating a Digital Reference Desk

Ann Marie Breznay
Leslie M. Haas

SUMMARY. This article explores digital reference and offers practical advice to those interested in implementing a digital reference desk in their library. Digital/chat/online reference services are defined and practical guidelines on staffing, selecting and troubleshooting hardware and software, training, and marketing are offered for those establishing such a service. *[Article copies available for a fee from The Haworth Document Delivery Service: 1-800-HAWORTH. E-mail address: <docdelivery@haworthpress. com> Website: <http://www.HaworthPress.com> © 2002/2003 by The Haworth Press, Inc. All rights reserved.]*

KEYWORDS. Online reference, chat reference, digital reference, practical tips, guidelines

---

Ann Marie Breznay (E-mail: AnnMarie.Breznay@library.utah.edu) is Electronic Resources Coordinator, and Leslie M. Haas (E-mail: Leslie.Haas@library.utah.edu) is Head, General Reference Department, both at the Marriott Library, University of Utah, 295 South 1300 East, Salt Lake City, UT 84112.

[Haworth co-indexing entry note]: "A Checklist for Starting and Operating a Digital Reference Desk." Breznay, Ann Marie, and Leslie M. Haas. Co-published simultaneously in *The Reference Librarian* (The Haworth Information Press, an imprint of The Haworth Press, Inc.) No. 79/80, 2002/2003, pp. 101-112; and: *Digital Reference Services* (ed: Bill Katz) The Haworth Information Press, an imprint of The Haworth Press, Inc., 2002/2003, pp. 101-112. Single or multiple copies of this article are available for a fee from The Haworth Document Delivery Service [1-800-HAWORTH, 9:00 a.m. - 5:00 p.m. (EST). E-mail address: docdelivery@ haworthpress.com].

http://www.haworthpress.com/store/product.asp?sku=J120
10.1300/J120v38n79_07

Reference librarians who are not in denial know that doing business as usual isn't working the way it used to.

–Serving the Remote User:
Reference Service in the Digital Environment
Anne G. Lipow from Strategies for the Next Millennium Proceedings
of the Ninth Australasian Information Online & On Disc Conference
and Exhibition, Sydney Convention and Exhibition Centre,
Sydney, Australia 19-21 January 1999

INTRODUCTION

Digital. Chat. Online reference. All phrases that have become more prevalent in librarianship in recent years. What is digital reference? How is it different from e-mail reference or virtual reference? Why are all these articles being written about it and is it something I want to do at my library? The purpose of this article is to explore digital reference and offer practical advice to those interested in operating a digital reference desk in their library.

DEFINING DIGITAL REFERENCE

For the purposes of this article, digital reference refers to the act of providing reference service via the web in real-time. Screen sharing, co-browsing, queuing patrons, canned answers and tracking software are features available in many of the software packages in today's market. While this method of delivering reference service is new to libraries, the format is very familiar to those who have been on the web for several years. Chatting or instant messaging are services that are provided by most Internet Service Providers. Text messaging is even available to those who have a cell phone. Digital reference is similar, extending the technology used in chatting with friends to the reference transaction, as a way of reaching users who are using library resources remotely. They may not be able to come to the reference desk to ask a question, but they often want a quicker response than one they might get via e-mail.

WHY DIGITAL REFERENCE?

Users have embraced the web and routinely turn to the Internet to find answers to their questions. Libraries have responded by placing databases, tutorials, catalogs and other tools on the web as a way to keep current resources available to users for their research needs. Libraries have FAQs, tutorials and pages where users can submit their questions via e-mail. While these services satisfy many user questions, none of them can provide immediate assistance at point of need.

With more tools available on the web, users are responding by accessing the library from their homes, offices, labs or other places besides the physical library. Librarians have created a structure for doing good research without having to come to the library. However, finding effective ways to reach remote users has been more difficult. Users expect immediacy and want to be able to get assistance at point of need, regardless of location. Moreover, many students have essentially grown up with instant messaging systems and are comfortable and facile with quick Internet communication.

Digital Reference is one of the solutions to raised user expectations. It makes assistance available to the users at point of need in an easy and convenient manner. Librarians are available when users have questions. Users don't have to leave their computer to get the help they need, regardless their location or time of day. Also, in a step beyond what can be done in a simple e-mail or phone call, many of the digital reference services allow the librarian to co-browse (your computers are in sync and you can take them to specific web sites); enabling the librarian to show the user how to search a database and not just describe it to them or point them to it.

Digital reference is also a boon to distance education students. More and more students are taking advantage of online or distance classes. Many times they are located hours away from the institution making it difficult to get to the library to use the collection. Digital reference programs give these students access to services usually available only to students who are able to come to the library.

LITERATURE REVIEW

The topic of digital reference services is very popular right now and there have been several articles written in various library journals. In the February 2003 issue of *D-Lib Magazine*, the entire issue is devoted to digital reference. This magazine is available online and the address is available in the bibliography at the end of this article.

THE TEAM

Setting up a digital reference services takes time and research. A successful launch requires a person or people to fill three critical roles:

1. *Manager/Coordinator:* There needs to be at least one person to shepherd the project from start to finish. They will be the cheerleader, scheduler, troubleshooter, and salesperson. In some libraries, depending on the size, this may end up being a small group, but this person(s) is important since they need to sell the service to the staff and patrons.
2. *Technical support:* The team should include someone who has technical skills and can help set up the service. They need to have rights and privileges (if necessary) to the library's server in order to get the program running properly. They are also essential in case there are technical difficulties requiring contact with the vendor's technical support staff.
3. *Web support:* Another important team member is the web person. Placing the links in the proper places, making sure that they work and designing the web pages and icons to make the project visible and successful is critical.

GETTING STAFF ON BOARD

Usually the initiative for a digital reference service comes from one person or a small group of enthusiastic staff. In order for the new service to get launched and continue as a viable service, there are two groups within the library that have to be sold on the idea: library administration and public services staff.

New services cost money and starting one means there will be both initial costs and ongoing costs that should be mapped out when talking to administration. Costs will vary depending on the program that the library decides to purchase (or subscribe to). Even when programs are available for free, there will be costs associated in staff time to load onto the library's server, training staff, publicity, etc. Other programs have one time set up costs in addition to ongoing monthly fees and these will vary depending on the number of seats you want. (A seat typically refers to the number of librarians who are online at a specific time to answer questions.)

In addition to the program costs other costs to keep in mind include:

- The cost of any necessary upgrades for the computers of those who will be offering the service.
- Money for publicity and marketing. It is not enough to place the service on the library's web page and hope users will find it. Marketing costs money, and while a press release in the local newspaper or library newsletter may help reach some users, the library will need to explore ways to let everyone know about this new service.

One way to keep these costs under control would be to join a consortium. There are several consortia of varying sizes and types around the country. If your library decides to pursue a consortium related program, be aware that most of these consortia choose specific digital reference programs which your library would be required to use in order to participate. There are advantages in joining a larger network of libraries: sharing costs, having more staff available to work during the hours the service is offered, making the service available more hours per day, name recognition and a support group. Drawbacks may include: having to learn library policies for other libraries in the group, no access to a database used by another library, assisting users who may not be in your area (this would depend on the size of the consortium; some are international), and the hours your library is assigned to cover may not be convenient (e.g., weekends or late evenings).

Once the go ahead has been given from library administration to explore the idea of a digital reference service, the next group to "sell" on the project will be the library's public service staff. Staff who already feel they have busy schedules may be reluctant to add yet another service. Questions they may ask include: Where do we do this? At the reference desk? If I have a patron standing in front of me and one online, who gets served first? If I am working away from the desk, is this in addition to the hours I already spend at the desk working with the public or does this replace those hours? How will this additional workload be shared? Can someone who is a part-time assistant do this? What hours is this going to be offered? Can I do this from home?

Staff may also fear transcripts. Since the reference transaction is written down, staff may worry that the record may be used against them during a performance review or that their transaction may be used as an example to others as a "bad transaction." Set guidelines for use of transcripts ahead of time. Early in the process you can strip off identifying information and use them as training tools; later you may decide to incorporate them as part of evaluation or training process. Guidelines should be written down so that staff will not be surprised.

The questions can go on from there and it will be important not just to have answers available but also be willing to discuss solutions to increase the level of interest and availability of staff to work on this new service. This would be the point to start developing policies to help define the service. Using current library polices as a foundation, the policies for the digital reference service should reflect existing policies.

SELECTING THE RIGHT SOFTWARE

As is frequently the case in library settings, choice of software often is determined by factors unrelated to the ultimate purpose of the software. Some questions to ask include

1. Does the parent organization support the software? Are you a Linux shop? Use Microsoft products only? Would the chat software you choose run in your environment? Happily, many are Internet-based and so this is less of a concern.
2. Are you required, due to site licenses, purchasing department constraints, or previous contracts, to limit your choices? You should understand what those would be.
3. What will you have to do locally? Will you install the software on a local server? Who will support it? Or will you run the software on the vendor's system? Do you have local technical support to help you, even if you don't host the software locally? You may find, for example, Java or cookie issues. If you don't understand those potential problems, do you have someone you can call on who does?
4. Can you afford the software? Many have pricing based on the number of 'seats' or concurrent librarian users and, based on your experience with other software in use in your library, you will need to determine the pricing and support costs.
5. Do you have the right computers? If you use Macintoshes or Unix machines, be sure the software is usable for you.
6. Does the software conflict with other software packages you use? Will you have to close down or remove software in order to make the chat reference software work? One of the potential benefits of chat software is that you can carry on other work while you're waiting for patrons. If you can't open the software you want, is this ok?

7. Do your library resources (catalogs, databases) work with the software? If you license the chat software to use on the vendor's machine, then that machine may control what you can access. For example, if access to your databases is IP-controlled, you will have to work with the database vendors so that the vendor's machine IP is included in your access.

8. How good is your online reference staff at computer trouble-shooting? Are they comfortable with checking Internet settings? Modifying them? Are they savvy enough to distinguish between an online patron who disconnects because they've had their question answered vs. one who has just gotten lost out there vs. one who is frustrated with the inevitable time delay between questions and answers vs. one whose own settings preclude a solid connection?

9. How comfortable is your online reference staff with typing, to put it plainly? Are they comfortable enough with the keyboard to be able to respond reasonably quickly and legibly to the patrons?

10. What about licensing issues? Do you have resources licensed for use on library machines only?

11. How do patrons typically connect? Slower dialup connections will mean problems with image-heavy web pages, PDF files, etc.

12. How is the information presented to end-users? Will they get confused trying to figure out which services are 'live chat,' which ones require an e-mail and which have web forms that need to be filled out? Clear web pages help a lot here.

WHO SHOULD STAFF THE DIGITAL REFERENCE DESK?

Who staffs the digital reference desk will be one of the first questions a library will need to answer. If the library is large enough, there may be enough staff interested in the service to staff during the hours that the desk is opened. In other libraries it may become part of the job description for all public service staff. When identifying staff to work, it is important to make sure that the staff are comfortable with the electronic databases and other electronic tools used by reference staff. Some libraries have designed digital reference web pages with all the resources grouped together to help the staff person find an answer in a timely manner. Training will be key to easing some of the fears that staff may have and will be discussed later in the article.

LOCATION

Location, location, location. Just like in real estate, location of the digital reference desk is key to its success. Not just the placement of the staff workstation, but also the placement of the service on the library's web page.

In deciding the placement of the workstation for the digital reference librarian, there has been a debate between placing it at the reference desk versus placing the workstation in a separate area. Generally speaking, most libraries have placed the workstation in a separate area. This allows the librarian's attention to be focused on one task and not be placed in a position of being asked to assist someone in person and having to leave them to answer a digital reference question (and vice versa).

Most digital reference software can be set up to work on an individual's computer workstation, allowing the librarian to work comfortably at their desk during their shift. This allows them to get other work done and when a question comes in they then can devote their full attention to working with the patron. Some libraries compromise and have the librarian also take on responsibility for answering the phone or e-mail questions during their digital reference shift. However, it appears to be the general consensus to place the workstation away from the activity of the general reference desk area.

The second key location is the placement of digital reference on the library's home page. Since many requests for assistance come at point of need, it will be necessary to place icons liberally around the website, to remind users about the service. Some libraries have icons placed on database portals and others use pop-up windows asking the patron if they need assistance. If the library is not able to run the service 24/7 it will also be important to include links to other services (e-mail, telephone, reference service hours, consultations, etc.) during the hours the service is not in operation so that patrons are not frustrated with the lack of available assistance.

HOURS OF OPERATION

The big advantage to digital reference services is that the library becomes more than a virtual collection but rather a digital public service. The next question to consider when designing the digital reference service then is; when should the service be offered?

What patrons like about digital reference is its availability at point of need, regardless of time. This is a dilemma for many libraries since that time may be at 11 p.m. at night after they have either shut down reference service or closed the building. How do you staff a service that ideally should be available 24 hours a day 7 days a week? Is this realistic? The answer is that not many libraries can afford to operate this type of service 24/7 and thus must decide what hours it can be available to patrons of their library. The hours may vary depending on your patrons and should be well advertised. Once again, it is important to make sure that e-mail or telephone reference services are displayed prominently during hours the operation is closed, to let patrons know of alternative ways to get assistance.

Not many librarians are willing to work an 8 p.m.-midnight shift on a regular basis and hiring someone may not be realistic. If your library chooses to join a consortium, though, one of the advantages may be that they offer 24/7 service and all you are required to contribute is a certain number of hours per week (in addition to using the same software provider). The disadvantage may be that the hours that you are asked to work may not be convenient in terms of staffing (e.g., 5-8 p.m. on a Friday or a Sunday afternoon). This will be a consideration if you choose to join a consortial arrangement.

TRAINING

Before opening the digital reference desk to the public, staff will need to be trained on the software and get used to answering questions in chat mode. In addition, many of the higher end software packages allow librarians and users to co-browse and this will take some practice on the part of the librarian.

Many of the companies will do some training on site. They will also provide handbooks and online assistance for libraries using their software. Take advantage of the onsite training. This is an excellent opportunity to ask lots of questions and practice with someone who is familiar with the product. In addition, getting the workstations set up in advance will also identify any technical glitches; having the trainer onsite may help solve some of those problems.

Once the training is over, staff should take time to practice, pairing up to allow each to play the roles of patron and librarian. During these sessions it may help in the beginning to use the phone to help each other in learning the software and getting used to "chatting" online. Also, if staff has access to the web from their home they should dial in and try the service from home. It will help to see how the service changes depending on what technology is being used at home. This will also let staff develop scripts and other techniques when they need to deal with slow modems, etc.

Once the digital reference service is up and running, it may be beneficial to have the company trainers come back for a "refresher" session. This provides staff a chance to ask questions that did not occur to them during the first session and it will also be a chance to introduce the service to more library staff who may be interested in participating.

Finally, staff should be reassured that there will be unanswerable questions. It could be that the patron will need to come to the library or talk to an expert to get the answer to their question. This is okay, the digital reference transaction has been successful because it has identified where they can go to get further assistance and the transcript can be forwarded to the appropriate parties for follow up. It is also okay to ask the patron if you can e-mail them the answer to their question, especially if it may take you a while to do the research. Many patrons are okay with receiving an answer within a few hours of the original transaction and this allows the librarian to do a thorough search without worrying about leaving the patron waiting while the research is being done.

TROUBLESHOOTING AND OTHER STUFF

Any time a new service is introduced, there are always some difficulties that were not foreseen. Online assistance and handbooks should be able to assist staff in finding answers to most of the basic questions they have. It would be a good idea to establish an e-mail list (or other form of communication) to let others in your local group know of any problems faced during a shift and how they were resolved. The liaison between the software company (or consortium) and the staff can monitor the list reports and look for patterns that might not be apparent in "one by one" reports to a help line, as well as to be alert for problems staff have which suggest need for additional training.

Most software packages allow staff to develop individual and group scripts. This is worth taking the time to develop these fully. Developing scripts to the most commonly asked questions will save time and allow the conversation to proceed in a more efficient manner. Sample scripts may include: how to find books or magazines in the library; library circulation policies; remote access, etc. Once again these will vary depending on the library, and studying the transcripts after a few months will identify the most commonly asked questions for your library.

MARKETING AND EVALUATION

Marketing is the key to the success of any new service and digital reference is no exception. When establishing the budget for this service, include money for marketing. Digital reference is not a service offered exclusively by libraries and many users turn to search engines and other Internet services before thinking about asking a reference librarian for assistance. Libraries need to educate users not just about this new service, but remind the general public about all the different services available at their local public or academic library.

There have been several books and articles written recently about the marketing of the library and marketing itself is a whole other article. Generally speaking, libraries should identify the best avenues to reach the public and use those avenues. These may include: press release to the local media; talking about the new service during instructional sessions; demonstrating it live to various audiences; screen savers; and links from related web pages (e.g., related university or city/county web pages).

Evaluating the service is the final piece to guaranteeing the success of this service. Many libraries review the written transcripts to identify question trends and evaluate the quality of service. In addition to the transcripts, many libraries ask users to fill out a questionnaire (via a pop-up window) at the end of the session to get their reaction. Just like with marketing, there are articles and books available on evaluation.

CONCLUSION

Every library is different and it is not possible to supply answers to all the different questions that may come up in the course of establishing digital reference. However, this checklist should help identify items to pay attention to and give librarians an idea of things to think about and discuss as they consider adding this service to their public services menu.

BIBLIOGRAPHY

Boyer, Joshua. "Virtual Reference at North Carolina State: The First 100 Days." *Information Technology and Libraries* 20, no. 3 (2001): 122-128.

Diamond, Wendy et al. "Digital Reference: A Case Study of Question Types in an Academic Library." *Reference Services Review* 29, no. 3 (2001): 210-218.

D-Lib Magazine 9 no. 2 (2003). Address: http://www.dlib.org/dlib/february03/02contents.html (February 15, 2003).

Hirko, Buff. "Live, Digital Reference Marketplace." *Library Journal* 127 (2002). *Available*: Academic Search Elite; Address: http://search.epnet.com/login.asp. (February 7, 2003).

Kenney, Brian. "Live Digital Reference." *Library Journal* 127 (2002). *Available*: Academic Search Elite; Address: http://search.epnet.com/login.asp. (February 7, 2003).

Meola, Mark and S. Stormont. 2002. *Starting and Operating Live Virtual Reference Services*. New York: Neal-Schuman.

Shamel, Cynthia L. "Building a Brand: Got a Librarian?" *Searcher* 10, no. 7 (2002). *Available:* Academic Search Elite; Address: http://search.epnet.com/login.asp. (February 7, 2003).

Stormont, Sam. "Going Where the Users Are: Live Digital Reference." *Information Technology and Libraries* 20, no. 3 (2001), *Available*: ABI/Inform: http://proquest.umi.com/pqdweb (February 7, 2003).

Whitlatch, Jo Bell. "Evaluating Reference Services in the Electronic Age." *Library Trends* 50, no. 2 (2001): 207-217.

CHAT SERVICES

Hurry Up and Wait:
Observations and Tips
About the Practice of Chat Reference

David S. Carter

SUMMARY. This article offers practical suggestions for doing chat reference, including setting up, using language, interviewing techniques, and composing responses. It contains comparisons to in-person, phone, and email reference techniques. *[Article copies available for a fee from The Haworth Document Delivery Service: 1-800-HAWORTH. E-mail address: <docdelivery@haworthpress.com> Website: <http://www.HaworthPress.com> © 2002/2003 by The Haworth Press, Inc. All rights reserved.]*

KEYWORDS. Reference, chat reference, real-time reference, digital reference, Internet reference, reference interviews

David S. Carter is Engineering Librarian, University of Michigan, Media Union Library, 2321A Media Union, 2281 Bonisteel Boulevard, Ann Arbor, MI 48109-2094 (E-mail: superman@umich.edu).

[Haworth co-indexing entry note]: "Hurry Up and Wait: Observations and Tips About the Practice of Chat Reference." Carter, David S. Co-published simultaneously in *The Reference Librarian* (The Haworth Information Press, an imprint of The Haworth Press, Inc.) No. 79/80, 2002/2003, pp. 113-120; and: *Digital Reference Services* (ed: Bill Katz) The Haworth Information Press, an imprint of The Haworth Press, Inc., 2002/2003, pp. 113-120. Single or multiple copies of this article are available for a fee from The Haworth Document Delivery Service [1-800-HAWORTH, 9:00 a.m. - 5:00 p.m. (EST). E-mail address: docdelivery@haworthpress.com].

10.1300/J120v38n79_08

We've been doing chat reference at the University of Michigan since September of 2002. I come to this chat reference service from a unique perspective: most of the planning for the service was done before I came to my current job, and my previous job was as the Director of the Internet Public Library (IPL), where we were influential pioneers in digital reference service, having mounted one of the first wide-scale email reference services (Lagace & McClennen 1998) as well as mounting an early experimental project in real-time digital reference (Shaw 1996).

It should be noted that the observations, opinions and suggestions in this article reflect my own experiences with the particular system and way of doing chat at the University of Michigan, and do not necessarily reflect the experiences or opinions of anyone else. In particular, as we use QuestionPoint (Quint 2002) as our chat reference system, your experience with some of the technical aspects of chat reference may differ depending on which system you are using at your institution.

SETTING UP

Ideally, your computer should have a display of 17″ or more set at a resolution of at least 1024x768–you'll want to be able to do several things at once and you'll appreciate the screen real estate.

Browsers: I recommend using a Mozilla-based browser (Mozilla, Netscape 7 or later, Camino, etc.) mainly because of an important feature that Mozilla has: tabbed browsing. (The latest beta release of Safari, Apple's browser for the Macintosh, also has a tabbed browsing feature.) By using tabs, you can have several Websites open at once, but only have to deal with one browser window. This greatly reduces the screen clutter when trying to respond to a question. You may find it helpful to use more than one browser, e.g., use Internet Explorer for the chat session and Mozilla to do your searching.

Turn up the volume on your computer loud enough so that you can hear the 'beep' when a new question arrives. If you're at home or some other private place there will be a strong tendency to crank up your iTunes (or other music player) to entertain yourself, but be sure that it's not so loud that you cannot hear the system beep.

Get comfortable. You'll be spending a long stretch of time sitting in front of a computer. Be sure to stand up occasionally and stretch. If you're going to have a shift longer than an hour, make sure there's a bathroom nearby (especially if you're going to be drinking coffee or Mountain Dew in order to stay alert!).

HURRY UP AND WAIT

So, now you're all set up and ready to take your first chat reference question. So you wait. And wait. And wait. Gee, weren't the questions supposed to be pouring in?

I've spoken with many people who have done chat reference at different places and in different situations, and the experiences seem to fall into one of two extremes: either they have so many questions that they need multiple people to keep up with demand, or the questions come in dribs and drabs, where if they're lucky they'll get one or two questions per hour. My personal experience so far has been the latter.

Unless you know you're going to be inundated with questions, you'll want to be sure to have something else to do—you don't want to be simply staring at the screen for an hour waiting for a question to arrive. The trick is to have it be something that doesn't take too much concentration. So (as I've found) it can be rather difficult to write an academic paper while doing chat reference, but catching up on some professional reading can be fine. It helps if the task you choose can be broken up into small chunks, so that when you're interrupted by a question you won't find it hard to return to your task.

LANGUAGE

Language used in chat rooms is often delightfully informal—long and/or common words are abbreviated (e.g., gr8 = great), capitalization is often foregone, and complete strangers are addressed as bosom buddies. While many of our patrons may employ such standard chat conventions, we should avoid employing them ourselves. Without the artifice of a building around us, a position at a desk, the clothes we wear, etc., the only thing we have to present our authority are the words we use. Thus, it is imperative that we not come across as just another buddy, but rather as the official face of the institution (library) that we represent.

On the other hand, don't sweat it out too much. If a misspelling or two creeps through, or your sentence structure isn't perfect, no one is going to hold it against you. You don't really have the luxury of time to compose a perfect response–it is more important to get your response back to the patron.

GETTING TO KNOW YOUR PATRON

You don't get to see (or hear) your patron when doing chat reference. In some ways this is beneficial: there are no opportunities for any prejudices or assumptions based on appearance to creep into the process. But by the same token you'll be missing many of the helpful conceptual clues (age, demeanor, etc.) as well. All you'll have to go on are the words the patron types.

After sending off the standard welcome greeting to a new patron, the first thing I do–while waiting for the patron to respond with his question–is to try to find out more about him. If he's from the University, I can quickly look him up in the online directory to discover his status (student, staff, faculty) and department affiliation. Another thing that can be done is to Google the patron with his name and/or email. It may seem a bit like snooping, but it is all public information, and done in the spirit of being able to more directly address the patron's needs.

DEALING WITH PAUSES

Pauses in conversations are natural, and reference interactions are no exception. Sometimes we need to think for a moment. Sometimes we need to look something up before continuing. In person, the patron can see a pensive look on our face, or that we have turned to the computer and are typing, or that we are walking across the room to grab a book. In chat reference, all the patron sees is a blinking cursor. If the pause goes on too long, she may start to wonder what is going on: perhaps we are looking for information, but maybe we have been disconnected, or we're choking on a biscotti, or someone else has come along with a more interesting question!

(Strangely, this problem doesn't seem to exist much with phone reference; I suspect that as a culture we are so used to being put on hold it doesn't phase someone to hear "Hang on a minute–I'm going to look this up for you," and then wait for five minutes until we continue the conversation.)

Thus, it's a good idea to periodically remind the patron that you are still there: every couple of minutes, send a short message–"still looking

. . . " seems to work well–to let her know that you remember that she is there and you are working on her problem.

We are just as likely to be faced with long pauses from the patron's side as well. The pauses can be for many reasons–including the same bad case scenarios mentioned above–but most likely are due to one of two reasons:

First, the patron may be multitasking. This is quite likely for a patron who is comfortable with chat as a medium. She may be continuing to work on her paper, or searching in Google, or chatting with a friend–all the while asking a chat question to the librarian. Just because you are hanging on the patron's every word doesn't mean that she is doing likewise.

Second, the patron may be unfamiliar with using chat, and may be typing a long response himself. Think about how uncomfortable you were the first time you did chat reference, and then remember that in all likelihood this is your patron's first time as well. He has not developed techniques for efficient chat reference that you have.

If the pause goes on too long you should probably send along a gentle prod ("Are you still there?") but it can be quite common for a patron to take several minutes to compose a response to a question you have asked, and we need to take care so as not to appear too impatient or pushy.

THE ART OF PRODDING

Just as with other forms of reference, some patrons will be more forthcoming with their questions and information needs in chat reference than others. Many of the same reference interview techniques that you are used to using in in-person and phone reference can be applied in chat reference as well. However, recall that brevity is a virtue with chat, so take care to construct your question so that they are not too complex, and will elicit short, direct answers from the patron.

(I have yet to encounter this in a chat reference system, but I'd be interested in seeing how a pre-interview to chat reference would work–besides asking for name and email, get some demographic information, ask them for their question up-front, ask where they've already looked, etc.–much like a good email reference form does. I've also always thought that it would be interesting to employ a chat bot armed with a battery of reference interview questions before sending the patron on to a real librarian.)

You can also use questioning to another useful end, one that is unique to chat reference: stalling for time! While you're trying to think of the best place to look, or are in the process of looking, instead of sending a 'placeholder' message (e.g., "still looking . . . ") you can give the patron a good Dervin and Dewdney (1986) neutral question to chew on (e.g., "How are you planning on using this information?") This not only helps to keep the patron engaged and interested in the question at hand, it can also help to supply additional potentially useful information.

STARTING THE SEARCH
WITH INCOMPLETE INFORMATION

The reference interview is a wonderful thing. Through it we learn better what patrons' true needs are and how best to meet them.

In the traditional reference interview, a librarian interviews a patron with a series of questions until the librarian comes to an understanding of what the patron wants. Once the questioning is completed, the librarian then goes to work, helping the patron find what he needs. While there may be some follow-up questions based on information found during the course of the search, the bulk of the interview is supposed to be done before the work of providing an answer commences.

This should not be the case in chat reference. Once you get a nugget of information to go on, get to work. Continue with the reference interview, but while you are waiting for the patron to respond, start your searching. If you need to make assumptions, go ahead–yes, the patron's further responses may show your initial assumptions to have been wrong, but all you've lost is the time you've spent searching, time that would have been lost anyway waiting for the patron to respond. But if your assumptions prove to have been correct, then you're ahead of the game and can respond to the patron that much sooner.

KEEPING YOUR RESPONSES SHORT

It is tempting to want to give lengthy, complete responses to chat reference questions. This is especially true for those of us with experience in e-mail reference, where we have the time and inclination to give exhaustive responses that include not only answers, but also a bit of bibliographic instruction as we go.

Alas, we do not have this luxury in chat reference. It takes time to craft a careful, well-thought out response and type it in, time during which all the patron sees is a blinking cursor until we hit send.

Thus you'll want to break up your responses into single sentences, and the simpler the better. Give the patron something to read while you're composing the next part of your answer. I usually try to put ("more . . . ") at the end of each sentence I send to indicate to the patron that my response will be continuing in the next message.

TO EVERY QUESTION ITS MEDIUM

There is a strong tendency towards wanting to answer all questions that come in by chat as chat questions. It's an understandable tendency– after all, when someone phones, we give them the answer over the phone; when they come in person, we give them the answer in person; when they email, we send back the answer via email.

Except sometimes we don't. Sometimes when someone phones, we tell them that they need to come into the library for help. When someone comes in person, we sometimes take down their email address so that we can look for information and email it to them later that day.

In the same way, we need not always use chat to answer a question that comes in via chat. We may think that because a patron is using chat, it is her preferred way of asking us that question–but that need not be the case. More probably, it is the first method that she found for getting in contact with the library. Don't be afraid to take note her email address, let her know that you'll do some searching and then email what you find. You're really not doing her any favors by keeping her waiting in the chat client while you spend 20 minutes tracking something down.

Similarly, if you're thinking to yourself, "Gee, this would be much easier to handle over the phone than it is over chat," why not ask if your patron is near a phone and call him up?

WHERE CHAT SHINES:
HELPING PATRONS WITH WEB-BASED RESOURCES

Anyone who has ever done phone reference knows the frustrations involved with helping patrons remotely who are using Web-based resources. Reading a URL over the phone is a nightmare, and you find yourself saying things that no sane human should ever have to utter

("Do you see down in the lower right hand corner of the page where it says 'Patents & Standards'? Click there. Now find where it says . . .."). With chat reference, a librarian can just copy and paste a URL from the browser's address bar into the chat message window, surround it with context, and send it. After the chat session is over, the user gets an email copy of the session, including all the URLs for easy reference in the future. Some chat systems even allow for co-browsing, wherein the librarian can take control of the patron's browser to allow the patron to see what the librarian is doing and where he is going online.

CONCLUSION

Like phone and email reference before it, chat reference offers the opportunity to expand reference services to others in our user populations. Like most aspects of digital librarianship, it is "the same but different"–the same basic concepts are there, but the applications are different and novel. Different applications require new techniques; this brief article demonstrates some of the techniques that I have found helpful, techniques I hope that others will find useful to employ, expand on, and even disagree. As long as we continue to employ chat reference in serving our patrons' needs, and share what we've learned, it will continue to grow as another useful component of the ever-growing reference toolbox.

REFERENCES

Dervin, Brenda and Patricia Dewdney. (1986). Neutral Questioning: A New Approach to the Reference Interview. *RQ* 25: 506-13.
Lagace, Nettie, and Michael McClennen. (1998). Questions and Quirks: Managing an Internet-Based Distributed Reference Service. *Computers in Libraries* 18(2): 24-28.
Quint, Barbara. (2002). QuestionPoint Marks New Era in Digital Reference. *Information Today* 19(7): 50, 54.
Shaw, Elizabeth. (1996). Real-Time Reference in a MOO: Promise and Problems. http://web.archive.org/web/20020202194450/http://www-personal.si.umich.edu/~ejshaw/research2.html.

Communication Strategies
for Instant Messaging
and Chat Reference Services

Jody Condit Fagan
Christina M. Desai

SUMMARY. Instant messaging (IM) reference is gaining in popularity but still faces resistance. Some librarians agree with some researchers in the field of computer-mediated communications (CMC) that it can never approach the complexity of face-to-face communication, and is therefore an unsuitable medium for reference. Librarians in face-to-face reference use nonverbal communication skills such as a welcoming expression and an interested tone of voice to encourage patrons to approach the desk and discuss their topic; they also interpret the nonverbal cues of patrons. This analysis of online reference conversations shows how online skills can substitute for many of these nonverbal cues. Some skills are unique to computer-mediated communication while others involve written language skills to encourage exploration of the topic, increase clarity, demonstrate approachability and empathy, and instruct. The study illustrates

Jody Condit Fagan (E-mail: jfagan@lib.siu.edu) is Assistant Professor and Reference Librarian, and Christina M. Desai (E-mail: cdesai@lib.siu.edu) is Assistant Professor and Science Librarian, both at Morris Library, 605 Agriculture Drive, Mailcode 6632, Southern Illinois University Carbondale, Carbondale, IL 62901.

The authors would like to thank Loraine Hunziker and the Office of Research Development and Administration for their support in this research, and the Morris Messenger staff, without whom the service would not be possible.

[Haworth co-indexing entry note]: "Communication Strategies for Instant Messaging and Chat Reference Services." Fagan, Jody Condit, and Christina M. Desai. Co-published simultaneously in *The Reference Librarian* (The Haworth Information Press, an imprint of The Haworth Press, Inc.) No. 79/80, 2002/2003, pp. 121-155; and: *Digital Reference Services* (ed: Bill Katz) The Haworth Information Press, an imprint of The Haworth Press, Inc., 2002/2003, pp. 121-155. Single or multiple copies of this article are available for a fee from The Haworth Document Delivery Service [1-800-HAWORTH, 9:00 a.m. - 5:00 p.m. (EST). E-mail address: docdelivery@haworthpress.com].

10.1300/J120v38n79_09

communication problems and solutions using actual conversations, giving particular attention to the reference interview. *[Article copies available
for a fee from The Haworth Document Delivery Service: 1-800-HAWORTH.
E-mail address: <docdelivery@haworthpress.com> Website: <http://www.
HaworthPress.com> © 2002/2003 by The Haworth Press, Inc. All rights reserved.]*

KEYWORDS. Reference services, instant messaging reference, chat,
live online reference, computer-mediated communication, reference interview

INTRODUCTION

Synchronous virtual reference services, particularly chat and instant
messaging (IM), have become as popular as they are controversial. Libraries have long provided access to large portions of their resources
electronically; they are now extending the idea of remote access to library services as well. Instant messaging (IM) and chat reference services are being introduced in hundreds of libraries, just as e-mail and
telephone services were started soon after those media became popular.
Pre-conferences and programs at the American Library Association
draw both excited proponents and recalcitrant skeptics. Issues surrounding the integration of this new medium into libraries are myriad,
but at the core of the maelstrom, librarians ultimately want to know if
high quality reference service can be offered within this unfamiliar territory. "It borders on the fatuous," writes Michael Gorman, "to propose
that technology can be employed to provide a satisfactory alternative to
the nuances of the interaction between librarian and user, knowledge of
the whole range of recorded knowledge and information, and the subtleties of information and knowledge seeking" (2001, 171). Gorman's
concern is valid, and his feelings are shared by many, but before a conclusion is made, the profession needs to take an objective look at the
substance of these new reference transactions. In the context of our
changing world, can new media for reference be used as effective tools
for meeting new challenges without creating new problems?

When Morris Messenger, an instant messaging reference service,
was started at Southern Illinois University in summer of 2001, library
staff felt uncertain about the new service. Some objected to offering a
new service when staffing shortages made it hard to staff the library's
physical Information Desk. Others thought that students need to come

to the library and interact with staff in order to learn how to do research, rather than have their questions answered remotely, with no effort on their part. They felt that students who are forced to interact with staff in person become more comfortable doing it and gain confidence in the process. Many simply felt it awkward and slow to answer questions by typing, copying, and pasting. They felt the reference interview could not be conducted adequately in this medium and librarians would not be able to gauge the students' needs without the visual and aural cues to age, educational level, etc., that come with a face to face encounter. Almost all the objections fell into two categories, one concerning users and the other, staff:

1. Users don't need this service; they should be made to deal with librarians face to face.
2. Librarians shouldn't have to work in the non-human environment of computer-mediated communication because it is not as good as the face-to-face environment.

These objections to instant messaging reference both stem from doubts about the possibility of communicating effectively in the medium. After four semesters of offering the service, staff who regularly participate have become much more comfortable conducting the reference interview, finding the resources, switching back and forth between various open windows, and pasting and posting responses. While the lack of nonverbal cues continues to offer challenges, experienced staff members have developed strategies to overcome this problem.

Students, Morris Library's primary users, seem to have no qualms about the effectiveness of the medium and are not put off by the text-only format of the medium. User survey results have been overwhelmingly positive (Ruppel and Fagan, 2002). Spontaneous comments during online conversations are filled with praise and gratitude.

Both the suspicions of librarians and the habits of students find broader context in a new field of inquiry called computer-mediated communication (CMC). This field of study followed on the heels of popular fears expressed in the media in the early days of the Internet that users would become disturbingly anti-social as they spent more and more time communing with their computers. The pervasiveness of the Internet today, both at work and home, has to some extent allayed these fears. However, the phenomenon continues to receive academic attention. For example, some researchers have studied the social perceptions of Internet communicators: do we idealize our Internet interlocutors as

Joseph Walther concludes? Do we present ourselves as better than we are, and do we form erroneous impressions of others since we cannot see or hear each other? (Walther 1996). Does CMC break down the barriers of social class, as Keisler, Zubrow and Moses suggest and does this lead to less inhibited behavior, again since the communicator is hidden from view? (Kiesler, Zubrow, and Moses 1985). The anti-social effects of Internet use were recently supported by findings of a large survey conducted by Norman Nie and Lutz Erbring to determine the social effects of spending time on the Internet. According to this study, "the more hours people use the Internet, the less time they spend with real human beings" (quoted in O'Toole 2000).

These various inquiries stem from one basic "problem" of computer-mediated communication: it lacks the non-verbal cues of face-to-face communication. There is no gesture, no tone of voice, no handshake, slap on the back, or wink online. The Nie quote above shows the tendency to conflate Internet communication with human-to-machine communication. The quote implies that communication via the Internet is not communication between "real human beings." For many, the text-only nature of CMC presents an insurmountable barrier to full and normal communication.

Despite these cogent concerns, the use of computers and the Internet for communication continues to spread across the United States, particularly among the young. Though the so-called "digital divide" is a reality, it is a divide based not so much on income as on age and education (Nie 2001, 427). Of those over 66, only about a quarter use the Internet, while an impressive 90% in the 16-18 year-old bracket do. Educational background also plays a key role. Less than a third of those who don't have a high school diploma use the Internet, whereas 86% of those with college degrees do. Internet use is not confined to surfing websites. Of all Internet users, according to the Nie and Erbring study, 90% use e-mail and 24% use chat (2000). Given these age and education trends, it is likely that those numbers are higher now, particularly among college students. From these statistics, we must conclude that for high school and college students, communicating on the Internet is as natural as picking up the phone. The question for librarians, then, is not whether students will become less sociable or less able to communicate the full range of information and emotions if we allow them to access reference services via instant messaging, but rather how to use the new medium to its fullest potential and overcome its inherent weaknesses with a population that is already quite comfortable communicating online.

This article will examine past Morris Messenger conversations to find examples of strategies for computer-mediated communication. Some of these techniques involve strategies unique to online communication and some are traditional methods of bridging the distance between the written and spoken word. First, we illustrate common communication problems and some solutions as applied to reference service. Next, we analyze the various parts of the reference transaction and show how effective communication styles may be adapted to the online environment. Texts of conversations illustrating good practice are included to give the flavor of this form of online conversation. Conversations were edited for length, but were otherwise left intact, including spelling mistakes, to preserve the essence of the medium. Some names of library staff were changed on request.

COMMUNICATION STRATEGIES

In his core reference text, *Introduction to Reference Work*, Bill Katz notes that maintaining "a good relationship" with the patron is crucial to the reference interview (1997, 165). The skills needed to do this are fairly different for online and face-to-face reference. Though working with text only, librarians using IM reference do not simply convey factual information. They must introduce social and even emotional elements and a high degree of interactivity through a seemingly impersonal medium. The idea of "personal space" exists online as well as face-to-face, but in different ways. Finally, the very language of communication can have some important differences in the instant messaging environment.

The Human Element

Those who don't use instant messaging might think of it as colder and less personal than face-to-face reference. In reality, the interaction can be just as personal, but the cues are different. Katz' exhortations about face-to-face reference include ensuring approachability, and this is usually accomplished by tone of voice, facial expression, and body language. This is so important that studies have shown that a helpful and friendly, albeit incorrect or incomplete answer can be more satisfying to a patron than a cold but correct answer. In a landmark study by Joan Durrance of 266 reference interviews, observers were found to be "far more forgiving when library staff members had weak interviewing skills or gave inaccurate answers than they were if the staff member made them feel uncomfortable, showed no interest, or appeared to be judgmental about the question" (1989, 35). Over a quarter of observers who indicated an answer was "largely inaccurate" were still inclined to return to the same librarian, while "nine out of ten observers who gave librarians either a one or a two on the interpersonal variables of friendliness, interest in the question, or comfort level said that they would *not* ask the offending staff member another question" (35, italics in original. For further application of Durrance's findings to IM reference, see Desai, 2003.).

With instant messaging, the online librarian is always equally approachable. Patrons can feel anonymous in asking a question they might otherwise be embarrassed to ask. Neither patron nor librarian can form judgments based on race, age, gender, or a busy or uninterested appearance. Yet welcoming body language and non-verbal cues are absent and must be compensated for by textual or typing techniques. Although instant messaging can be very human and friendly, it does take some effort and knowledge of techniques to put a smile or an interested look into typed words.

As with face-to-face interaction, giving positive feedback about the patron's topic or skills is one way to add warmth. In the following example, Alice shows interest in the patron's topic and willingness to be educated about it. This makes for good give-and-take in the reference interview and a good evaluation by the patron in the follow-up survey.

Patron:	*Where would I look for books/journals about crack cocaine v powder cocaine contraversy*
Alice:	hi there . . . .
Alice:	OK I would try EBSCO and I would start with a search like this: (crack or crack cocaine) and powder n5 cocaine
Patron:	*just to be sure, you understand what I am talking about?*
Alice:	maybe I don't–go ahead and explain more about what you mean?
Patron:	*the sentencing disparity between crack and powder and the fact that there is roughly a 100:1 ratio, i.e., 500 grams powder v 5 grams crack = same sentence*

Patron: *minorities (who use crack more than whites claim it is racial bias)*

Alice: Wow! neat topic. Yeah, there seem to be articles about that. And there are articles about the race angle in there, too . . .

The following conversation shows the difference a caring attitude can make in patron satisfaction. One night, a patron rang in looking for "ITER," a database Mary was unfamiliar with. After a lengthy discussion of a patron's topic and suggesting some alternate databases, Mary turned to the humanities division for help in locating the elusive ITER. By commiserating with the patron's plight, Mary really connected with this person even though the library doesn't subscribe to the database.

Patron: *i did find numerous results in MLA, but since he keeps pushing ITER I just thought I'd try to figure out what it is . . .*

Mary: I am calling the humanities division now.

Patron: *Thanks*

Patron: *i might have to break down and ask him, but i was trying to avoid looking stupid since he seems to assume I know what it is already, you know what i mean?*

Mary: I will send you an email if I find anything. The librarians aren't there now, but one will be in this evening. If it makes you feel better, the staff person I talked to had never heard of this either.

Patron: *Ha ha ha . . . those professors think they know everything, don't they?*

Mary: Actually, I think I found something. Try this web site. http://iter.library.utoronto.ca/iter/iter1a3.htm [opened the page http://iter.library.utoronto.ca/iter/iter1a3.htm]

Patron: *Mary, you rock! That has to be it*

Patron: *yep . . . middle ages and renaissance . . . i'm sure that is it!*

Mary: Let's here it for the Internet! But don't tell anyone that librarian said that!

Patron: *ha ha ha . . .*

Patron: *Thanks so much for your help! I really appreciate it.*

Patron: *You helped me save face with one of my disseratation directors!*

Staff can also add warmth to a conversation by offering additional ways to get help. In the first example, after helping the patron find several business resources, Nicole finds a friendly way to let the patron know she has reached the limit of her expertise (at least through the instant messaging medium) and offers her own information and that of the business specialist:

Nicole: That is all I could find for now. Jody Fagan is the Business Librarian. Don't hesitate to contact her (or me) if you have further questions. Her contact info: jfagan@lib.siu.edu, 453-5844.

Nicole: My contact info: mruppel@lib.siu.edu, 453-2706

Nicole: Oh, and my name is Margie Ruppel

Patron: *I'm sure that will help me. If I have any further questions I will be sure to contact one of you two. Thanks very much*

Nicole: Great! Bye.

In a similar example, Roland promises to contact the patron later by email so as not to leave the patron "hanging," and the patron responds with warm appreciation:

Patron: *how do I locate a "symposium"*

Roland: If you have a title, you may search the SIUcat by that. Let me know more details, please.

Patron: *It's called "Forum for Applied Research and Public Policy," and it's listed document type is Symposium. I searched SIUcat, but didn't find it readily*

Roland: It may take me a few moments to do some checking. Have you an email address I could get back to you?

Patron: *yes. It's xxxx@hotmail.com The specifics say Vol 14, no 1, Spring 1999. That's why I originally thought it was just a journal. Thank you for your help!*

Roland: Don't go away. I think I'm close.

Patron: *still here*

Roland: I have a reference that says we should have this title, but I haven't located it yet. I don't like to leave you hanging. Is there a way I can get back to you later?

Patron: *you can just e-mail me at the hot mail address whenever you find it. I'd like to pick it up today sometime if possible? Thanks again!*

Humor is a delightful way to keep instant messaging reference conversations light and fun–and it is often contributed by patrons. The following conversation begins with frustration. Chris responds by taking immediate action to get an answer instead of starting with the usual greeting or welcome. However, the patron finds the book first, yet still thanks Chris, probably just for her willingness to dive right in and help:

Patron: *where in the world is canterbury tales?!*

Chris: Hold on. I'll look it up.

Patron: *FOUND IT !!!! =D*

Chris: good for you!

Chris: need anything else?

Patron: *big mac and fries?*

Chris: coming right up;.]

Patron: *keke~~~~~~ thanks*

Roland's self-deprecating humor is also appreciated by this patron who signs off "laughing out loud" (LOL) after Roland suggests a face-to-face visit at the information desk to provide instruction on using ERIC:

Patron: *I see. Okay, I'll come to you if Ican't find what I need. Thanks :-)*

Roland: Look for a skinny blond guy with glasses. I won't have ERIC on my forehead, though!

Patron: *By the way, are article in ERIC primary source?*

Patron: *LOL @ ERIC on forehead*

As with face-to-face reference, the diverse personalities of the staff can come through in their conversational style. Both formality and informality can work equally well, transcending analysis. In the first example, Alice's casual manner works well, but in the second, Roland's polite erudition seems to work effectively, too:

Patron:	*I wanted to know if the computers on the fourth floor had word*
Alice:	hi there . . .
Alice:	nope, I am sorry, only the 1st floor computers do
Alice:	sorry I know it is a bummer
Patron:	*Thanks you anyway*

Patron:	*i would like to read a book entitled "the duality of men" but i dont know the author . . . and i can not figure out this new system . . . help?*
Roland:	Have you a reference to this title? I don't find that we have such a title, but I wonder if it might be off a bit or a spelling problem?
Patron:	*all i really know its a widely known concept . . . i was maybe trying to figure out who wrote it and if that's what its title was*
Patron:	*thanks for helping*
Roland:	So that isn't the title, just a concept. We may be able to pursue other means. I'd be glad to keep trying if you stay on.
Patron:	*alright man. . . . cool enough with me . . . i'd appreciate it*

Showing interest in the patron's topic, sympathizing with the patron, adding some humor, and referring the patron to other sources of help are all possible in both the online and face-to-face environment. Three additional ways of adding interpersonal content to electronic communication include emoticons (also called smileys), exaggerated typographical features such as repeated punctuation or bold type, and mood comments, such as 'chris smiles' or <giggle>. These techniques reflect the origins of chat as an entertainment medium, and increase the element of informality and fun in what could be a sterile medium. Librarians can use this expectation to encourage participation. Shy students who wouldn't normally ask questions at a reference desk may feel freer to take a risk in an online environment. This element of fun, experimentation, and risk taking can help remove the forbidding atmosphere attached to libraries (Koh 2002). It can make librarians seem more approachable.

Here Rita simulates facial expression by using a frowning smiley.

Rita: I have only come up with one video on Health Professions.

Rita: Do you have a specific career you are thinking about?

Patron: *no that is the general topic thanks*

Rita: Sorry, I couldn't help more. : (

Alice uses ellipses to simulate a pause, and makes her advice more urgent by adding additional exclamation marks:

Alice: You can click right on it and it should take you there. . . . don't try to type it in!!! too long!

In the following example, which began with the question, "I am looking for Quantum Mechanics by David Liboff, 3rd Edition," Alice helps the patron request the book through interlibrary loan. Later she uses the mood comment ("feeling stupid") and gets a thanks from the patron, who solved the problem without her help.

Patron: *so how do i put the # from 1 to 10 . . . or i don't need it*

Alice: I'm not sure what you mean–the edition number? you don't need that one . . .

Patron: *no they have this priority no;'*

Alice: oh. (looking.)

Patron: *when i request it from them. . . . they enter it . . .*

Alice: (feeling stupid) I'm still like, not getting this. . . . did ILLINET ask you for this priority number?

Patron: *no i've got it . . . working on it . . . thanks . . . bye*

Alice: Sure, anytime!

In the following examples, use of tone and mood words, capital letters, and repeated punctuation reveal a lot about the writer's state of mind:

"I'm feeling lost"

"Where in the world is Canterbury Tales??"

"Thanks for your help. It is greatly appriciated (hope I spelled it right)."

"THANK YOU VERY MUCH NANCY!"

Traditional methods of introducing emotional content and friendliness into written media are also used in chat. If text alone could not convey emotion, then old-fashioned letters sent by mail would never have caught on, and the movie would always be better than the book. Tone of voice is certainly an important element of communication, but it can be conveyed to a surprising extent by words alone. Compare the tone of the alternatives below:

"Select a periodical index." vs. "I suggest you try ERIC."

"Hello." vs. "Hi!"

"Consult volume 5 of the Library of Congress Subject Headings, Call Number: Q.025.3 U58S for the proper subject heading. (INPUT Q.025.49U58L FOR 8 AND LATER VOLS.)" vs. "Let's start with a subject search in the catalog."

"Enter search terms here." vs. "Hi! Can I help you find something?"

In online conversations, as in face-to-face reference, the goal is to speak the patron's language, to sound like an approachable human being. That means avoiding library jargon and robot-like instructions, like those above often found on library Web pages.

A final consideration when trying to increase the human element in an instant messaging conversation is interactivity. Remote patrons who use instant messaging have chosen it in lieu of email. They want a synchronous connection with the person on the other end. Approachability and interactivity can be missing even from face-to-face reference. In a study of unobtrusive observation of reference interviews, Dewdney and Ross (1994) stressed the importance of eye contact, clarifying questions, and welcoming body language, to the success of the reference transaction, and concluded that reference staff need training in communication skills. One observer in their study wrote that the online catalog was being used as a shield, because the library staff member's first action "was to type for a minute 'without anything being said or without any eye contact'" (227). Even though this interactivity may add to the response time, it is a major key to humanizing the medium.

One technique to increase interactivity online is to be sure to send messages every couple of minutes or so to update the patron as to what is happening behind the scenes. When instant messaging, a couple of minutes of silence can seem like forever and patrons often assume the librarian has disconnected. In a survey conducted by Ruppel and Fagan, patrons indicated they were sometimes unsure whether the librarians were "doing what they were supposed to be doing" because they couldn't see them (191). Some software allows library staff to create a selection of "pre-formatted answers" (stored responses) that address common situations and questions. Sometimes the answers can be edited before sending. Other software sends pre-formatted answers at the click of a button without the possibility of editing. This is an example of a pre-formatted answer: *"I am still searching ... Please stay connected. Will return soon."* This feature allows the librarian to send updates quickly and often, while continuing to search. Patrons are far more patient than many staff expect, as long are they are kept updated about what is happening. They know all too well that computers can be slow and that searching can be difficult. Here, Mary's comment that begins "Hang on" is a pre-formatted answer she created to keep the patron informed about the progress of the search and the reason for the delay. Note the time each line was sent to see the delay in response.

Patron: (6:10:00 p.m.)	*Which SIUC computer labs have telnet/fatman server access and where are they located? I need a computer that does SAS for my stats EPSY 506 class*
Mary: (6:10:39 p.m.)	Let me work on that . . . It may take a few minutes.
Patron: (6:10:46 p.m.)	*thanks:)*
Mary: (6:13:17 p.m.)	Hang on, my computer is being slow but I think I've found something.
Patron: (6:13:42 p.m.)	*ok . . . no prob . . . you will know more than me!*

The next example shows how ellipses can be used at the end of lines to indicate that Alice is taking action and will be writing more just as soon as her fingers can handle it. In the middle of a line, ellipses show a pause in the conversation.

Patron: *where can I find a magazune article from the 1940's about fasion*

Alice: like Glamour or Cosmo but from the 40's?

Patron: *yea preferable vogue*

Alice: ok looking . . .

Patron: *or anything like from 30's to the 40's is fine*

Alice: chug chug chug chug (my computer)

Patron: *i mean 20's to 40's*

Alice: ok bad news we only have those earlier years on microfilm . . .

Alice: but not for all fashion magazines . . . want me to try another or do you want the vogue microfilm?

In face-to-face reference, one can frequently tell if patrons are following along simply by facial expressions. With instant messaging, this is more difficult. Even if your library has software that allows "co-browsing" or "escorting," at some time you will have to rely on text-only conversations to know whether or not patrons are keeping up with your messages and instructions. The capabilities of the patron's computer and internet connection may prohibit you from co-browsing effectively. Or, the database you want to show may not allow co-browsing. Another consideration is the educational issue: patrons presumably learn how to navigate the databases better when they perform all the steps themselves than when the librarian controls the screen. This is more cumbersome to accomplish with text alone, but it can be done. It is important to break down complex processes such as searching in a database–or even navigating a web site to enter a database–into discrete steps, and to make sure the patron is keeping up. In the following example, Magda gives the patron just a bit of information at a time and checks to make sure her directions are clear:

Magda: First make sure you are at the library's home page which is www.lib.siu.edu.

Patron: *i've got that*

Magda: Next, you will want to click on the icon labelled "Find Articles, Journals and More." Do you see that?

Patron: *alright . . .*

Magda: You will see near the top two links labelled "Proquest" and Ebsco. Please press the link next to Proquest that says magazines & Journals.

Patron: *i've got it*

Patron: *i think i can handle it from here, thanks for your help*

Magda: Thank you for using online reference . . . let us know if you need more help.

Patron: *i will . . . thanks again*

Magda: [Connection was closed]

In a similar example, Chris offers the quick answer in case the person just wants a push in the right direction, but asks about the patron's familiarity in case the student is new to searching the library. It turns out this case requires step by step directions:

Chris: Okay, I suggest you start with Art Index to find articles.That's one of the Silverplatter databases. Are you familiar with that?

Patron: *Silverplatter????*

Chris: Okay we'll do this step by step . . .

Chris: From the library's home page, click on Find Articles . . .

Patron: *I'm ready*

Chris: Type in Art Index in the first text box.

Patron: *do you want me to write this info down or do it as we go?*

Chris: Sorry, it's art abstracts.

Chris: Do it as we go

Chris: First open a new window by pressing control N.

Chris: Are you still with me?

Patron: Yes, I am on Silverplatter

This type of guidance becomes integral to the online reference interview, and will be discussed again in a later section.

The textual nature of instant messaging doesn't hide a librarian's caring attitude, sense of humor, or distinct personality when efforts are made to include these elements in a conversation. By being interactive, friendly, and helpful, online librarians can develop the same sort of relationships with patrons that they enjoy cultivating at the reference desk. Just as some librarians need to be taught to make eye contact, look available, and smile when at a physical desk, some staff may need to be trained or re-trained in human-to-human reference when they enter the online environment.

Personal Space

In face-to-face reference, the spatial relations between patron, librarian, computer, and other material objects can be important. Does the librarian turn a shared computer screen toward the patron so that both can see well? Does the librarian get up out of the chair to assist a user with the encyclopedia set on the standing table? These kinds of actions and choices have a role in making the patron feel comfortable–or uncomfortable. Online reference has a parallel to this: how does the librarian act in the shared virtual space?

With instant messaging, "maintaining a good relationship" with patrons in their virtual space includes providing warnings before doing something that will affect them, such as pushing a page, disconnecting them from the service, or redirecting them to another online librarian. In face-to-face reference warnings are less necessary, because the librarian will still be there to address any confusion or additional questions.

In the following example, Chris is wrapping up the conversation after providing directions for an online database:

Chris: Does this help?

Patron: yes, i'm finding some good stuff (finally)–thanks

Chris: Good, anything else you need?

Patron: *not right now*

Chris: Okay, I'm going to disconnect because someone else is waiting.

Patron: *Ok*

Chris: [Staff Disconnected]

Some patrons may often use instant messaging and other applications simultaneously, so they may not assume they will be disconnected just because their initial question was answered. Often is it unclear whether the patron is still attending to the reference interview, as below:

Patron: *fines*

Anne: Hi, please give me a minute . . .

Anne: Can you tell me a little more about your request?

Anne: Are you still there?

Patron: *How much fines on late books are per day*

Anne: The fine is 15 cents per day per book. Some special items are 25 cents per day.

Also, it isn't always clear to the online librarian whether or not patrons have asked all the questions they have. At the reference desk, it's usually obvious from body language whether there are additional questions, but it's impossible via IM without asking directly. In the following example, it seems that Alice has wrapped it up, until she asks if there's anything else she can help with:

Patron: *where are there books on oprah*

Alice: hi there . . . looking . . .

Alice: do you mean like a biography?

Patron: *Anything*

Alice: Okay I am looking for a specific call number but basically you need to do a subject search in ILLINET Online on winfrey, oprah

Alice: Here is one call number: 791.45 W786. It will be on the 2nd floor

Patron: *yes that is right, thank you for your help*

Alice: anything else I can help you with today?

Patron: *yeah can you help me find info on the right brothers?*

Another important aspect of virtual space that librarians must be conscious of is technological constraints. They must remember that some patrons have slow computers or are connected to the Internet through a modem. Some will be using Macintosh computers or different Web browsers. Some may not have the same plug-ins that the librarian may take for granted. In the following example, the patron has asked for a list of computer labs on campus. The only online list is in PDF format, and the patron has trouble opening the file. Mary remembers that Google can display PDFs as HTML files, but this would be pretty complex to explain. Luckily, she can push the patron's browser directly to the translated page. Notice that she sends a warning and checks to make sure the page was actually transmitted. Sending an email backup wasn't a bad idea, either:

Mary: Hang on a sec, I just thought of something . . .

Mary: Google, the search engine, will display this page as an HTML file. (Although download the Acrobat Reader eventually, you'll need it for online journals). Do you want to know how to do this? Or, I can just send you the file via your email . . .

Patron: *xxxx@hotmail.com*

Mary: OK. I will try to push your browser to the HTML page. [opened page]

Mary: Did it work?

Patron: *Yes*

Mary: Good. I also sent a link to your email account.

Patron: *Thanks*

Something else to remember is the physical size of the screen. Results sets and full bibliographic records will not fit in most online reference interfaces. It's best to condense the information to the most crucial elements or offer to send entire citation records through email. In the following example, Alice isolates the title and call number:

Alice: On second floor, look for this book:
The times are never so bad: a novella & eight short stories/
Andre Dubus. call number: 813.54 D821T

Sometimes the physical screen display makes it tough for students to deal with long URLs. Librarians may need to explain that they don't have to type in the URL but can click directly on it:

Alice: Here is a video that we do not own but is DIRECTLY on your topic . . . you would have to interlibrary loan it. The URL is really ugly, sorry:
http://newfirstsearch.oclc.org/WebZ/FSFETCH?fetchtype=
fullrecord:sessionid=sp01sw01-35415-cskpy95c-m1h1aw:
entitypagenum=7:0:recno=1:resultset=3:format=FI:
next=html/record.html:bad=error/badfetch.html::
entitytoprecno=1:entitycurrecno=1:numrecs=1

Alice: You can click right on it and it should take you there. . . . don't try to type it in!!! too long!

Something that can be tough with instant messaging is providing suggested search terms in a way that makes sense to patrons. Enclosing a search statement in quotes may lead them to think that they, too, need to use quotes. A line break before the suggested search terms can convey the message better:

Alice: I found even more results with
(gun or guns) and (felon or felons)

Line breaks can reduce confusion in other situations also. For example, line breaks between the fields in bibliographic and holdings records help the patron interpret the information fields (title, location, call number, etc.) better than one big jumbled sentence. And when giving instructions, it's helpful to use line breaks and number each step:

To fill out the Interlibrary Loan form:
1. Go to the Morris Library home page (www.lib.siu.edu).
2. Click on "INTERLIBRARY LOAN" under the list of Quick Links.
3. Click on the gray bar near the bottom to access the form.

Another aspect of virtual space is privacy. Although IM reference software may display (but hopefully not store) information about the workstation, including the location of the patron's computer and what URL they linked from, librarians should be careful how much of this to reveal. Obviously, we don't want the patron to feel that Big Brother is watching. This would be the online equivalent of leaning silently but intrusively over a patron's workstation. In the following example Chris already knows the patron's location, because the software identifies which floor of the library the computer is on, yet she asks anyway.

> Patron: *how do I type a paper on this computer?*
>
> Chris: hi. Where are you?

Anonymity is one of the features that attracts many patrons to the service, as our evaluation surveys have shown. Many patrons are shy or too embarrassed to approach the traditional reference desk.

Nuts and Bolts: Typing and Spelling

Typographical features can be used to show emotion or reduce the formality of the conversation, taking the place of tone of voice or other nonverbal cues, as discussed above. They can also be used for the sake of clarity or emphasis, in place of stressing important words or concepts verbally or physically demonstrating features on the screen in a face-to-face interview. Asterisks can be used to highlight important words, while capital letters can be used to denote web site buttons when giving directions (as in the second example). If overused, however, they lose their impact.

Here, Alice sets off the words "currently subscribe" with asterisks because the database does not include cancelled subscriptions, and she wants to make sure the patron notices.

> Alice: okay . . . there are a few steps . . .
>   1. From the library home page, www.lib.siu.edu, click on Find Articles, then scroll down to the second section. Here, you can type in keywords from your journal titles. This will tell you if we *currently subscribe* to them in print or electronic (full text) versions.

Note, however, that patrons may use asterisks to correct errors–this is a common IM formatting custom:

· *Patron:* *hold up lemme get a pen and penci*

Patron: *pencil**

Capital letters can also be used to denote text that appears on a graphical button or will serve as a hyperlink:

Nicole: SIUCat is Morris Library's catalog; it tells you what the Library owns and where things are located. You can also renew items online. To use SIUCat:
1. Go to the Morris Library home page (www.lib.siu.edu).
2. Click on the Quick Link that says "SIUCat."
3. Click on MY ACCOUNT in the long black navigation bar.

Katz advises, "Be sure to talk the language understood by the user," whether it's technical jargon or street talk (1997, 165). In instant messaging, this takes on a new dimension. Grammarians and spelling-conscious librarians may have trouble accepting the fractured English that comes across through chat, and in replying, may or may not choose to emulate the users.

When all you've got to communicate with is typed text, spelling can make a difference. But spending too much time to get the spelling and grammar perfect may try the patron's patience–or worse, make the response sound like a computer. Misspellings and abbreviations, though they may introduce confusion, can lend an air of informality that can make the librarian seem more approachable or less robotic. In ending a conversation, for example, we need a polite way to disconnect without offending: "Good night." might sound somewhat dismissive, whereas "g'night!" sounds friendly. Using shortcuts like "u" for "you" and "i" for "I" conveys an accepting environment where it's all right to be informal and make mistakes.

Most importantly, online librarians need to be receptive to patrons' chosen language, style, and spelling. They may use all caps, no caps, or even no spaces, as in the following examples:

Patron: *Ineedtorenewabookthenumberisisbn0-69232485-5*

Nicole: You can renew books online, by phone or in person. Which do you prefer?

Patron: *Onlineandthebookisfromanotherlibrary*

Patron: *DISCRIMINALTION JOURNALS*

Chris: Hello. Are you looking for articles about discrimination?

Patron: *YES. I AM INTERESTED IN ASIAN AMERICANS MOSTLY.*

Misspellings are important only if they confuse the question at hand. It may help to say words out loud to figure out what they mean–they may be spelled phonetically. For example, the following question didn't make sense until Jody read it out loud:

Patron: *how do i get to a resamay builder*

Jody: hi there . . .

Jody: are you wanting help writing a print resume or do you want to construct and post one online?

Patron: *just help on building one*

Using "copy and paste" from the patron's query is usually a good time-saver. However, in this case it backfired because the patron misspelled the title. Explaining why the original search failed meant pointing out the patron's error. Whether or not to call attention to misspelling, so as to help patrons avoid the problem in future searches, is a judgment call that is probably easier to make in person than online.

Patron: *how can i find the journal of college student devolopement?*

Chris: Hi.

Chris: I'll check in our catalog for that title

Patron: *Thanks*

Chris: I checked our catalog and Ebsco but it looks like we don't have that journal. Do you need a particular article from it?

Patron: *yes i do i got the title of it from my psychology teacher it is for a library assignment actually.*

Chris: Okay, the spelling was wrong, but I found it now. It should be on the fourth floor. Correct spelling is Journal of college student development.

Patron: *ok thanks*

Another technique to save time typing is to use "pre-formatted answers" for initial greetings and common responses. Care must be taken to assure that pre-formatted answers sound spontaneous rather than machine-generated, by editing for the specific situation if necessary. In the example below, the patron enters a phrase rather than a complete question, as if using an automated search. Anne's greeting, although a pre-formatted answer, is personal enough to let the person know she is real. Better yet would have been a response that included some reference to the patron's query about yoga.

Patron: strengh yoga

Anne: Hi, please give me a minute . . .

Anne: Do you want books on this topic?

As the examples above show, one doesn't have to be the best (or most correct!) typist to make a success of instant messaging reference.

THE REFERENCE INTERVIEW REVISITED

Although the above examples show strategies to address many of the problems of computer-mediated communication, the reference interview is a specialized form of communication. How can librarians incorporate standard reference interview techniques when using instant messaging? According to Bill Katz, the first step to a successful reference interview is to "obtain the greatest, most precise information about what is needed" (1997, 165). In face-to-face reference, the interpersonal engagement allows the librarian to ask as many open-ended questions as needed to find out what exactly is needed. With instant messaging, this approach may make patrons feel they are being "interrogated" by a barrage of questions with no sign of an answer in sight. Librarians need to use professional judgment to determine which clarifying questions are of the highest priority, and how many questions the patron will tolerate before getting impatient.

In the following example, the patron's initial entry is fairly specific–specific enough that the first order of business is finding out what kind of information the person needs about their topic. After the patron asks for videos, Alice goes back and attempts to get the patron to restate their topic.

Patron: *empathetic and counselor traings*

Alice: Hi there . . .

Alice: I can help you find information if you tell me a bit more about what you're looking for–articles? books?

Patron: *Videos*

Alice: okay, about counselor training? just general or in a specific field?

As the conversation continues, we can see an example of one of the drawbacks to instant messaging: because interaction is limited to alternating lines, it can take quite a bit of restatement to clarify the patron's information need:

Patron: *i want to do a seminar on training professionals in empathy training*

Patron: *also, enything that would show an example of the beginning of empathy in children*

Alice: wow! are you looking for a video about that, too? And about the training professionals bit, do you mean training professionals to use empathy when counseling children?

Patron: *no I want to show that empathy occurs at an early age*

Alice: oh, okay. so you're looking for a book about the beginning of empathy in children and for a video that is about counselor training?

Patron: *A video to show empathy training in action*

Patron: *Yes*

Nicole's conversation below shows how an experienced librarian asks a somewhat leading question about format, following a hunch which turns out to be correct, i.e., Nicole surmised that the patron had been told that newspapers are stored on microfiche, but didn't necessarily need a microform source:

Patron: *How do i find my particular subject on microfiche*

Nicole: Hi . . . I am a librarian at Morris Library. Thank you for contacting our "chat" reference service. Can I help you find something?

Nicole: What is your subject?

Patron: *Erik Erikson, a psychologist*

Nicole: Does the information you find *have* to be on microfiche or are you just assuming it will be?

Patron: *It is for an assignment, an annotated bibliography and he would like us to havve one source on mucrofiche, if possible*

Nicole: To find microfiche materials on Erik Erikson, you will first need to use an index . . .

Patron: *I misundersood his notes, we just need a newspaper article, can you direct me how to find that and forget the microfiche, sorry and thanks*

Nicole: Okay. So just a newspaper article. I will be right back . . .

In the following conversation, Chris couldn't proceed very far without more specifics but notice that the patron only answered the question about the topic, not about format.

Patron: *Toxic Chemicals*

Chris: Hello. What do you need?

Patron: *I need to find toxic chemicals*

Chris: You mean articles about toxic chemicals? books? any particular chemical?

Patron: *I need info on the chemical Sodium Lauryl Sulfate*

When this happens, librarians just have to take a guess as to what is usually the most helpful for their patron community. In our case, an academic library, the best bet is peer-reviewed journals. After getting the patron started in the most likely resource, Chris checked back to make sure this is the kind of resource needed.

The second characteristic of a successful reference interview, according to Katz, is to "understand at what level the material is needed and how much is required." A good way to achieve this through instant messaging without sounding overly interrogative is to simply ask the person how they will be using the information. Since a limited number of questions may be asked, it is especially important to avoid library jargon that a patron might not understand. Asking "What type of resources do you need" assumes the patron would know what "resource type" means. In the following example, the patron clearly identifies the topic, so Mary can then ask a question to figure out what type of resources her patron needs.

> *Patron:*   *What was life like in Ancient Sumerian cities?*
>
> *Patron:*   *i really want to know some stuff regarding the social structure, occupations, buildings, and the political system. . . .*
>
> Mary: How will you be using this information? It will help me know what resources I should suggest.
>
> *Patron:*   *i will be using these resources in writing a paper*

In a similar example, Mary found out how much information to provide by determining whether the patron was an undergraduate or graduate student. Mary also gives the reason for the question, to assure the patron that there would be no difference in service for an undergrad and give the patron a chance to comment on how much information is needed.

> Mary: Are you a grad or undergrad?
>
> *Patron:*   *i'm not asking you for all the answers . . . jst a general idea*
>
> *Patron:*   *Under*
>
> *Patron:*   *first semester here*
>
> Mary: I understand, but sometimes I go overboard in making suggestions.
>
> *Patron:*   *Oh*
>
> *Patron:*   *it's ok. . . .*
>
> *Patron:*   *i can hadle them*

Another technique for finding out the level of information required is to ask more pointed, if sometimes leading questions. Although in person, it is usually better to ask open-ended questions, with instant messaging, it can be more constructive to provide some foreshadowing of what information is available. In the following example, instead of asking more open-ended questions, Alice provides a few probable alternatives and examples.

Patron: *Rattlesnake, timber*

Alice: Hi, How are ya?

Alice: might you be looking for books? articles on rattlesnakes?

Patron: *journal articles*

Alice: the kind in popular magazines (like Nature) or some other type? (scholarly? experiments?)

Patron: *scholarly, research project is what i am working on*

Alice: OK I would try "Biological Abstracts" which is an index to journals . . .

Alice: you may need to figure out what the scientific name of the timber rattlesnake is and use that in your search.

Patron: *okey dokey*

Alice: anything else I can help you with today?

Patron: *nope, thanks*

After determining the information need, good reference practice includes restating it to make sure our understanding is correct. Summarizing the question, or as Katz puts it, the "art of restating and paraphrasing the main points of the interview, in order to achieve a maximum of mutual clarity" (1997, 168) is a sometimes difficult but important step in the reference interview that should precede any actual searching. In the following example, Nicole has to spend several lines determining what it is the patron wants to know, but she also explains why she needs to know and promises that the answers will lead to the books and articles the patron needs. Her summary of the query shows she's got it and sets a transition point for the rest of the conversation.

Patron: *MTV*

Nicole: Do you need to find information on MTV?

Patron: *Yes*

Nicole: What type of information do you need to find about MTV?

Patron: *video shooting style*

Nicole: Specifically, who is shooting the videos?

Patron: *the style in which productions are made*

Nicole: I am just trying to figure out how MTV fits into it. Then we can start looking for some books, articles, etc. . . .

Nicole: I know MTV shows videos, but do they do the shoots?

Patron: *no, but they spearheaded a new video style in productio of their Promos, and the way they present their television*

Patron: *It is actually called the MTV style*

Nicole: Okay, so we want to find information on the MTV video shooting style. . . .

"No matter how the gambit is analyzed," writes Katz, "the best advice in the reference interview is to turn a tight yes and no discussion into a relaxed conversation about the topic" (1997, 169). Although it's a little more difficult with instant messaging, it is true in this medium as well.

Another important variable in composing an answer to a question is the amount of time the user wishes to spend on finding and using the information. With any reference medium, librarians are generally willing to help to the extent that the patron is willing to listen and learn. We enjoy our craft and enjoy helping others learn to use the library. If the patron is willing, we would like to add to their library skill level as well as provide good directions for their current task. With face-to-face reference, social interaction provides librarians with an idea of how interested a patron is. Helping a patron find a journal can range from pointing to the periodicals stacks to intricate explanations of serials titles and shelving practices. Some patrons want to know; other patrons want to GO! Impatience becomes evident through body language, eye contact, and facial expressions. With instant messaging, it is tougher to tell how much information patrons are ready to handle. Do they want a quick and basic answer or do they want to spend some quality time with an expert searcher? If they were hoping for a quick answer, the librarian who tries to be thorough and instructive may overwhelm them. However, one common misconception about instant messaging is that all patrons want a quick answer. This is not the case. And although Instant Messaging is not the best medium for complex library instruction, many patrons do want to learn how to use the library and choose chat reference as their medium.

The examples below show how librarians may gauge the patrons' interest by observing how they react to initial responses. The first conversation is an example of a patron who is interested in taking action rather than learning about the process. The patron could probably have benefited from more time with Michelle, but disconnected after her initial question.

Patron: *i need a journal article pertaining to middle school advisory hour*

Michele: Hello

Michele: Have you checked the ERIC database?

Patron: *hello Michele*

Patron: *no i'll try thanks*

Michele: ERIC Firstsearch has some full text.

Patron: *[patron disconnected]*

In the next example, Chris draws the user in, giving answers but implying that the search can be even more targeted. When the patron replies with a very general request for musical scores, she offers to find one, hinting that the patron could do the same by using the catalog. After finding several scores, Chris explains how to limit to musical scores in the catalog. This conversation demonstrates a good balance between giving an immediate answer and gauging interest in instruction.

Patron: *sheet music*

Chris: Hi, need a particular piece?

Patron: *musicals?*

Chris: All the music scores are on the second floor, but you can look up titles just like a book.

Patron: *any musical scores*

Chris: They would listed in SIUCat, our library catalog. Let me try looking for one.

Patron: *Finian's Rainbow?*

Chris: Oklahoma is Call Number: M1503R62 O31943X. I'll try Finian now.

Chris: Finian's Rainbow, vocal score: Call Number: M1503L366 F51968X

Patron: *Phantom of the Opera?*

Chris: SIUCat is under Quick Links on the home page and you can limit to Musical Scores (menu under Quick Limits).

Chris: We had that one but our copy is lost.

Chris: You could request it through Interlibrary Loan.

Chris: Anything else? I have another person waiting.

Patron: *Cabaret*

Chris: M1620B74 C21980X

Patron: *or Annie*

Chris   Annie is M1503B4726 A51947X

Patron: *Thanks*

Chris: Any more?

Patron: *No*

Chris   Bye then.

A suggested instant messaging best practice would be to give a brief and correct answer initially, but to indicate that more searching may be fruitful, and that more help is available. The question of providing the right amount of information and indicating that more help is available is related to another issue: how much instruction can be provided in the online reference conversation. A step-by-step approach works well, as it gives the patron the chance to show interest or lack of interest in the instruction. This conversation is an example of first providing an immediate answer, then introducing some instruction in the follow-up response.

Patron: *Indus Valley civilization*

Chris: Hi. Can I help you find something?

Patron: *I'm looking for a book with a chapter or two on The Indus Valley civilization and the Indo-European Civilization*

The first book meets the patron's need quickly. . . .

Chris: Here's one with a chapter on Indus civilization:
        Author: Kennedy, Kenneth A. R.
        Title: God-apes and fossil men: paleoanthropology of South
        Asia/Kenneth A.R. Kennedy.
        Published: Ann Arbor: University of Michigan Press, c2000.
        Location, 6th floor, 599.9 K35g 2000

Patron: *Thanks, I'll give it a try*

. . . . while the second book, along with the browsing tip, allows the patron to explore further if he or she chooses. The patron is pleased enough to stay connected, giving Chris a chance to check the location, explain why it might be a problem, and do a bit of instruction on the meaning of the "Q" prefix.

Chris: Here's another:
        Author: Possehl, Gregory L.
        Title: Kulli: an exploration of ancient civilization in Asia/
        Gregory L. Possehl.
        Published: Durham, N.C. : Carolina Academic Press, c1986.
        Call number: Q. 935.01 P856K

Chris: Also browse around those call numbers for similar books.

Chris: The second book may be hard to find because we have moved all the 900's. I'll check the location. Just a sec.

Chris: Okay, the Possehl book will be on the second floor. Note that "Q" books are oversized and are shelved in a separate section.

Patron: *OK man, Thanks!*

To summarize, it is probably best to clarify the information need by asking more about the topic, but put off questions about format until after giving the patron some concrete direction or citations. It is also clear from many examples that patrons online, as in person, either have an unclear idea of what they are looking for, or express their needs in vague terms. Yet they usually have a very specific information need and assume it will be clear to a librarian. The online environment presents more of a challenge to clarifying the information need because asking too many questions leads to impatience and a feeling of being put off. Although instant messaging users are often quite willing to wait for an answer to their question, they do expect a high level of interactivity and frequent feedback about the progress of the search. The librarian must continually "test the waters" of the patron's patience. The librarian should also test the patron's willingness to be instructed but not assume that instruction is not welcome in this medium.

One of the strengths of instant messaging is that patrons have a greater role in defining the nature of the interaction. They can disconnect when they please, they can ignore the librarian while they take a cell phone call, or they can send multiple threads simultaneously and expect the librarian to multi-task. This is complemented by a disadvantage: the patron, looking at a window on a computer screen, has even less of an expectation of how the conversation will proceed than in face-to-face reference.

Despite some feeling of loss of control, however, the librarian can still use his or her professional skills to direct the way the conversation progresses, and foreshadow the possibilities for the patron. Without this direction, important aspects of the reference interview will be lacking and the interaction will ultimately be unhelpful to the patron. In an even broader sense, the librarian needs to structure the interaction within the context of the larger reference environment. This means making the patron aware of other places to go get help, perhaps from subject specialists or even from the same librarian later that day, perhaps by phone or email. Although the patron chooses the medium of instant messaging to initiate the conversation, the librarian has a good deal of control in deciding the outcome.

One concern that librarians commonly have is wondering if they will get the chance to explain the complexity of an information problem to the patron. In the next example, Roland perceives that there are several avenues for getting help. He essentially provides a "menu" of what kinds of help are available. The user's query requires a long response, but Roland prepares the patron for the wait and promises more after the first long answer. This provides structure to the conversation and alerts the patron that there is more to come. Although Roland's replies were lengthier than some instant messaging conversations, he was able to explain completely, and the patron was thankful for the time and care he spent on the explanation.

> *Patron: I need to find lesson plans and activities for certain children's books. How do I do this?*

Roland: Hi, Im a librarian reading your query. Ill respond again in just a moment.

Roland: There are several approaches, none perhaps perfect. To find lesson plans for a particular book may not be possible, but there are resource materials on the fourth floor, some of which pertain to particular authors. There also are books (see the catalog under the author name as subject). For the resource materials, check with the staff on the fourth floor or, if no one is there, come to the Information desk on first. I'll be back in a moment with more . . .

Later in the conversation Roland suggests the Web as yet another source and gives suggestions on how to search there. Although instant messaging can make the reference interview more challenging, it is clear that adhering to traditional tactics increases the effectiveness of the interaction. Since patrons have more control over the length and quality of the session than in face-to-face reference, there are times when librarians can do little to encourage them to participate fully. However, as librarians become more familiar with the medium, they can learn strategies to increase the amount of professional guidance they can provide to instant messaging reference conversations.

CONCLUSION

The conversations quoted above show that instant messaging is a valid form of communication and furthermore, a valid medium for reference service. Instant messaging is not an impersonal technology but a person-to-person service using technology as a go-between. Although instant messaging introduces new challenges, it also addresses some of the problems found in past studies in the reference literature, such as patrons being too shy to approach the reference desk or perceiving librarians as "too busy" to help. It builds on the history of chat as an informal, intimidation-free medium for communication.

Even given these and other advantages, instant messaging is admittedly not the ideal medium for reference in all circumstances. Not all patrons get the service or answers they are looking for, and some choose to disconnect mid-conversation. Instant messaging is particularly limiting in regard to instruction. We must concur with Michael Gorman that at the present time, instant messaging frequently fails to fully capture all "the subtleties of information and knowledge seeking" (2001, 171). However, we do feel that a great many of these nuances can be expressed through instant messaging, and that this medium can be used to provide many aspects of reference quite well. Just as poor face-to-face reference can turn patrons off of asking for help, good instant messaging reference can turn them on to an unfamiliar library service.

A surprising number of longstanding reference standards and best practices still apply to instant messaging reference conversations. This is encouraging in two ways. First, it is clear that librarians' skills are still crucial in the online environment for effective communication. Traditional reference interview rules are still frequently valid. Secondly, the similarities imply that instant messaging reference is a valid form of reference, even though clues to interpreting the communication and the techniques for responding may be different.

Just as knowing how to use computer technology is not the same as knowing how to do research online, so knowing how to use instant messaging is not the same as knowing how best to use it to provide reference help. Our experience is that it is possible to improve one's online reference skills by paying attention to the communication dynamics described above. Reading others' conversations is a great way to see what works and what doesn't. Talking with other online staff members about them is even better. The idea of reviewing reference transcripts as a group can be intimidating, but if everyone in the group brings some of their own good and not-so-good conversations to share, it is less threatening. While it is, of course, useful to improve in mechanics like cutting and pasting, and typing speed, online communication skills are far more crucial to the success of the instant messaging reference transaction.

REFERENCES

Desai, Christina M. (2003), "Instant Messaging Reference: How Does It Compare?" *The Electronic Library* 21(1), 21-30.

Dewdney, Patricia and Catherine Sheldrick Ross (1994), "Flying a Light Aircraft: Reference Service Evaluation from a User's Viewpoint." *RQ* 34 (Winter), 217-30.

Durrance, Joan C. (1989), "Reference Success: Does the 55 Percent Rule Tell the Whole Story?" *Library Journal* 114 (April 15), 31-36.

Gorman, Michael. (2001), "Values for Human-to-Human Reference." *Library Trends* 50 (Fall), 165-182.

Katz, William A. (1997), *Introduction to Reference Work*, Vol. II, 7th ed. New York: McGraw Hill.

Keisler, Sara, David Zubrow, and Anne Marie Moses (1985), "Affect in Computer-mediated Communication: An Experiment in Synchronous Terminal-to-Terminal Discussion." *Human-Computer Interaction* 1, 77-104.

Koh, Stella. (2002), "The Real in the Virtual–Speech, Self and Sex in the Realm of Pure Text." *Asian Journal of Social Science* 30(2), 221-238.

Nie, Norman H. (2001), "Sociability, Interpersonal Relations, and the Internet." *American Behavioral Scientist.* 45(3), 420-35.

Nie, Norman H., and Lutz Erbring (2000), *Internet and Society: A Preliminary Report.* Stanford Institute for the Quantitative Study of Society. Feb. 17, 2000. Available: http://www.stanford.edu/group/siqss/Press_Release/Preliminary_Report.pdf. Viewed Mar. 4, 2003.

Ruppel, Margie and Jody Condit Fagan (2002), "Instant Messaging Reference: Users' Evaluation of Library Chat." *Reference Services Review* 30(3), 183-197.

O'Toole, Kathleen (2000), "Study Takes Early Look at Social Consequences of Net Use." *Stanford [Online] Report.* February 16, 2000. Available: http://www.stanford.edu/dept/news/report/news/february16/internetsurvey-216.html. Viewed Mar. 4, 2003.

Walther, Joseph B. (1996), "Computer-mediated Communication: Impersonal, Interpersonal, and Hyperpersonal Interaction." *Communication Research* 23(1), 3-43.

Real-Time Chat Reference
and the Importance of Text-Chat

Steven Ovadia

SUMMARY. One of real-time chat reference's strengths is the options it gives the librarian in terms of answering questions. Librarians can use text chat, send over a Web page (push pages), or let a patron watch them work over their computers. Options come with a price, though–transaction speed. While most librarians work from a speedy connection, patrons chatting with them are probably using slower dial-up connections. Chat software features are expanding quicker than most patrons can handle, so now it's time to focus on how to best serve the most patrons, instead of inadvertently catering to a select group of technologically savvy patrons with fast computers. Text chat is an excellent way to make sure the most patrons get the best results from real-time reference chats. *[Article copies available for a fee from The Haworth Document Delivery Service: 1-800-HAWORTH. E-mail address: <docdelivery@haworthpress.com> Website: <http://www.HaworthPress.com> © 2002/2003 by The Haworth Press, Inc. All rights reserved.]*

KEYWORDS. Real-time chat, reference service trends, public librarianship, virtual reference

Steven Ovadia is Project Coordinator, Brooklyn Public Library's *Live Reference Database Help* real-time chat reference project, and a student, Palmer School of Library and Information Science.

Address correspondence to: Steven Ovadia, 2422 33rd Street, Astoria, NY 11102 (E-mail: steve@popupdate.com).

[Haworth co-indexing entry note]: "Real-Time Chat Reference and the Importance of Text-Chat." Ovadia, Steven. Co-published simultaneously in *The Reference Librarian* (The Haworth Information Press, an imprint of The Haworth Press, Inc.) No. 79/80, 2002/2003, pp. 157-161; and: *Digital Reference Services* (ed: Bill Katz) The Haworth Information Press, an imprint of The Haworth Press, Inc., 2002/2003, pp. 157-161. Single or multiple copies of this article are available for a fee from The Haworth Document Delivery Service [1-800-HAWORTH, 9:00 a.m. - 5:00 p.m. (EST). E-mail address: docdelivery@haworthpress.com].

Virtual reference is growing by leaps and bounds. As librarians learn more about serving patrons electronically, the software they use to provide the service gets better and better. Where the earliest real-time virtual reference was a text-based virtual reality chatroom,[1] current real-time chat systems can stream video, send patrons Web pages, and share computer screens with patrons.

Like any new idea, though, it takes a while for industry professionals to figure out how to effectively implement it. Consequently, there's not a lot of literature about handling actual real-time chat reference transactions. As JoAnn Sears reported in the fall of 2001, the literature of virtual reference can be divided into three camps: (1) surveys of what's available in terms of chat software; (2) articles on how virtual reference projects were implemented; or (3) articles predicting the future of virtual reference.[2] Even the Reference and User Services Association is still trying to make sense of the technology and concepts and develop some kind of guidelines for the future of virtual reference services.[3] But right now, there is not a lot of practical literature on how librarians should act after their chat services are set up and they find themselves in a chat session with a patron.

Librarians have some time to think about and discuss how to help patrons in real-time chat transactions. Patrons are just starting to discover real-time virtual reference, and while some patrons need their answers right away, a significant number seem content to get their answers e-mailed to them a day or so later.[4] So there is a window of opportunity to open a dialogue about how to best serve patrons in the real-time chat environment–albeit a small window before patrons start expecting virtual reference answers almost instantaneously. So now the question is not *if* libraries should offer real-time chat reference, but *how* they should offer it. Now is the time for librarians to seriously debate the content of real-time chat reference transactions, because the precedents librarians set now will define the service for years to come.

One of real-time chat reference's strengths is the options it gives the librarian in terms of answering questions. Librarians can use text chat, send over a Web page (push pages), or let a patron watch them work over their computers. Options like these come with a price though–transaction speed. While most librarians work from a speedy connection like a T1 or DSL, patrons chatting with them are probably using slower dial-up connections.[5] And even if a public patron is connecting from a fast connection, that doesn't necessarily mean they have an above-average understanding of how to use their computer or of how to navigate the Internet–especially if the patron is connecting from a branch computer because she doesn't have a computer herself. Chat software features are expanding quicker than most patrons can handle, so now it's time to take a breath and focus on how to best serve the most patrons, instead of inadvertently catering to a select group of technologically savvy patrons with fast computers. An important concept of virtual reference is that unlike face-to-face reference or even telephone reference, there are other factors that need to be considered when answering questions. It's not just about the patron and their question. Real-time chat librarians must also consider the hardware of the patron they're helping. Real-time chat librarians must quickly assess the patron's computer situation, too, and provide help based on that assessment.

So is public virtual reference impossible or implausible? Not really. It just means librarians must try to think a little more like the patron. Here are some suggestions:

Text chat doesn't need a super-fast computer over a super-fast connection. When vendors show librarians chat software, it's invariably between two good machines over a fast connection. That causes librarians to picture every future transaction like those early test ones, with tons of windows open, video streaming, and information popping up in a matter of seconds. Unfortunately a lot of patrons don't have machines that good or connections that fast. So by trying to share applications (the online process of a librarian sharing her computer screen with the patron, so the patron can watch as she searches) and push pages (sending Web pages to the patron's computer), librarians are really just slowing the patron's machine and making him wait minutes for pages to pop up, which can be very frustrating and counterproductive. Instead, librarians should try to use as much text chat as possible. Text chat is quick. Text chat works pretty consistently over different speed connections and computers. Of course, text chat is harder on the librarian and it's not always as clear as showing the patron via application share. All things being equal, it's often not the best way to educate the patron. But all things (computer quality and connection speed mostly) aren't equal yet, so it's up to the virtual librarian to be the equalizer and put patrons with less computing power on equal footing with patrons with a lot of computing power.

Text chat transcripts are a manual. Another advantage to relying on text chat is the transcript at the end of the session, which becomes a manual to the user. It's great to show a patron how to search a database, but if they don't remember after seeing it once or twice, they have no recourse but to call back virtual reference. If you provide written instruction to the patron via text chat, though, the patron always has instructions to consult–the librarian's step-by-step text chat instructions. In addition to keeping call volume down, which isn't an immediate concern for most public virtual reference initiatives, it empowers the patron by letting them help themselves. It also lets patrons become comfortable with electronic resources at their own pace, without worrying the librarian will have to end the session for another call.

Text chat is more interactive. One of the challenges of virtual reference is determining what the patron is understanding. In face-to-face reference transactions, there are physical cues an alert librarian can pick up on, telling him when the patron is getting frustrated or confused or when information is clicking. Those cues don't really exist for virtual reference as most libraries use it now. Text chat is a great way to gauge the patron's level of understanding. Instead of just showing the patron how to do something, with no real idea what the patron is thinking, text chat lets you question him as you go along. Text chat also engages the patron. Instead of passively watching the librarian search for him (that's at best–at worst the patron is playing solitaire or watching TV out of boredom instead of watching the search), text chat forces the patron to participate in the transaction. Now obviously you can use text chat and application share together, but then you run the risk of splitting the patron's attention, forcing him to move between screens, or worse, to only watch one screen missing half of what he needs to know. Leaning on text chat keeps the patron in the transaction. (Once the patron's attention is firmly focused by text chat, occasional use of application share becomes a lot more effective and helpful to the patron.)

Also, as Marsteller and Mizzy reported in their study of digital reference interviews, patrons are quite responsive to answering questions about their queries in a real-time chat environment,[6] so librarians should not be afraid to engage the patron.

Text chat focuses the librarian and the patron. Reference librarians can become swamped very quickly, almost like a flash flood. With live, in-person patrons, it's hard to ignore a waiting patron. They're standing in front of the librarian, a reminder that a line of real people needs real answers. With virtual reference, though, it's very easy to forget that you're dealing with real, live patrons. Instead they become more a function of your computer screen that needs to be dealt with. When the patron isn't in front of the librarian, it's tempting to try to clear the queue. And most librarians have scripts of some kind in their chat client, so instead of typing, they just have to choose the best answer, like a multiple-choice test. Instead of thinking about the query and then explaining the answer to the patron, librarians can just show the patron what to do, omitting any meaningful explanation. But by focusing on text chat, librarians are forced to keep their head in the transaction, serving the patron better. Text chat, while time-consuming, gives the less techno-logically sophisticated patrons a better product.

Also, the give and take between a patron and librarian via text chat helps to focus the patron's request. Writing is an act of discovery and by getting the patron to write, the librarian is helping him to figure out what he needs. By focusing on the text chat aspect of the virtual transaction, librarians give patrons a chance to think about what they need. Patrons might not get that chance if they type a question and librarians start opening different windows in order to answer the question.

These ideas are intended as guidelines, not as absolute rules. The im-portant thing is to evaluate each reference transaction at the line of scrimmage and not plan how it will progress before the patron is even logged on. More advanced chat client features aren't necessarily better for the patrons. Virtual reference librarians, especially those serving the general public and not a specific population, need to think about more than the reference question. They also have to think about the technol-ogy, both physical and mental, that the patron is using to ask the ques-tion. Every virtual transaction is different (much like every face-to-face transaction), but text chat is a large umbrella that allows librarians to help the most patrons.

REFERENCES

1. Henderson, Tona. "MOOving Towards a Virtual Reference Service." *The Refer-ence Librarian* 41/42 (1994): 173-184.

2. Sears, JoAnn. (2001). Chat Reference Service: An Analysis of One Semester's Data. In Issues in Science and Technology Librarianship [electronic journal]. [cited 20 August 2002]. Available http://www.library.ucsb.edu/istl/01-fall/article2.html.

3. Oder, Norman. "The Shape of E-Reference." *Library Journal* 126 (2001): 46-50.

4. Lankes, R. David, and Shostack, Pauline. "The Necessity of Real Time: Fact and Fiction in Digital Reference Systems." *Reference and User Services Quarterly* 41(2002): 350-355.

5. Business Week Online. Daily Briefing. <http://www.businessweek.com/technology/content/jul2002/tc20020723_7717.htm> July 2002.

6. Marsteller, Matt and Mizzy, Danianne. "Exploring the Digital Reference Inter-view: It's Still Okay to Answer a Question *With* a Question." Paper presented at the an-nual meeting of the American Library Association, Atlanta, Ga. 16 June 2002.

Opportunities
for Real-Time Digital Reference Service

Matthew R. Marsteller
Jackie Schmitt-Marsteller

SUMMARY. This article explores the opportunities that real-time digital reference service can offer to a variety of library settings from the independent public library to the large multi-campus university or the multi-national corporation. There are many occasions when a real-time digital reference service will be the optimal solution for a portion of a library's reference service. The authors' goal is to offer their original ideas, and examples from the literature, that will stimulate thought about real-time digital reference services that could be offered by your librar-

Matthew R. Marsteller is Physics and Math Librarian, Carnegie Mellon University, Engineering & Science Library, Room 4400 Wean Hall, Pittsburgh, PA 15213-3890 (E-mail: matthewm@andrew.cmu.edu). Jackie Schmitt-Marsteller is Director, South Fayette Township Library, 515 Millers Run Road, Morgan, PA 15064 (E-mail: schmittmarsj@eiNetwork.Net).

[Haworth co-indexing entry note]: "Opportunities for Real-Time Digital Reference Service." Marsteller, Matthew R., and Jackie Schmitt-Marsteller. Co-published simultaneously in *The Reference Librarian* (The Haworth Information Press, an imprint of The Haworth Press, Inc.) No. 79/80, 2002/2003, pp. 163-181; and: *Digital Reference Services* (ed: Bill Katz) The Haworth Information Press, an imprint of The Haworth Press, Inc., 2002/2003, pp. 163-181. Single or multiple copies of this article are available for a fee from The Haworth Document Delivery Service [1-800-HAWORTH, 9:00 a.m. - 5:00 p.m. (EST). E-mail address: docdelivery@haworthpress.com].

10.1300/J120v38n79_11

ies. The numerous ideas and examples should provide the reader with workable methods for extending the reach of reference service to under-served populations. *[Article copies available for a fee from The Haworth Document Delivery Service: 1-800-HAWORTH. E-mail address: <docdelivery@ haworthpress.com> Website: <http://www.HaworthPress.com> © 2002/2003 by The Haworth Press, Inc. All rights reserved.]*

KEYWORDS. Real-time, synchronous, digital, virtual, chat, electronic, live, reference, kiosks, public libraries, academic libraries, special libraries, school libraries, information, referral

INTRODUCTION

The literature and the listservs are flooded with information about real-time digital reference service. Discussion of the topic has increased during the last five years, but the idea is not particularly new. On the DIG_REF listserv, veteran real-time digital reference providers who worked for a company called Telebase discussed the birth of their real-time digital reference product that occurred nearly twenty years ago.[1] Because of the current glut of information, the authors felt that a focus on practical applications was needed.

There have been attempts to dismiss the need for real-time digital reference. Lankes and Shostack conducted a study of an e-mail based Ask-A service that only focused on the satisfaction of its users, with no attempt made to gage the desire for a real-time service. Their argument was more of a defense of e-mail reference than a refutation of any need for real-time digital reference.[2] The authors of this paper agree with Lankes and Shostack that e-mail reference has its place in library reference services, but do not propose that the utility of e-mail reference is a reason not to pursue real-time digital reference. An op-ed article by McKinzie and Lauer warned that real-time digital reference was overrated and fraught with administrative difficulties, another opinion that the authors of this paper disagree with.[3] One argument against real-time digital reference service that McKinzie and Lauer make is that librarians ". . . model habits of information trolling and gathering"[4] and "[t]his modeling is almost impossible to develop over fiber optics."[5] However, it would seem that any sound demonstration of real-time digital reference software that offers cobrowsing would immediately refute this. Page pushing, interspersed with search strategy suggestions, is a step down from cobrowsing (also referred to as escorting) on the scale of personal interaction, but it can also effectively model the librarian's search behavior and thought processes. In a post to the DIG_REF listserv, Nancy O'Neill indicated that she used the page push feature of 24/7 Reference–a feature rich tool for real-time digital reference–more than 60 percent of the time.[6]

The main argument for the provision of real-time digital reference is to have the librarian available to the patron at their time of need. In 1999, Tennant stated: "The digital library is a lonely place."[7] Some people may prefer the privacy and loneliness of independently using electronic resources, while others find it desirable to have a level of mediated help that doesn't include face-to-face 'or telephone interaction. Real-time digital reference enables the patron to have immediate acknowledgment and assistance instead of being isolated in the complex electronic resource world or facing the unknown timeline and reliability of sending questions via e-mail. The provision of real-time digital reference service has made the Internet a far less lonely place. However, real-time digital reference service can also make the Internet a place where many people will find their highest level of personal comfort with the library. Tenopir states "Having multiple options for communication means being able to help patrons more appropriately."[8] Libraries, individually and in collaboration, are assembling vast digital collections for their patrons' use. Are we to ignore the users of these collections, or should we insure that we are there to help them effectively utilize these expensive resources? The answer would appear to be obvious.

This article will review opportunities for real-time digital reference where this medium is the optimal choice for provision of reference service. The review is structured by library setting, a choice made only to lend form to the article and not meant to dissuade collaboration by different types of libraries. Indeed, there are already several multi-type collaborative efforts that serve as shining examples. The readers are cautioned not to overlook the possibility that an idea expressed in one setting may be applicable in another. The authors have not focused on the details of starting up real-time digital reference services. The goal is to offer their original ideas, and examples from the literature, that will stimulate thought about real-time digital reference services that could be offered by your libraries.

OPPORTUNITIES IN THE PUBLIC LIBRARY SETTING

Everything today is about speed and convenience, for better or for worse. People are overloaded–overloaded with responsibilities, technology, visual and auditory stimulation, brands–there is so much of everything that it is hard to sort it all out. It is only when something stands far above the maddening crowd that its superiority is achieved. Librarians must face the fact that this is the society in which libraries must function. Each library must carve a niche for itself based upon the needs of its users and what strengths it has developed to fulfill those needs. Call it continuous quality improvement, reinventing one's self, commitment to change, or any other organizationally savvy phrase. Whatever it is called, the fact remains that money–and people's attention–are not limitless resources, and the competition for both is ferocious. Libraries must be ferocious competitors with other service providers, and with each other, in order to remain relevant and worthy of continued funding and patronage. Libraries that provide real-time digital reference services should remain competitive in today's information marketplace.

Whether librarians like it or not, the Web is now a huge part of reference service. Many people think that they will be able to find all of the answers and information they need on the Web. How sad for them, but it represents a tremendous opportunity for librarians to make sure that our patrons are using reputable sources, and are instructed in how to use them correctly and effectively. A reference librarian's job is not as different today as some people would think or lead the profession to believe. Put simply, the Web is just one gargantuan library of excellent, marginal, and disreputable resources, and librarians must help people determine which resources to use and how to use them. Librarians do this on a regular basis within the library building. It is our non-users that we must concern ourselves with in terms of how we best reach them and get them to use library services. Fortunately, real-time digital reference can help libraries reach users and non-users regardless of where they are located or when they are in need.

A must-read for library professionals interested in the future of libraries and their use of technological innovation for service provision is the proceedings of 3M Library System's 1998 summit "Vision 2008." For librarians considering the implementation of real-time digital reference, there are great lessons to be learned from the results of the summit. Making this service available and keeping its costs down allows the library to be a competitive step ahead of fee-based information services, which fits right into a "best future scenario." Deciding whom the end users will be, and analysis of those users, results in the implementation of only the services that are needed. Again, this fits well into the best future scenario of market analysis and keeping costs down for the user.

Finally, the provision of real-time digital reference remotely and at varying times, as well as the training of users via page pushing and cobrowsing, also conforms to the best future scenario.[9]

Generic Services

Small to medium sized public library directors and reference staffs need not believe that offering real-time digital reference service in their libraries is impossible. At the 2002 Virtual Reference Desk (VRD) Conference, Sathan delivered a presentation about Memorial Hall Library's 24/7 reference project. Although the authors would hesitate to call it a small library (thirty public Internet terminals were available), Memorial Hall Library's collaborative real-time digital reference project is definitely of interest to public librarians wondering if it is possible to provide 24/7 reference in their libraries.[10]

"Sunday Night Live!–An Experiment in Real Time Reference Chat– On a Shoestring Budget," describes the year 2000 real-time digital reference project of the Suffolk County New York Library System. The system chose Ticketsmith for its log on and statistical tracking capabilities, and HumanClick for its chat and page-pushing capabilities. Suffolk County had little problem recruiting librarians for the project because the project was perceived as new and exciting, and the real-time digital reference librarian was provided with a laptop that had special connectivity to the library's server. One reason for establishing the service was the system's purchase of an extensive collection of digital products, many of which had diverse search interfaces and features that might overwhelm the patron. It was felt that real-time digital reference would help to insure an adequate and increasing level of patron use of these expensive resources. The library system found that the reliability and functionality of the software were vital to the success of the service. This included the ease of patron log on, the lack of patron requirements to have special software or to complete downloads, and the ability for librarians to use automated responses. The librarians found it difficult to handle multiple sessions simultaneously and the addition of a "Leave a Message" feature resulted in an increased number of e-mail questions which necessitated a daily check and resolution of e-mail. Many case studies of real-time digital reference indicate that libraries experience a marked increase in e-mail questions. As a result of their Sunday night experiment, Suffolk County planned to extend the service to other evenings and to increase publicity, committed to the idea that the service would become as normal for libraries to provide as telephone reference.[11]

Another project worthy of attention is the LSTA-funded Washington Statewide Virtual Reference Project. Although the project's definition of Virtual Reference Service includes e-mail and online forms along with real-time digital reference, its focus on the development of best practices, methods, standards, and cost/benefit models should have wide and useful application to libraries considering implementation of real-time digital reference services.[12]

One opportunity that should never be overlooked is the chance to market library services. For the time being, real-time digital reference enjoys the status of being "cool." The provision of such a service may act to break down non-users' misperceptions of the library. The mere existence of a library Web site that describes it may enlighten the Internet savvy non-user who has no knowledge of the library's services and resources (or perhaps even its existence).

Geographical barriers have long been a challenge for library services. Real-time digital reference in conjunction with digital resources can be extremely important to segments of the population that have no library located in or near their community, such as children in rural areas and people with limited transportation options. Libraries in large cities also find it difficult to serve children when busy streets are between the child and the library, or when the child is not allowed to travel alone.

Because the authors are not children's specialists, examples of real-time digital reference services such as homework help services are not included in this article. If the reader has identified a need for such services–and it is safe to say that the need exists in many public libraries–a significant amount of library and non-library literature is available.

Low use of libraries because of inadequate physical facilities such as minimal seating, lack of a quiet study area, or bad lighting can be partially overcome by building digital collections and relying on the patrons to supply the ambiance for their library experience. Building renovations can also result in a situation where physical facilities may be unavailable. Providing the local community with access to the library's digital resources and real-time digital reference service during renovation projects may help to insure continued state funding even though the building is closed. Offering after hours real-time digital reference services will serve patrons who are unable to use the library during normal operating hours or whose information needs emerge at inconvenient times.

Kiosks

Some public libraries have placed ATM-like kiosks in remote locations from library buildings in order to connect with under-served populations. In 2001, the Platteville Public Library (CO) spent $50,000 on an e-Branch Library kiosk manufactured by Public Information Kiosk, Inc.[13] Although the kiosks are expensive, they are less expensive than building branch libraries, staffing those libraries, and paying overhead. The kiosks, which can be found in such locations as schools, grocery stores, and malls, provide patrons with access to libraries' web sites and card catalogs, enabling materials to be reserved and reference questions to be asked. The machines have the capability to scan and read library cards, send faxes, take money, and enable access to e-mail and the Internet. The machines can also be adapted to serve the needs of the physically disabled. PIK assesses an annual fee to the libraries for the cost of maintenance and web site services. In 2002, PIK and LSSI entered into a partnership to offer LSSI's "Virtual Reference Services" on PIK's e-Branch Library kiosks. The possibilities of using kiosks to provide real-time digital reference, particularly to under-served segments of the population, are numerous and exciting to public librarians. Mathies states,

> One of the great benefits of the e-Branch Library kiosks is that they help level the playing field between the 'haves' and the 'have-nots' by making many of the library's electronic services available to those who don't own a computer or an Internet connection. This is of particular concern to libraries running virtual reference services, because–up until now–these new and innovative services have largely been limited to those who had the computers and technology to access them. But not any longer. Now any member of your community can access live library reference services (as well as your catalog, databases, and other electronic services) 24 hours a day, 7 days a week, from any eBranch Library kiosk.

Mathies goes on to describe how the kiosk and the interaction works:

> Patrons simply touch a button on the eBranch Library screen to connect with a librarian any time of the day or night. The librarian opens up a shared browser on the kiosk which she can use to send Web pages to the patron, 'escort the patron' through searches on

the library catalog, databases, or statewide information resources, and the librarian can even send photocopies or scanned images from books, journals and print resources to the patron–all live and real time. The librarian and patron may communicate via 'chat' or simply by talking over the phone that's built into the kiosk. Once the interaction is completed, the patron is emailed or faxed a complete transcript of the session for future reference.

The "Virtual Reference Services" feature of the kiosk can be set up so that services are totally provided by LSSI, or LSSI is used to cover some hours of the library's real-time digital reference service, or LSSI software may be purchased and used by the subscribing library to provide the service via the kiosk.[14]

Another example of the use of library kiosks is the Millennium Library of Cerritos, California. The mission of this 2002 project, designed through collaboration by Hewlett-Packard and the city's IT and building contractor staffs, was "to create an e-learning experience for kids and adult . . . beyond just providing Internet access to patrons through kiosks . . . create a library that everyone would enjoy as a gathering place for the community for a shared learning experience."[15] The technologically-rich kiosk provides the ability to interact via real-time streaming video, enabling such uses as real-time digital reference via video-conferencing and provision of informational programs in real-time to remote locations.

Other public libraries involved in the use of kiosks for providing real-time digital reference services include the State Library of Hawaii Public Library System,[16] the Brevard County, FL Library System,[17] and the Connect IT Omaha project of the Omaha Public Library, NE. The Connect IT Omaha 2002 Community Technology Fund Grant Application could be used by other libraries as a model for similar kiosk-related projects.[18]

It is also important to note that kiosks provide a partial solution to the problem that some real-time digital reference software products have with non-Microsoft operating systems. At least libraries will know that all patrons, regardless of the type of computer they own and the operating system used, will be able to reach them via the kiosks.

Information and Referral

Information and referral services are traditionally provided by public library reference departments to connect patrons with other community information and service providers. The advent of real-time digital reference services provides a host of opportunities for enhancements to this important aspect of public library service.

A librarian in an urban setting whose library allows telephone use by, and on behalf of, patrons may have occasionally made phone calls for people needing information on social services such as food banks and homeless shelters. Making this telephone call or allowing the patron to use the telephone is not typically within the realm of library services. Tying up the library's telephone line, allowing the patron to access staff areas, the lack of privacy afforded to the patron who is using the library's telephone, and the potential embarrassment caused when the telephone call is made by a staff member on the patron's behalf, are all issues of concern. It is possible that real-time digital reference technologies can be utilized for these and other types of information and referral while adequately addressing the concerns expressed above. For example, free or inexpensive chat software–or already-existing Internet chat rooms–can be used by service providers to make themselves available to library patrons and community members in need. Patrons may access these providers through the library's computers, home computers, or kiosks. Thus, information and referral can be provided by community and government agencies via real-time digital reference technologies hosted by the public library, without the need for telephone access. Taking this idea a step further, let us assume that the patron in need of a social service cannot type, or cannot read. With the addition of relatively inexpensive software and peripherals, voice communication using voice-over Internet protocol (VoIP) technology can be provided. The possibilities of using this medium for information and referral are numerous when considering the ability to reach and easily interact with people who cannot type, read, or for some other reason cannot use chat. Public libraries will often have the Internet connectivity capable of supporting VoIP.

Citizen Information and Participation Services

Public libraries may want to consider using real-time digital reference technology to host a citizen information and participation service for local government in order to enhance citizen involvement and strengthen neighborhood initiatives. An example of services that public libraries could become involved with are the LUV (Linking Up Villages) initiatives of Dorchester, MA and Newark, NJ. Low-cost, graphics-capable software called MUSIC (Multi-User Sessions in Community) is used to provide the following capabilities to residents: Access information about community activities and services; Organize neighborhood coalitions; Offer input and express concerns to local government officials; Create and access community databases; Post help wanted ads; Apply for jobs; Participate in online discussion groups; and Conduct real-time informational chats. The system is easy to use and the technology is inexpensive.[19]

Another interesting citizen information and participation service that libraries could model their initiatives after is the Blacksburg (VA) Electronic Village (BEV). In 1996, Andrea Kavanaugh envisioned the service including "broader use of chat services . . . to support carefully focused and scheduled online meetings to discuss specific issues and topics," and "extensive, broad-based training to ensure citizens have the skills and expertise needed to effectively use the new channels for civic communication."[20] A forward-thinking public library might propose to collaborate with local government to host the village and/or provide training to the public in how to use such a resource. Not only would the library be using a proactive and creative approach to fulfill its educational and informational missions, but collaborating with local government might have a positive effect on government officials' perception of, and financial support of, the public library.

Real-Time Digital Reference Services for Senior Citizens

Results of a survey of one hundred residents of Warrensburg, MO ages 65 and older found: 70 percent of survey respondents considered the computer to be a companion; More than 50 percent participated in electronic gatherings such as chat-rooms, and; 94 percent expressed a desire to learn new technology.[21] Although these numbers cannot be said to be representative of a larger group, the authors of this article have observed that the willingness of senior citizens to use computers and learn new technologies has grown as the popularity of E-mail and the Web has grown. Also, many of today's retirees participated in the advent of the computer revolution. This has opened up great new potential for library services to senior citizens, and the old notion of the "library without walls" is taking on an exciting new meaning. Homebound services, which traditionally included only the delivery of books and other library materials, can now be enhanced with any real-time digital reference service that has been identified as needed or desired.

An interesting example of a public library's real-time digital service to senior citizens is the Palchat service of Acacia Ridge Community Library (Brisbane, Queensland, Australia). Seniors use the service primarily to communicate with friends and family, as well as make and maintain friendships with people around the world. The library provides weekly Palchat lessons and even provides microphones so that seniors who can't or don't want to use the keyboard can still chat.[22]

Let's take this idea a step further and consider outreach services that public libraries provide to nursing homes, assisted living centers, residences and senior centers. The authors have provided library services to seniors and have seen first-hand the benefit that these services, particularly ones that include a reader's advisory interaction or other intellectual stimulation, can provide. It's somewhat surprising how seniors with mild Alzheimer's or dementia may forget many details of daily life, but remember precisely what day and time the monthly library visit is. Popular and professional literature has suggested that interpersonal interaction and intellectual stimulation are important to well being as one grows older. Add to this the growing interest among senior citizens in new technologies. The result is a great opportunity for public libraries to enhance their outreach services to seniors through the use of real-time digital technologies.

A public library might consider collaborating with a group of nursing homes, assisted living centers, residences and senior centers–or with a senior service provider like a county Agency on Aging–to place computers in locations where seniors live and gather. The library can set up chat rooms on health, current events, books or whatever is of interest to its seniors. A real-time digital reference service can be incorporated into the project, enabling seniors to get immediate access to information and receive help in using the library's resources. The library can also offer training sessions on location.

Real-Time Digital Reference Service for the Disabled

Australian public libraries are highly involved with the provision of online services to people with disabilities. A literature review by Monash University written in conjunction with the Commonwealth's Access-Ability project "Online Services for People with Disabilities in Australian Public Libraries" provides some very important information that justifies, and demands, public library efforts in providing digital services to this audience. The report keenly states,

> As online technologies and information services become more and more prevalent and an integral part of everyday life, it is vital that people with disabilities can participate equitably in the information

economy. Online services have particular benefits and potentialities for people with disabilities. The opportunities for communication and information acquisition are likely to be significantly expanded through online services, especially for people who are isolated by their disabilities . . . one of the major issues and applications of the new information technology is the potential for seamless communications and life-styles for people with all sorts of disabilities . . . For people with disabilities, the degree to which they can participate in the new information age depends upon the degree to which the information age makes itself compatible with their needs. History has shown that the presentation of information has not shown much consideration for the needs of people with disabilities . . . the sense of companionship achieved through . . . private chat modes and the more public conferencing modes cannot be overemphasized . . .[23]

From personal experience with a hearing impairment, one of the authors can readily recognize the advantages of a real-time digital reference service for persons with this particular disability. A profound hearing loss impeded his ability to perform a face to face reference interview, but his involvement with real-time digital reference allowed him to continue to share the reference workload. Thankfully, his situation has improved with surgery and he now enjoys the ability to participate in all modes of reference with confidence. Real-time digital reference offers a tremendous alternative to regular users of TDD services.

On the DIG_REF listserv, there is a posting that will change anyone's view of the value of real-time digital reference. Lise Dyckman, Library Director of the California Institute of Integral Studies, tells the story of a patron with MS who was taking online courses and using a real-time digital reference service.[24] This anecdote lends additional credence to the use of real-time digital technology to extend the reach of reference services, and should give its readers additional ideas of how to market the service to people whose lives will benefit from it. Librarians need to keep in mind that there are services available for the disabled to gain Internet access. Libraries only need to complete the connection for them.

In addition to physical disabilities, real-time digital reference can provide a breakthrough for those with anxiety, emotional or personality disorders. There are situations where shyness or self-consciousness can prevent a patron from using traditional reference service. Many veterans of real-time digital reference service have noticed that there are some patrons that will use the service from within the library in lieu of approaching the reference librarian in person.

OPPORTUNITIES IN THE ACADEMIC LIBRARY SETTING

In the academic library setting, there are a number of occasions when the normal routines of patrons disrupt their access to the reference librarian. These disruptions can be viewed as opportunities for the expansion of reference services.

The Needs of Travelers

Faculty may be required to travel for conferences or testimony, or students may be required to travel for sporting events. As a result, they may be in a travel status for extended periods of time. In these cases, as well as others, there is a compelling need for real-time digital reference service in conjunction with digital resource use. Satisfying these needs in real-time can have a profound effect on quality of work or study.

Distance Learning

When an educational institution opts to expand their product via distance learning, it is imperative that provision of library services to the students is considered. Once again, real-time digital reference is the optimal solution for providing instruction in the use of digital resources because the user can see the librarians' information seeking behavior. Powell and Bradigan asked an important question about e-mail reference that can also be asked of real-time digital reference: "Should distance education students be 'penalized' because of choosing to take advantage of this new way to attend classes, though they may pay the same tuition as on-campus students?"[25]

Support to Remote Research Facilities

At universities like Carnegie Mellon, there are remote research facilities that might be well served by real-time digital reference. Carnegie Mellon's remote facilities include the Driver Training and Safety Institute an hour away, Carnegie Mellon's West Coast Campus (located in the NASA Research Park at Moffett Field, California), and the Athens

Institute of Technology in Greece. In addition, there are more than fifty research centers affiliated with Carnegie Mellon in the city of Pittsburgh but not at the Carnegie Mellon campus. Serving these affiliates is a problem that is common for universities in urban settings. An example outside of Carnegie Mellon is provided by Jana Ronan of the University of Florida, who recounts a chat with a graduate student who is temporarily located in Tennessee.[26]

The Role of the Regional Resource

A large academic library may be designated a regional resource and receive funding to assist all who approach them for service. Gray notes this in the conclusion of her article: "Large research libraries whose collections hold unique items that are of a broader interest to those outside the institution have global or regional responsibilities to serve outside users. Virtual reference services provide an excellent opportunity to communicate with these users."[27] Early experience with QuestionPoint at Carnegie Mellon illustrates this type of opportunity with the added bonus of QuestionPoint's ability to track question status.

Limited Service to Alumni

Alumni frequently contact Carnegie Mellon with their information needs. Although we're not legally permitted to use our own resources to help them, we can use real-time digital reference to introduce them to resources in their new surroundings and point them to publicly available resources.

Service to Emeritus Faculty

Emeritus faculty members often decide to stay active within the department, but sometimes find themselves mobility impaired or geographically removed from the campus. They can still contribute and collaborate with long-time colleagues by remaining within virtual reach of the library's resources.

Bibliographic Instruction

Another opportunity exists within the realm of instructional software like Blackboard or WebCT. Professors can easily include librarians as guest lecturers via the chat function of the software. It would be interesting to survey librarians to determine the extent to which this is being done.

Service to Branch Campuses

Many academic libraries provide services to branch campuses. Although print collections may exist at the branch facility, the multiple campus institution will often negotiate access to digital resources for the entire system. Again, real-time digital reference service allows academic librarians to be where and when their patrons need them. Reference staff from the entire system can be involved with providing the service.

Collaboration

Involvement of reference staff from multiple institutions (including other types of libraries) allows for the sharing of hours and expertise. Real-time digital reference service provides a mechanism for this to occur. An example would be children's and young adult librarians from nearby public and school libraries using real-time digital technology to provide reference service to education majors who are focusing their studies on these age groups. Keep in mind that many academic institutions will have a sole education librarian (who may be assigned other disciplines as well) trying to provide reference on his or her own. In return, subject specialists at the academic institution can provide specialized real-time digital reference assistance to the harried public library reference staff.

OPPORTUNITIES IN THE SPECIAL LIBRARY SETTING

The special library setting can provide opportunities that echo those already discussed, but there are also opportunities that might be considered unique to this setting.

Support for Branch Offices

One opportunity that exists in the special library setting is reference support for small branch offices. Many special libraries that are part of for-profit companies remain hampered by licensing issues with publishers of digital resources. In a recent e-mail discussion with Denise

Callihan of PPG Industries, the authors were given at least one solution that publishers could consider: the idea to price digital resources in a manner that charges the company based only on the number of employees who will want to make use of the resource. At the present time, many publishers charge amounts based on overall FTE. In addition, many publishers still try to charge corporate libraries for small branch offices (local area versus wide area pricing). Because of this, digital collection development in corporate libraries has been slower than what many corporate librarians had envisioned. Until these concerns are realized by publishers, only digital resources that are meant for a broader corporate audience will be purchased en masse. There are sales opportunities for publishers of scientific and technical information, if only publishers would make an effort to develop pricing that recognizes the logical level of use (perhaps FTE of the R&D personnel) and get past their stringent views on what truly constitutes a second sale to a particular company. If this transpires, the authors envision a burgeoning need for real-time digital reference in corporate libraries–not to mention better bottom lines for the companies and the publishers. For now, real-time digital reference to branch offices remains limited by licensing issues.

Librarianistic Teleswarms

Years ago, one of the authors envisioned what he called "librarianistic teleswarms"–and yes, probably neither of the character strings in the phrase could be considered words at this point in time. What he meant was the idea that one large facility of a company (or research facility in this case) would provide backup for another of the company's large facilities in times of need. Special librarians are frequently pulled into projects or time sensitive research that will put a major stress on the quality of reference service at that particular facility. If their counterparts at another facility could swarm in to the rescue via real-time digital reference, then there you have it–"librarianistic teleswarms!" Somebody alert the folks at Merriam-Webster.

The Needs of the Business Traveler

Another reference need to consider is that of the business traveler. Employees that are traveling don't necessarily like to fall behind in their absorption of new information. And, when they return home, they may have family needs to look after. If their information flow is disrupted, catching up will unnecessarily cut into their quality of life. It would logically follow that librarians should be able to provide reference assistance in real time. It can be very inefficient to attempt a high level of assistance without features like cobrowsing or page pushing. Even the use of simple chat software is a better way to pass along a URL or a search strategy than the use of a telephone.

OPPORTUNITIES IN THE SCHOOL LIBRARY SETTING

The Needs of Teachers and Administrators

In Pennsylvania, there are support facilities for teachers, administrators, and librarians called Intermediate Units that are located throughout the state. Intermediate Units provide, among many other things, reference service to the school workforce. There's usually a geographic barrier challenging the support that the Intermediate Units can provide. The rapid shift to digital resources offers an opportunity for enhancements to the reference service that is being provided.

The Traveling Librarian

Many school librarians find themselves in situations where they must provide support to students at more than one school. These traveling librarian assignments afford a great opportunity for school librarians to employ real-time digital reference service. Just because the librarian is not present at a particular school on any given day does not mean that his or her reference skills have to be absent from that school.

CONCLUSION

The authors hope that this article promotes the use of real-time digital reference services in all types of libraries. Acting on opportunities to provide these services with the hope of improving the quality of life of users and extending reference services to previously under-served populations will help to keep libraries fulfilling their educational and informational missions. If the reader is inspired to adopt any of these ideas, the effort will have been successful.

NOTES AND REFERENCES

1. A discussion on the first real-time digital reference service took place on the DIG_REF listserv in August of 2002. Three postings that discuss the earliest known service of this type are contributed by Susan Ware, Lise Dyckman and Sam Stormont. These postings are available from the World Wide Web @ http://groups.yahoo.com/ group/dig_ref/message/5853, http://groups.yahoo.com/group/dig_ref/message/5856, and http://groups.yahoo.com/group/dig_ref/message/5859.

2. R. David Lankes and Pauline Shostack, "The Necessity of Real-Time: Fact and Fiction in Digital Reference Systems," *Reference & User Services Quarterly* 41, no. 4 (2002): 350-5.

3. Steve McKinzie and Jonathan D. Lauer, "Virtual Reference: Overrated, Inflated and Not Even Real," *The Charleston Advisor* 4 no. 2 (2002): available from the World Wide Web @ http://www.charlestonco.com/features.cfm?id=112&type=ed.

4. McKinzie and Lauer.

5. McKinzie and Lauer.

6. Nancy O'Neill, posting to the DIG_REF listserv: available from the World Wide Web @ http://groups.yahoo.com/group/dig_ref/message/6246.

7. Roy Tennant, "Of Human and Humane Assistance," *Library Journal* 124, no. 11 (1999): 30.

8. Carol Tenopir, "Virtual Reference Services in a Real World," *Library Journal* 126, no. 12 (2001): 38-40.

9. Don Leslie, "Industry Experts Gather to Map Future of Libraries," available from the World Wide Web @ http://www.3m.com/market/security/library/archives/ pts/vision2008.jhtml.

10. Eleanor Sathan, "Can a Small Library Provide 24/7 Reference Service?" available from the World Wide Web @ http://www.vrd.org/conferences/VRD2002/proceedings/ sathan.shtml.

11. Edana M. Cichanowicz, "Sunday Night Live!–An Experiment in Real Time Reference Chat–On a Shoestring Budget," *The Charleston Advisor* 2 no. 4 (2001): available from the World Wide Web @ http://charlestonco.com/features.cfm?id= 59&type=fr.

12. "The Washington Virtual Reference Project Overview" is available from the World Wide Web @ http://wlo.statelib.wa.gov/services/vrs/aboutvrs.cfm.

13. Melinda Patterson Grenier, "E-Branch Library Machines Help to Bridge Digital Divide," available from the World Wide Web @ http://www.digitaldividenetwork. org/content/news/index.cfm?key=413.

14. Jennifer Mathies, "Library Kiosks to Get Virtual Reference," posting to the PubLib listserv available from the World Wide Web @ http://sunsite.berkeley.edu/ PubLib/archive/0201/0226.html.

15. Paula Musich, "A Futuristic Library," *eWeek* (2003): available from the World Wide Web @ http://www.eweek.com/article2/0,3959,508960,00.asp.

16. Leila Fujimori, "Libraries Propose Public Internet Kiosks: The Terminals Would Be Fully Equipped and Serve Areas with Little Access to State Libraries," *Honolulu Star-Bulletin* (Tuesday, September 26, 2000): available from the World Wide Web @ http://starbulletin.com/2000/09/26/news/story12.html.

17. "Brevard Library Foundation–Future Projects," available from the World Wide Web @ http://www.brevardlibraryfoundation.org/future.html.

18. Ronald R. Heezen, "Nebraska Information Technology Commission, Community Technology Fund 2002, Application Form, Project Title: Connect IT Omaha," available from the World Wide Web @ http://nitc.nol.org/cc/grants/2002/applications/ctf50connectomaha.pdf.

19. "Strengthening Neighborhoods," In *States & Communities Building the Future from the Ground Up*, available from the World Wide Web @ http://www.benton.org/Library/Stake/states/states-full.html.

20. Andrea Kavanaugh, "The Use of the Internet for Civic Engagement: A View from Blacksburg, Virginia," a luncheon address to the Virginia Municipal League, October 21, 1996, available from the World Wide Web @ http://www.bev.net/about/research/reports/docs/VAMuniLeague.address.pdf.

21. Godavari Devendrappa Patil, "Computer Access and Utilization Patterns of Older People," (Warrensburg, MO: Central Missouri State University, 2002), abstract available from the World Wide Web @ http://wwwlib.umi.com/dissertations/fullcit/1407333.

22. "Seniors Get Pally on the Net," *Southern Star* (March 13, 2002), available from the LexisNexis™ Academic database.

23. "Online Services for People With Disabilities in Australian Public Libraries. A Review of the Literature by Information and Telecommunications Needs Research (ITNR), Monash University," (January, 2000): available from the World Wide Web @ http://www.infotech.monash.edu.au/itnr/reports/review1.pdf.

24. Lise Dyckman, posting to the DIG_REF listserv: available from the World Wide Web @ http://groups.yahoo.com/group/dig_ref/message/4799.

25. Carol A. Powell and Pamela S. Bradigan, "E-mail Reference Services: Characteristics and Effects on Overall Reference Services at an Academic Health Sciences Library," *Reference & User Services Quarterly* 41, no. 2 (2001): 170-8.

26. Jana Ronan, "Chat Reference: An Exciting New Facet of Digital Reference Services," *ARL* no. 219 (2001): 4-6.

27. Suzanne M. Gray, "Virtual Reference Services: Directions and Agendas," *Reference & User Services Quarterly* 39, no. 4 (2000): 365-75.

Usage and User Analysis
of a Real-Time Digital Reference Service

Kelly M. Broughton

SUMMARY. This paper presents the results of a use analysis and the results of a user survey of Bowling Green State University Libraries' "Chat with a Librarian" service for the academic year 2001-2002. When appropriate, the results are compared with the results of other libraries' services. Information examined includes when and from where users ask questions via the services, how users find out about the service, and what types of questions the users ask, the status and affiliation of the users, and user satisfaction with the service. Most of this information can be compared to findings from at least one other academic library's study of a

Kelly M. Broughton is Reference Coordinator and Associate Professor, Jerome Library, University Libraries, Bowling Green State University, Bowling Green, OH 43403 (E-mail: kmoore@bgnet.bgsu.edu).

[Haworth co-indexing entry note]: "Usage and User Analysis of a Real-Time Digital Reference Service." Broughton, Kelly M. Co-published simultaneously in *The Reference Librarian* (The Haworth Information Press, an imprint of The Haworth Press, Inc.) No. 79/80, 2002/2003, pp. 183-200; and: *Digital Reference Services* (ed: Bill Katz) The Haworth Information Press, an imprint of The Haworth Press, Inc., 2002/2003, pp. 183-200. Single or multiple copies of this article are available for a fee from The Haworth Document Delivery Service [1-800-HAWORTH, 9:00 a.m. - 5:00 p.m. (EST). E-mail address: docdelivery@haworthpress. com].

somewhat similar service. With a few exceptions, the findings are similar from service to service. *[Article copies available for a fee from The Haworth Document Delivery Service: 1-800-HAWORTH. E-mail address: <docdelivery@haworthpress.com> Website: <http://www.HaworthPress.com> © 2002/2003 by The Haworth Press, Inc. All rights reserved.]*

KEYWORDS. Digital reference service, user satisfaction, use statistics, academic libraries

INTRODUCTION AND REVIEW OF THE LITERATURE

The nature of synchronous digital reference services (text-based and in real-time) allows for much easier studies of reference transactions than are possible in face-to-face situations. It allows us to more easily capture a great deal of information about any single transaction, such as exact times and length of transactions and even the entire dialog between the user and librarian. Librarians evaluating existing digital reference services or considering implementation can benefit from information provided by those of us who have some experience in this new reference medium. To this end, this article offers some basic information from an analysis of an academic year of our use data, as well as the results of our user survey. This article will also attempt to make useful comparisons with recently published similar literature. There is a growing body of literature on digital reference services and of course, not all of it is applicable to every library's situation. It is most useful to examine the results of studies from libraries having similar missions and patrons. To that end, there are seven available articles, reports, and presentations that have examined synchronous, online reference services in academic settings and are useful for comparison here.

Use data was studied and reported by Kibbee et al., who examined over 600 online reference questions received at the University of Illinois at Urbana-Champaign (UIUC). Sears studied and reported on the use of a semester's worth of online reference questions received at Auburn University Libraries. Sloan reported on 613 transactions received by the Ready for Reference project of the Alliance Library System, a consortium of 8 diverse colleges and universities. Many of the variables he reported can be compared here, although that project involves multiple libraries. Granfield reported on over 300 transactions received by Ryerson University in Toronto. Marsteller and Neuhaus reported on analysis of the logs of seven months of transactions at Carnegie Mellon.

The results of user surveys were also reported by Kibbee et al., Granfield, and Marsteller and Neuhaus. Foley reported on the results of completed surveys by users of the instant messaging system at the General Libraries at the University at Buffalo. While use data was captured in Foley's study, it reflects only those sessions where users submitted the survey. Finally, Ruppel and Fagan reported on the results of two user surveys, totaling 392 surveys, about the instant messaging system at the Morris Library at Southern Illinois University.

ABOUT OUR USER ENVIRONMENT AND DIGITAL SERVICE

Bowling Green State University (BGSU) is a residential university located in rural northwest Ohio. BGSU has an enrollment of over 17,000 undergraduate students and nearly 3,000 graduate students (Office of Institutional Research, BGSU, *BGSU Fact Book 2002-2003*). Only 6% of first-year students are over 24 years old and the average age of all undergraduates is 21. The university has a residential requirement for main campus, full-time undergraduates in their first two years, unless they live with their parents within a 50-mile radius of the university. Ninety-one percent of first-year students live on campus (Office of Institutional Research, BGSU, "Student Life").

Despite the fact that our university does not have large numbers of commuting students or distance learners, library gate counts and in-person reference statistics have been declining steadily as our electronically available resources and the amount of information on the Internet has grown. All residence halls have Internet-accessible computer labs and all residence hall rooms are equipped with high-speed access if students own personal computers. There are twelve additional computer labs on campus outside of the residence halls.

So, the BGSU student is very much your stereotypical mid-western college student. Many of them have high-speed access to the Internet on their own computers or computers very nearby and many don't visit the library as often as their counterparts did five or ten years ago. This information is useful to keep in mind as one examines our statistics and attempts to make comparisons with data from other institutions.

Background on Our Service

Librarians in the reference unit of the Jerome Library at BGSU began offering synchronous reference service over the Internet in May of

2000. In January of 2001, we began offering this service using LSSI's Virtual Reference Desk (VRD) software (for more information on the early months of our service, see Broughton). During the 2001-2002 school year, we offered the service all hours librarians staffed the reference desk. Normally this is Mondays-Thursdays 9:00 a.m.-10:00 p.m., Fridays 9:00 a.m.-5:00 p.m., Saturdays 1:00 p.m.-5:00 p.m., and Sundays 1:00 p.m.-10:00 p.m., with reduced hours on holidays and breaks. The service was staffed at the reference desk while performing in-person and telephone reference. The service was open to anyone, although the entry page did state that the service was intended for the use of BGSU students, faculty, and staff or others with questions about the BGSU Libraries and its collections.

USE ANALYSIS

This analysis was based on the database of information collected for each digital reference transaction by the VRD software. This data was exported into a Microsoft Access database created by a staff member in our office. Much of the analysis could have been performed using VRD's querying capabilities, but the author wanted to eliminate testing and other superfluous transactions. After the data was exported, the author examined the transactions and eliminated the information associated with testing, training, and demonstrations so that the results would more accurately reflect actual user transactions.

Use by Month

From September 1, 2001 through May 31, 2002, there were a total of 642 sessions with users of our service. The graph in Figure 1 shows monthly usage as a percent of the total. May is the lowest month (spring semester ends before mid-May), with only 32 sessions, and March is the peak month, with 99 sessions. The graph nicely illustrates the crescendo of user interactions we experience each semester in the library. Fall semester reference transactions peak in October and November; spring semester peaks right after spring break in March. This reinforces the findings of Granfield, ". . . service levels peaked during the peak library usage months . . ." (p. 8).

Use by Week of the Semester

It might also be useful to take a different look at traffic patterns and consider use by week of the semester. Figure 2 compares the number of

FIGURE 1. Percent of Usage by Month

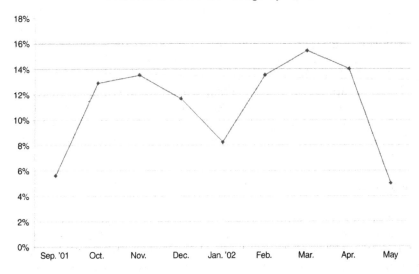

FIGURE 2. Use by Week of the Semester

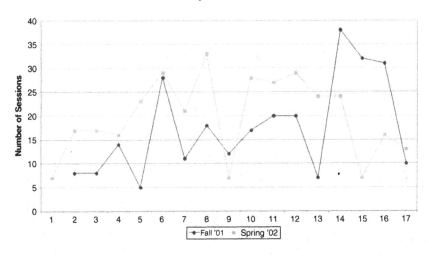

sessions by week of each semester. The dip in fall semester's week thirteen is the Thanksgiving holiday. The dip in week nine of spring semester is spring break. Other dips and peaks may or may not be representative of patterns of assignments given by instructors. Sears found that sessions peaked in weeks 8-10 of the semester and Sloan stated that a gradual progression of numbers by week through April, and then a subsequent decline, ". . . appears to parallel the use of academic libraries in general as a semester progresses." While that appears to hold with our data for spring semester (ignoring week 9), it is not so for fall semester. Only further study will determine if there is a pattern and if it is unique to BGSU.

Use by Day and Hour

In examining questions by day of the week, we can also see interesting parallels with in-person reference service. Figure 3 shows sessions by hour of each day, offering totals for each day of the week and each hour of the day. Tuesdays (166) and Wednesdays (140) are the busiest days on our digital service. Kibbee et al. (p. 31) also found numbers highest on Tuesdays and Wednesdays, ". . . likewise follow[ing] the pattern for in-person service," at UIUC. Eighty-two percent of our sessions took place Monday through Thursday. Sears found that the users of their InfoChat system ". . . [asked] more questions during weekdays

FIGURE 3. Sessions by Hour and Day of the Week

	Mon	Tue	Wed	Thu	Fri	Sat	Sun	TOTAL
9 a.m.	3	6	4	6	12			31
10 a.m.	7	6	9	10	10			42
11 a.m.	11	13	9	9	2			44
12 p.m.	6	10	12	7	7			42
1 p.m.	12	16	15	12	8	1	3	67
2 p.m.	11	23	14	12	5	3	6	74
3 p.m.	9	23	13	12	7	3	8	75
4 p.m.	10	11	16	13	3	2	4	59
5 p.m.	8	11	6	6			3	34
6 p.m.	11	9	16	6			6	48
7 p.m.	11	14	15	6			6	52
8 p.m.	6	12	6	9			13	46
9 p.m.	4	12	5	5			3	29
TOTAL	109	166	140	113	54	9	51	642

than on weekends." Sloan found that 74% of the Alliance system's digital reference sessions took place from Monday through Thursday. This is especially interesting, since the Alliance system offers service 24 hours a day, seven days a week, so there is no limit imposed on when students may seek assistance, unlike the services provides by BGSU, InfoChat, and UIUC, which all had fewer hours of librarian assistance available on the weekends. While it appears there may be some demand for weekend service, it doesn't appear that offering unlimited access brings in huge numbers, either.

The total number of questions asked by hour of day for BGSU's service can also be seen in Figure 3. What is most interesting about the hourly information is how much it varies by day of the week. Tuesdays and Wednesdays are the most similar with heavy numbers beginning after lunch and lasting until dinner, and then with a couple more heavy hours of traffic in the evening. Kibbee et al. (p. 31) reported technical and other difficulties that skewed some of the results of their hourly figures. However, there appears to be fairly clear evidence that usage falls over the lunch hour, peaks in the middle of the afternoon, falls again over the dinner hours, spikes around 7 p.m. and then steadily declines over the rest of the evening, similarly to BGSU's Tuesday and Wednesday usage. Thursday's hourly use pattern is not surprising. It appears that BGSU students are working hard to complete their work so that they can go out Thursday night. Monday's usage appears to be fairly steady from about 10:00 a.m. until 8:00 p.m., although compared to use at the reference desk, the lower total number was surprising. Sloan's data does not show any dips over lunch or the dinner hours, but it is not broken out by day of the week. It does show morning hours with lower use and afternoon and evening hours being more active. It would be interesting to know if our Thursday use pattern of overall high numbers, but concentrated in the afternoon, is unique to BGSU.

User Affiliation and Status

The affiliation and status of our users was self-reported on the brief questionnaire each was asked to complete at the beginning of their session. It was the only required element on this questionnaire. This information was captured by the VRD software and can be found in Figure 4. By far, this service appeals to our undergraduates (74%) more than others. Kibbee et al. (p. 31) also reported a vast majority of their users as students, although they do not differentiate between undergraduate and graduate students, and quite a significant number (15.7%) did not iden-

FIGURE 4. User Status

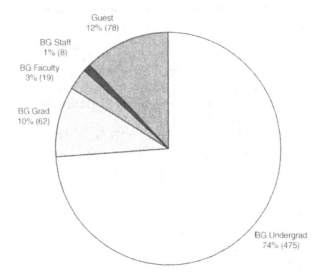

tify their status. It is interesting that so many (12%) of our users were not affiliated with BGSU. Some of these sessions involved users with specific questions about our holdings or events at BGSU, many were librarians interested in our service, and some were people from around the world seeking assistance with research. Given the time-consuming nature of reference transactions in this medium and this era of tight budgets, service to significant numbers of non-affiliated users has to be seriously weighed against the costs. Similarly, Granfield found that about 82% of their users were students, 6% faculty, 1% staff, and 10% "other." Marsteller and Neuhaus report very different findings at Carnegie Mellon, where only 23% of their users were undergraduates, compared with 43% graduate students. They suggest two possible explanations. "The greater amount of time spent on research by graduate students may naturally lead to more questions," or since their findings were based on a voluntary survey, with a 20% response rate, graduate students are more likely to complete it.

Question Types

The eight categories of question types were determined after discussion with the librarians. We considered our 15 months of experience in answering questions on the service that we thought might be most useful for our service evaluation. After these categories were determined, LSSI added them to our software profile. Librarians were asked to select a category from a pull-down menu in the software before they logged out of a session with a user. Often, librarians forgot this last step, as it was something that was added after having used the software for nearly nine months. In these instances, the author reviewed the transcripts of the session and assigned a question type. Categorization of the questions can be found in Figure 5. While the category "other" (49%) might seem less than useful, we were unable to construct any other meaningful breakdown of this large set of extremely diverse questions. Beyond known-item questions (where the user knows the exact item they are looking for and simply just needs to know if we own this item), we get very, very few ready reference questions, although in retrospect, perhaps a category to prove this point would have been worthwhile!

The "articles on . . ." category (22%) represents users asking specifically for articles on a particular topic. This is what seems to be the most often asked question at the reference desk, too. "Patron record" questions (6%) involve users asking about renewing books, or checking when items from other libraries have arrived for pick-up. Four percent of our questions were categorized as "BGSU info." This question type

FIGURE 5. Question Types

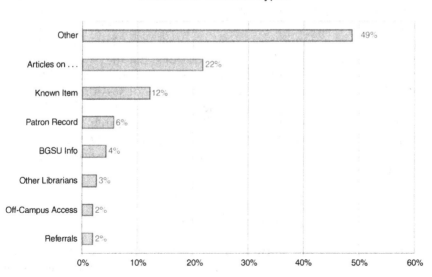

includes information about campus events and a variety of other questions related to the university, such as, "Where can I buy a BGSU sweatshirt online?" The "referrals" (2%) category includes questions posed by users that needed to be answered in other areas of the main library, such as circulation, or in a branch library or special collection. Because of our experience with this service, and because we often received other librarians or library students investigating on the service, we included a special category for them called "other librarians" (3%). Finally, the "off-campus access" category (2%) includes questions about accessing proprietary resources from off-campus.

Determining useful, specific categories for reference questions seems to be a common problem. Granfield reported that 56% of their questions were "reference," as opposed to "borrower information," "technical assistance," or "other." Kibbee et al. (p. 33) reported that 33.2% of their users asked for assistance "finding specific library materials" and 20.2% asked "subject based research" questions. Another 9.1% of their questions were categorized as "ready reference." Sears provided perhaps a more useful breakdown of reference questions types, following categories outlined by Katz (p. 11-15). Reference questions (55.6%) were segmented into ready-reference, specific search, and research questions. Their remaining questions were categorized as "directional" or "policy & procedural." Sloan lists in his report 116 actual questions from the Ready for Reference service. Beyond noting that 8% of the questions concern "access to library databases" and 5% deal with citing resources, he properly notes "the remarkable diversity of questions asked." Marsteller and Neuhaus broke down sessions by broad discipline (science, humanities, social science, business), general, and other. Their "other" category consisted of 51% of their total sessions, but they went further to break down these into ILL, circulation, OPAC, about chat, and technical problems. They also looked at the entire set of sessions and categorized how librarians responded to the questions, using ready reference, referrals, source suggestions, and "librarian does search" as their categories. Referrals were 20% of their responses and ready reference represented 25%. Both of these are much higher percentages than what we found at BGSU.

THE USER SURVEY

The VRD software allowed us to offer a web-based survey at the close of every transaction with a user. We began offering the survey on

October 1, 2001 and continued through May 2002. When either the librarian or the user ended the session, the survey opened in a pop-up browser window on the user's desktop. If the user chose to submit the survey, the answers were sent anonymously to a group email account administered by the reference unit. The survey contained no information identifying the patron or the session, other than information the user may have provided in the open text fields. The information from the completed surveys was retrieved from the email account and manually entered into Excel spreadsheets.

Some of the survey questions provided users with multiple-choice answers only, others allowed for open text comments in addition to selecting from a multiple-choice list, and one question allowed for an open text answer only. The questions on the survey were developed by the librarians and were designed to help us assess the value of the service and to determine the answers to various questions that were unavailable or too difficult to extract using the statistical information provided by the software. In addition to asking about user satisfaction with the help and resources received on the service, we sought to discover how users learned about out service, their location, and what they believed they learned during the session. During this eight-month period 209 surveys were submitted, while 606 sessions took place, representing slightly more than a 34% response rate.

How Users Learned About the Service

Figure 6 shows that 57% (121) of our users indicated that they learned about the service from the libraries' home page. The libraries' home page includes an "Ask a Librarian" link under "Help." This link gives users the full range of possibilities for contacting reference librarians, including chat. The home page also included a rotating text banner that advertised events and new services, including this service.

Over 10% (22) indicated that they learned about the service through a help link within a research database. A core set of about 40 of our research databases are provided via our consortia, OhioLINK. OhioLINK develops and maintains the interfaces for these databases. When BGSU users click on a help link, they are offered text help, as well as information about BGSU reference assistance. This information includes how to contact us in person, by phone, over email, and by "Chat with a Librarian." Interestingly, almost 18% (37) of the users selected "other." With this high of a response, it would have been useful to allow the users to explain further. One assumes this includes users who learned

FIGURE 6. How Did You Learn About This Service?

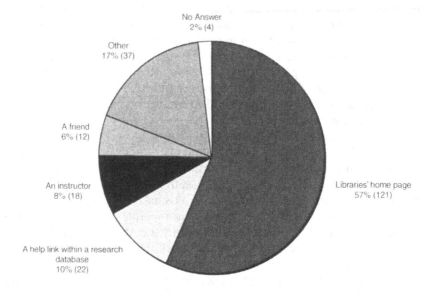

about the service in a library instruction session or from a web page other than the libraries' home page.

Granfield also asked users how they found out about their service and found that the vast majority (67.5%) found the service through the library website, but no further breakdown is offered. She also found that 11.3% learned about the service from library instruction. Kibbee et al. (p. 31-32) did not ask users how they found out about the service, but examined the addresses of the referrer web sites for each session and found that 50% of their users accessed the service from the library's home page, and another 27% came from the online catalog. During the period covered by this study, BGSU did not have links to the service embedded in our online catalog, and Kibbee et al. did not have links embedded in their databases. Clearly students do access the service at their point of need, and links embedded through a library's website, OPAC, and proprietary databases will increase use.

Location of the Users

Forty percent of our users were on campus but outside of the libraries (Figure 7) when they accessed our service. This is not surprising since

FIGURE 7. When You Initiated Your Chat Session, Where Were You?

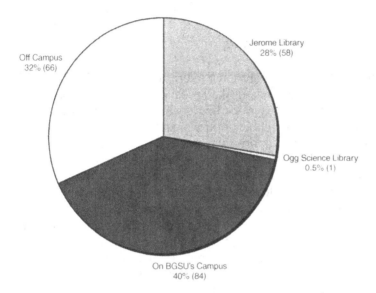

so many of our students live on campus. What is surprising is that almost as many users accessed the service from within the libraries (29%) as from off campus (32%). Only one other study reported on the location of their users. Granfield examined the IP address of users of their service, and found that 20% were located in the library. However, she notes that this figure does not exclude librarians practicing or testing the software, and therefore is more "inflated" than other location numbers. Compared to our users, a much larger percentage of Granfield's users (67%) were off campus.

It would be interesting to know if this difference in the percentages of in-library users of digital reference services is an anomaly, or if it reflects something more specific about our users or the layout and approachability of our physical reference desk. Some light may be shed on why users in the library select a digital reference mode over an in-person visit to the reference desk by results reported by Foley, as well as Rupple et al. Foley (p. 43-44) asked users why they chose instant messaging over another mode of reference and users cited reasons related to convenience and anonymity. Ruppel et al. (p. 190-192) also asked users what they perceived to the advantages of a digital reference service. Again, user responses show that some prefer the anonymity of digital reference service, as well as the convenience, whether it is not having to physically come to the library, or not having to get up from their computer.

User Perception of Learning

One of the ideas we are most interested in exploring is teaching and learning at the reference desk. To gauge user perceptions on whether and what they may have learned during their transaction, we offered them seven multiple-choice options, and a free-text comment space to answer. These seven options were determined by the librarians as skills that we often teach over the service and on the reference desk. The numbers of users indicating what they learned are shown in Figure 8. Some users selected multiple answers and some did not answer at all. Most of the identifiable results involve using proprietary databases or the online catalog. This is not surprising given the significant amount of questions we get related to the questions type "articles on. . . ." User selecting the "other" category (47) often offered comments in the free-text section. This ranged from comments like, "How to get to Eres," to "more information to create a work cited page."

FIGURE 8. What Did You Learn as a Result of Your Chat Session?

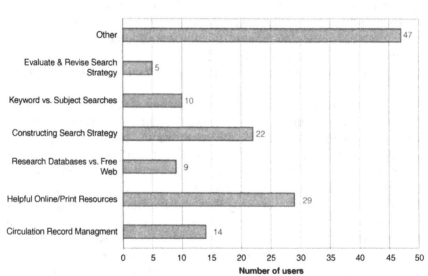

User Satisfaction

To examine user satisfaction with the service, we asked them four different questions. These questions ask users to consider their satisfaction with the service, as well as the information or materials they discovered as a result of their session, how helpful they felt the session was overall, and whether they intended to use the service again. Figure 9 details the responses to three of our satisfaction questions. Obviously, users are very happy with this service. Overall satisfaction ratings were highest, with 92% of the users responding "yes." Getting the expected help received the lowest "yes," with 83% and the highest "partly" with 14%. A look at the user comments for this question reveals some users noting technical problems, and others less than thrilled that they were referred somewhere else in the libraries. One user stated, "She referred

FIGURE 9. User Satisfaction

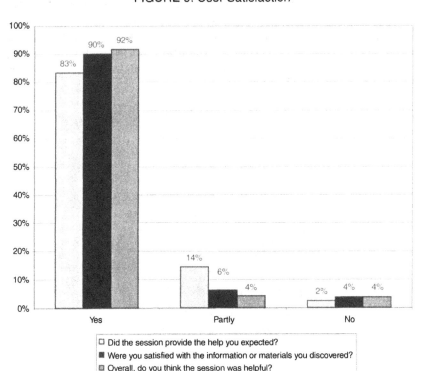

me to the right department but I couldn't get hooked up through the internet [sic] with the librarian on the third floor. I wish that I could have." Figure 10 shows how users responded when asked if they will use the service again. Like the other satisfaction questions, the positive response rate was very high (91%). Seven percent said they would not use the service and some of these were other librarians investigating the service.

Our satisfaction results are similar to the results of other user surveys. Ruppel et al. (p. 188) reported that a large majority of users found their service "very helpful," and 90% of their users said they would use the system again. Kibbee et al. (p. 34) found that "90 per cent of the respondents reported the completeness of the answer to their question as very good or excellent. Nearly 85 per cent found the service easy to use and would use it again." Marsteller and Neuhaus reported that about 88% of their users indicated that they would use the service again and about 75% said they had received the information they needed.

We also asked users how we might be able to improve the service. Here we received many comments such as, "It's great," and "The service was wonderful." We also received a few comments that the librarians could be faster or that we could use more librarians, e.g., "Maybe more librarians so it doesn't take as long. Since they have other people to help and stuff [sic]." Slowness of the librarians might be attributable to staffing the service at the reference desk, where interruptions are

FIGURE 10. Will You Use This Service Again?

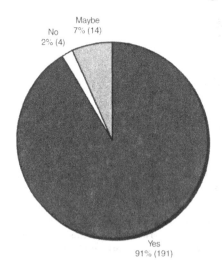

common and should be improved by staffing the service away from the public service points, if possible.

CONCLUSION
AND IMPLICATIONS FOR FURTHER RESEARCH

Our data and the results of the other studies indicate that digital reference services are appreciated by our users and that many of them find these reference transactions to be highly satisfactory. As this medium evolves, it will be interesting to continue to study the similarities and differences from institution to institution. Are our users and their needs too unique to our institutions to follow similar patterns? If we change their expectations (that we are not available after 10:00 p.m.), does that redistribute use or will it add significantly more users we are currently not reaching? When do the traffic patterns on a digital service parallel the traffic at the desk, and when don't they?

While a subject breakdown of question types might be useful for luring subject specialists into participation, hopefully further investigation and discussion on this issue could determine more meaningful categories of reference questions that will assist generalists in training and preparation for staffing their digital reference services. Transcript examination could also be helpful when considering revision to a library's web site. Are there recurring questions that may be better answered with a better web design? If the location of the link to the service is the best way to expose users to the service, how can we integrate this throughout our web sites and into every place a user may have a question?

Perhaps most intriguing is: why does it seem that users are *so* satisfied with this service compared to what we know from prior research about their satisfaction with service at the reference desk? Can we find out more about why users, especially users in the library, would pick a digital reference service over the librarian at the reference desk, and can we change this? Is there a relationship between why users would select digital reference over in-person when they are in the library and why they are so satisfied with this service?

REFERENCES

Bowling Green State University. Office of Institutional Research. (2002). *BGSU Fact Book 2002-2003.* http://www.bgsu.edu/offices/ir/factbook/coverpage.htm (February 27, 2003).
Bowling Green State University. Office of Institutional Research. (2002). "Student

Life." *Common Data Set, Fall 2002.* http://www.bgsu.edu/offices/ir/cds/studentlife. htm. (February 27, 2003).

Broughton, K. (2001). "Our Experiment in Online, Real-Time Reference." *Computers in Libraries,* 21(4): 26-31.

Foley, M. (2002). "Instant Messaging Reference in an Academic Library: A Case Study." *College & Research Libraries* 63(1): 36-45.

Granfield, D. (2002). *McConnell Funding Project Final Report. A Digital Reference Service for a Digital Library: Chat Technology in a Remote Reference Service.* May 15. http://www.ryerson.ca/library/ask/McConnell.pdf (March 3, 2003).

Katz, W.A. (1987). "Reference Questions." *Introduction to Reference Work, Volume I: Basic Information Sources.* 5th ed. Boston: McGraw-Hill, pp. 11-16.

Kibbee, J., D. Ward, and W. Ma. (2002). "Virtual Service, Real Data: Results of a Pilot Study." *Reference Services Review* 31(1): 25-36.

Marsteller, M. and P. Neuhaus. (2001). *The Chat Reference Experience at Carnegie Mellon University.* Presentation at American Library Association Annual Conference, 2001. http://www.contrib.andrew.cmu.edu/~matthewm/ALA_2001_chat.html (March 6, 2003).

Ruppel, M. and J. C. Fagan. (2002). "Instant Messaging Reference: Users' Evaluation of Library Chat." *Reference Services Review* 30(3): 183-197.

Sears, J. (2001). "Chat Reference Service: An Analysis of One Semester's Data." *Issues in Science and Technology Librarianship.* 32. http://www.library.ucsb.edu/istl/01-fall/article2.html (November 26, 2001).

Sloan, B. (2001). *Ready for Reference: Academic Libraries Offer Live Web-Based Reference. Evaluating System Use.* July 11. http://www.lis.uiuc.edu/~b-sloan/r4r.final. htm (December 5, 2001).

Going Where the Students Are:
Live/Web Reference at Cal Poly Pomona

Kathleen Dunn
Ann Morgan

SUMMARY. Increased student use of the Internet and declining reference desk statistics are factors encouraging academic reference librarians to look for new ways to reach patrons. Web-based customer contact center software gives librarians the tools to provide interactive, 24/7 reference service to Internet users. This article describes how the library at California State Polytechnic University, Pomona developed its live/web reference service. We discuss the factors that encouraged us to launch the service, the challenges that we encountered along the way, and examples of our experiences to date. *[Article copies available for a fee from The Haworth Document Delivery Service: 1-800-HAWORTH. E-mail address: <docdelivery@haworthpress.com> Website: <http://www.HaworthPress.com> © 2002/2003 by The Haworth Press, Inc. All rights reserved.]*

KEYWORDS. Reference service, academic libraries, library consortiums, live reference, electronic reference, digital reference, *24/7 Reference*, marketing, California State Polytechnic University, Pomona

Kathleen Dunn (E-mail: kkdunn@csupomona.edu) is Assistant University Librarian, Reference, Instruction, and Collection Services, California State Polytechnic University, Pomona, and Chair, California State University Live/Web Reference Task Force. Ann Morgan (E-mail: aemorgan@csupomona.edu) is Reference Librarian and Liason for askNow, both at California State Polytechnic University, 3801 West Temple Avenue, Pomona, CA 91768.

[Haworth co-indexing entry note]: "Going Where the Students Are: Live/Web Reference at Cal Poly Pomona." Dunn, Kathleen, and Ann Morgan. Co-published simultaneously in *The Reference Librarian* (The Haworth Information Press, an imprint of The Haworth Press, Inc.) No. 79/80, 2002/2003, pp. 201-213; and: *Digital Reference Services* (ed: Bill Katz) The Haworth Information Press, an imprint of The Haworth Press, Inc., 2002/2003, pp. 201-213. Single or multiple copies of this article are available for a fee from The Haworth Document Delivery Service [1-800-HAWORTH, 9:00 a.m. - 5:00 p.m. (EST). E-mail address: docdelivery@haworthpress.com].

INTRODUCTION

It is unmistakable and the signs are everywhere–in waiting lines for in-house computers, in database usage statistics, and in the changing use of library collections and services. Our students love the web, and so do we. Who wouldn't like the 24/7 access, the wealth of facts and information that span the world? As librarians we know, however, that much essential reference information is not free on the web and that there is more to research than Google. The time is right to experiment with new ways to bring our reference expertise to students who use the Internet for class-related research.

In summer 2000, before live/web reference was widely embraced by academic librarians, a few adventurous Cal Poly Pomona Librarians decided to seriously consider what it would take to implement a live, interactive web-based reference service. This article presents the factors that encouraged us to launch an Internet counterpart to the reference desk, the challenges that we encountered along the way, the elements of our askNow service, and examples of our experiences to date.

ESSENTIAL DEFINITIONS

Live/web reference goes by many names–live reference, live/web reference, chat reference, virtual and digital reference. Each of these designations has drawbacks, and the term "live reference" in particular elicits guffaws from librarians ("What, reference wasn't live before!"). In this article we use "live/web reference" to indicate the real-time, interactive nature of this service. The definitions for the concept and the technology that makes it possible are as follows:

Live/web reference: the provision of real-time, interactive personal reference assistance via web-based customer contact center software.

Web-based customer contact center software: software that enables questions to be asked and answered in real-time over the World Wide Web in a secure, private environment, using text-based chat, voice over IP and video, web pages, slide shows, and other materials that can be sent to the patron's browser, including web forms that can be filled out by both the patron and librarian; and that enables patrons to receive a transcript of the transaction with the referenced web sites embedded.

RATIONALE FOR A LIVE/WEB REFERENCE SERVICE

A member of the 23 campus California State University system (CSU), California State Polytechnic University Pomona (Cal Poly Pomona) currently enrolls approximately 17,000 full time equivalent students (FTES). Following the model of all CSUs, Cal Poly Pomona supports one library to serve the entire campus. The University Library has a strong commitment to the use of emerging information technologies and focuses on remote access to services and collections as well as on quality on-site services. The collection currently exceeds 2.4 million items in all formats, including a substantial number of ejournals, ebooks, and electronic databases.

Like most academic libraries we offered a number of options for reference service: walk-in at the Reference Desk, in-depth subject-specific assistance by appointment, email reference, and telephone reference. By the summer of 2000, however, several factors impelled us to investigate adding a real-time, Internet reference service. Substantial database use statistics and extensive use of our in-house computer workstations indicated that students were eagerly using the Internet. Analysis of our reference desk statistics confirmed a significant decline in questions asked at the Reference Desk over a five year period, with an even greater decline over ten years. The University Library offered a rich variety of resources and services on the Web, making it attractive for students to visit the library from remote locations. The availability of web-based customer contact center software in use by groups such as LSSI and 24/7 Reference made a sophisticated Internet reference service a real possibility. Both products also offered an opportunity for us to be part of a consortium that would extend the hours of our service.

BUILDING KNOWLEDGE AND ACCEPTANCE

Our first challenge was to make sure that all reference staff, both librarians and support staff, understood the basic concept of live/web reference and how it differs from traditional desk-based reference assistance.

The concept was introduced to our reference staff via a tape recording of the ALA 2000 Annual Conference session on digital reference entitled "24/7 Reference: High Tech, High Touch." This was followed by a visit from Susan McGlammery, Director of the 24/7 Reference Project located nearby in Los Angeles. After her dynamic presentation and demonstration of the 24/7 Reference software nearly everyone was enthusiastic about beginning our own experiment with a live/web reference service. Seeing the software in action made visible the potential of the Internet for delivering reference service to a greater percentage of our students.

Research and testing also built knowledge and acceptance. We discovered how academic libraries were incorporating live/web reference into their service plans and we developed a general knowledge of the various software options currently in use. Research activities included reading articles, monitoring listservs for digital reference discussions, and perusing web sites of libraries providing digital reference services. Reference staff tried out the services from the patron side by asking questions at various library websites and some of us also tried commercial services such as Lands' End Live. These activities generated enthusiasm for a live/web reference service.

SOFTWARE AND SUPPORT

Software and support proved the least of our concerns. Cal Poly Pomona as a member of the Arroyo Seco Library Network of the California State Library was entitled to participate at no cost in the *24/7 Reference* grant project.[1] A significant advantage of joining *24/7 Reference* was the opportunity to participate in a consortium. We knew that on our own we would never be able to offer enough hours to make the service viable to our campus community.

In order to authenticate our site-licensed databases we decided to purchase, at a cost of about $3,000, a dedicated server that is housed and maintained in the library. This is the only significant cost that we have incurred to date for this project. The ability to use our databases in live/ web reference sessions boosted confidence in our ability to provide a quality service.

TRAINING

We decided that everyone who worked on the Reference Desk would participate in this new service–seven Reference Librarians, three Library Assistants, and the AUL who started us off on this adventure. This decision enabled us to distribute the work and upgrade everyone's skills on an experimental, but potentially essential method of delivering reference assistance to university students. Therefore, all reference staff participated in the following training activities:

Expert training with 24/7 Reference staff. The first session, in May 2001, focused on using the software effectively. The October 2001 session focused on policy and service issues and on resolving problems with our use of the software;

Training through organized practice. Throughout July and August 2001 we scheduled our staff in teams of two, with one team scheduled to practice one hour each day. During the hour each partner spent half the time as librarian and half the time as patron. Partners rotated so that each person had the opportunity to work with a variety of people; and

Training through "real-life" experience. Before going "live" to the public we went "live" to our library. We sent out an email announcement to all library staff describing our project and inviting them to submit questions during specified hours. This practice experience was more "real-life" in that we did not know if or when a question would be coming and we did not always know which staff member was at the patron end.

Lessons Learned in Training and Practice

During the training and practice period we learned that there was more to preparing for a live/web reference service than just learning about the software. In theory, live/web reference is simply the provision of reference in another format, and that is certainly true. Yet, we observed and later experienced the fact that doing reference on the Internet is truly different. It is a different modality that is entirely technology-based and requires learning new skills. It takes considerable experience to become comfortable with the difference. Ample time for training, testing, and keeping in touch with others involved in this developing area of reference service proved essential to our willingness to keep our experiment on track. We also used Lipow and Coffman's manual on establishing a live/web reference service which includes practice exercises and a helpful section that outlines the differences between live/web reference and face-to-face reference.[2] Here are the highlights of lessons learned.

Communicating in a new way. None of our staff had experience with chat services, so we had to learn about communicating in the chat environment, for example, using short sentences, letting the patron know what you're doing, reminding the patron that you're still there, managing the pressure to work fast and respond quickly, and working without audio and visual cues.

Working effectively with the software. The software has multiple features and functionalities. Librarians must be comfortable working with multiple windows and there are many details to keep track of within each window. Basic procedures like logging in and picking up the patron require several steps that must be done in a certain order. The software is somewhat "touchy," for example, clicking at the wrong time or re-clicking because you're not sure you already clicked can cause screens to freeze. It is important to work methodically, to concentrate and pay attention to detail, and to work as quickly as possible without making mistakes.

Working with limitations. It is necessary to find creative ways around limitations and software glitches beyond our control. For example, before we had our own *24/7 Reference* server we could not use most of our subscription databases during live/web reference sessions; however, we were still able to suggest appropriate databases and advise on search strategies. When the Escort or co-browsing feature does not work properly, this same strategy is effective in getting people started on their research.

ISSUES FOR STAFF

While most of our reference staff were interested in a live/web reference service, some areas of concern emerged that are likely common to all librarians who consider a live/web reference service.

The primary issue was workload. Cal Poly Pomona has a small reference staff for a campus of its size. In addition to reference responsibilities, all of our reference librarians participate in instruction, collection management, library and campus committees, and professional development activities. How would we find time for another service? Fortunately, we were able to join the *24/7 Reference* consortium which limited the number of hours per day that we needed to devote to the service.

Secondly, there was concern about whether this was a good way to provide quality reference service. Wouldn't patrons get better service at the reference desk or even over the phone or by email? We are still in the process of addressing this concern as we continue to answer questions and study the transcripts generated by the *24/7 Reference* software.

Third, how much would people use this service? All available reports from other academic libraries indicated low to moderate use of live/web reference services. What if the use was so low that we could not get sufficient expertise with the software? On the other hand, what if the service was really popular? How would we handle it?

People also expressed concerns that proved unfounded, for example, that patrons would want photocopies, or that the question would require a print resource. In fact, most questions are easily answered with web-based resources.

HOURS AND STAFFING

A descriptive name for marketing and easy identification can increase the use of a new service. We settled on *askNow*, a name that implies immediate opportunity. *askNow* was first offered to the campus during Winter Quarter 2002, 4:00 p.m. to 6:00 p.m., Monday through Thursday. In Spring Quarter 2002 *askNow* became a 24/7 service, with Cal Poly Pomona staff providing service 7:00 p.m.-9:00 p.m. Monday and Noon-2:00 p.m. Tuesday through Thursday, with *24/7 Reference* covering all other hours. How did we settle on these schedules and with what success?

With a staff already stretched with many established responsibilities, staffing a live/web reference service was going to be a challenge. We decided to start by providing the service for limited hours–two hours a day, Monday through Thursday for a total of eight hours a week. Each person would be scheduled to staff the service about once every two weeks or so–not much of an addition to anyone's workload.

Our goal was to reach as many students as possible during the few hours the service was available. Reference desk use statistics pinpoint the hours of greatest use at our Reference desk, but preferred hours for a digital reference service would not necessarily coincide with heavy traffic times at the Reference desk. Reports from other libraries offering live/web reference[3] suggested more use in the late afternoon and evening, encouraging us to settle on 4:00 p.m. to 6:00 p.m. We maintained this schedule for Winter Quarter, yet even with an intensive marketing effort, the service averaged barely a question a week.

Rethinking Hours and Going 24/7

Offering the service during very limited hours was not much help to students. In addition, enthusiasm among reference staff would not remain high unless more people used the service. We needed feedback from our own students on preferred hours and we had to find a way to offer more hours.

Toward the end of Winter Quarter, a brief survey was distributed from the Reference Desk asking people to indicate the blocks of time that they would mostly likely make use of the service. Based on the survey results, we changed our service hours to Mondays 7:00 p.m. to 9:00 p.m. and Tuesdays through Thursdays, 12 Noon to 2:00 p.m.

The solution to more hours came from the *24/7 Reference* grant project. They were willing to monitor *askNow* around the clock, excluding the eight hours staffed by Cal Poly Pomona librarians and library assistants. We gratefully accepted their offer! Our campus community would now have true 24 hour access to reference assistance. The Reference staff benefited as well. Gone was the pressure to add more service hours to our busy schedule. We could continue to gain experience with the software and tap into the expertise of librarians with more experience in remote reference assistance.

MARKETING

Common wisdom suggests that marketing is essential to generate use of any new service. Here is what we did to advertise *askNow*:

- Placed a prominent link on the Library home page and added links to our "Ask a Librarian" page, the Library Catalog homepage, and the primary databases menu page;
- Created bookmarks with a color reproduction of the *askNow* logo on one side and a short description and hours on reverse side;
- Placed table tents, similar to the bookmarks, in the library and in other campus buildings;
- Advertised through campus electronic message boards, library website, and the Library listserv–"Latest News from the Library";
- Placed an article in *PolyCentric*, the campus newsletter;

- Produced a one page *askNow* FAQ that was posted in study rooms. We also asked the academic departments to post the FAQ on their bulletin boards; and
- Promoted the *askNow* service in Bibliographic Instruction sessions.

Was our marketing strategy effective? Use of *askNow* did not increase as a result of marketing; however, the limited hours were also an obvious factor in the lack of use. Point-of-use advertising is likely the most effective. Web-based services like *askNow* require links on the Library home page, the library catalog, and the database pages as a constant reminder to users that the service is available when needed. The central purpose of all other advertising is name recognition and to indicate hours of operation, if the service is not available 24/7.

USE OF *askNow*

We have very little data as yet on how much students or other users really like the service. Based on comments recorded in transcripts of sessions, some using the service expressed appreciation with comments like "this is great" and "cool service." Also, we do have some repeat users, which is a good sign. Some patrons send questions, but hang up or disconnect before receiving an answer. We have also had some very rude patrons. We do, however, have data on use of *askNow*. The following information is based on statistics and other data available through the reporting function of the *24/7 Reference* software.

During Winter Quarter 2002, when *askNow* was only available 8 hours a week, we averaged about 1 question a week. In Spring Quarter 2002, with the addition of round-the-clock service, we averaged 10-15 questions a week in the busiest months. As Figure 1 demonstrates, the use of *askNow* continues to grow with natural declines in use during summer months and vacations.

Initially, the lack of questions generated frustration and concerns about gaining sufficient experience with the software. It also made us question whether or not people really wanted this type of service. However, staff satisfaction with the service increased as it received more use, and particularly when they had a successful interaction with a student.

Types of Questions and Users

Transcript date, for example, email addresses and types of questions asked, indicate that most of the questions come from Cal Poly Pomona

FIGURE 1. *askNOW* Questions 2002

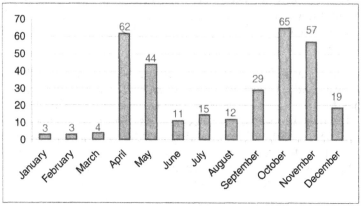

students. Students from other schools often identify themselves as such, for example, "I'm a student at . . ." These students often want to know if they can check out books from our library or if they can access our databases. A few questions have come from high school students and at least five from librarians or MLIS students asking questions about the service or the software. Since September 2002 we have been getting questions from students at other California State Universities as well as from academic libraries across the country that are participating in *24/7 Reference*. The questions fall generally into the following categories:

- Fifty percent reference questions, for example;
  - What are the best databases for journals concerning American foreign policy?
  - I'm looking for a source that discusses how 9/11 has impacted the religious faith of people.
  - How can I go about looking for critical essays on *The Great Gatsby*?
  - I need statistical information on what people think about the legalization of marijuana.
  - How many times was the Taft-Hartley Act invoked?
- Twenty-nine percent questions about library policies or technical problems encountered when accessing electronic resources, for example;

- Problems connecting to databases: interpretation of error messages, trouble getting into a specific database, or problems with library PIN (Personal Identification Number, required for off-campus access to databases and electronic resources).
- Course reserves: how to find materials professors had put on reserve or how to retrieve documents on our electronic reserve system.
- Library hours, renewals, fines, and other policy issues comprised about half the questions in this category.

- Sixteen percent known item or quick lookup questions, for example;

  - I need an article from *Journal of Bacteriology*, 1992, v. 174, 7419-7427.
  - Does the library have any books on how to learn French?
  - Is it possible to see the *California Manufacturers Register* online?

Some questions are not suitable for a remote question/answer service, even if it is real-time and interactive. People with in-depth research questions will still need to come to the library and talk to a librarian about the range of available resources, including print and microform resources.

It takes longer to answer questions through *askNow*. We are not using audio or video technology, though it is available in web contact center software. The need to type everything out and push web pages in a sequential manner, plus the pauses and overlaps of the Internet conversation between librarian and patron, adds time to the interaction that is not necessary in a face-to-face encounter.

Questions Answered Through a Multi-Types Consortium

The *24/7 Reference* consortium is comprised of public, academic, community college, and special libraries. Prior to Sept 2002 questions from Cal Poly Pomona students were answered mostly by *24/7 Reference* staff (mostly public librarians), except for the 8 hours when our librarians staffed the service. Currently members of the *24/7 Reference* Academic Category, including the Cal Poly Pomona University Library, answer questions for each other.

Overall other librarians have responded well to questions asked by Cal Poly Pomona students. They do good reference interviews and make excellent use of our library web pages to find answers to policy questions. They tell our students to contact our library directly for policy questions that can't be answered from our web pages. On the down side, students have sometimes been directed to public libraries instead of to our own catalog, or directed to the Internet when we might have recommended another approach such as searching a particular database. Also librarians not working in our library don't recognize questions that we routinely field, for example, a professor's peculiar assignment or questions generated by a workbook used in remedial English classes. But for the most part they worked hard to provide appropriate assistance.

THE FUTURE OF askNow AT CAL POLY POMONA

What is the future of *askNow*? It is uncertain, and dependent on more than just our enthusiasm and willingness to provide the service. To be really successful, such a service must be available many hours a day. It must be reliable as well, always there when needed. It is important that users believe they have received useful, accurate answers to their questions, and within reasonable time limits. Furthermore librarians and library administration must believe that such a service offers enough added value to be worthy of the time and money required to support it.

If our library can continue to share the workload within a 24-hour consortium, it is likely that *askNow* will continue and use will increase. For example, *24/7 Reference* is currently so busy that they have multiple questions at the same time. Fortunately, the libraries of the California State University system are testing a consortium approach to a live/ web reference service. Cal Poly Pomona University Library is one of six CSU libraries participating in the *24/7 Reference* part of CSU Live/ Web Reference Pilot Project.[4] The pilot project began in September 2002 and ended in May 2003. A live/web reference service offered by a consortium of CSU libraries with after-hours contractual assistance from a service like *24/7 Reference* may be an ideal model for delivering real-time, interactive reference assistance to CSU students, all 300,000 of them!

It may be a while before we know if a service like *askNow* will really catch on with university students, or if they will continue to take the "do it yourself" approach that the Internet enables so well. One thing is essential, however. Librarians must continue to experiment with ways of providing quality reference assistance in the Internet environment.

REFERENCES AND NOTES

1. *24/7 Reference* is a project of the Metropolitan Cooperative Library System (on-line, <http://www.mcls.org/nonmembers/index.cfm>), supported by Federal Library Services and Technology Act funding, administered by the California State Library. *24/7 Reference* is a set of software tools enabling librarians to provide real-time reference assistance over the Internet, and a consortium of multi-type libraries, mainly located in California, that provide 24 hour reference service to patrons of participating libraries. Online, <http://www.247ref.org/>.

2. Lipow, Ann Grodzins and Steve Coffman. *Establishing a Virtual Reference Service; VRD Training Manual.* Berkeley: Library Solutions Press, 2001.

3. Sloan, Bernie. *Ready for Reference: Academic Libraries Offer Live Web-Based Reference; Evaluating System Use.* July 11, 2001. Online, <http://www.lis.uiuc.edu/~b-sloan/r4r.final.htm> Accessed: 1-6-2003.

4. In December 2001, the Council of Library Deans/Directors of the California State University system established the CSU Live/Web Reference Task Force to investigate the feasibility of establishing a system-wide live/web reference service for the CSU. The Task Force subsequently initiated a pilot project for academic year 2002-2003 to test two products, *24/7 Reference* and *Convey.* Six CSU libraries, including Cal Poly Pomona, participated in the *24/7 Reference* pilot study, testing the technical capabilities of the software and the consortium features of the *24/7 Reference* service. CSU Live/Web Reference Task Force website: http://www.csupomona.edu/~kkdunn/livereftaskf/livereftfmain.htm.

Virtual Reference at Duke:
An Informal History

Phil Blank

SUMMARY. This article examines the history (2000-2003) of the virtual reference program at Duke University and covers the efforts involved at determining need, evaluating and selecting software, implementing policies and experimenting with the applications. Attention is paid to librarians' perception of virtual reference service as compared to other services. Future trends and consortium possibilities, both academic and across North Carolina, are also considered. *[Article copies available for a fee from The Haworth Document Delivery Service: 1-800-HAWORTH. E-mail address: <docdelivery@haworthpress.com> Website: <http://www.HaworthPress. com> © 2002/2003 by The Haworth Press, Inc. All rights reserved.]*

KEYWORDS. Virtual reference, LSSI, Duke University, North Carolina, Perkins Library, academic

THE BEGINNING: 2000

It is hard to remember the beginning of virtual reference at Duke, but it is much easier to remember the students who came into the library not to drink coffee or talk with friends but to "chat" on the computers. They

Phil Blank is Reference Librarian, Perkins Library, Duke University, Durham, NC 27708 (E-mail: phil.blank@duke.edu).

[Haworth co-indexing entry note]: "Virtual Reference at Duke: An Informal History." Blank, Phil. Co-published simultaneously in *The Reference Librarian* (The Haworth Information Press, an imprint of The Haworth Press, Inc.) No. 79/80, 2002/2003, pp. 215-224; and: *Digital Reference Services* (ed: Bill Katz) The Haworth Information Press, an imprint of The Haworth Press, Inc., 2002/2003, pp. 215-224. Single or multiple copies of this article are available for a fee from The Haworth Document Delivery Service [1-800-HAWORTH, 9:00 a.m. - 5:00 p.m. (EST). E-mail address: docdelivery@haworthpress.com].

10.1300/J120v38n79_14

tended to sit as far from the reference desk as they could and have a permanent smile on their face as their eyes were transfixed to the screen and their fingers poised on the keyboard. At the same time, the Internet was burgeoning with customer service initiatives and ideas, spurred on by the now infamous bubble of the late 1990s. Many of us were already completing tasks like buying airline tickets, banking and buying books online. Some popular companies began to offer live help online through chat software.

The adoption of this technology to the academic reference setting seemed obvious. In fact, for a few it seemed like the salvation of reference service. Duke, like many research libraries around the country, was seeing a significant decline in the number of reference questions. Attendance count was declining slowly. Gradually, we were starting to wonder if, for a significant group of users, the "library" was not a beloved building but a website, www.lib.duke.edu. Certainly some of these invisible users were abroad but we suspected many were students and faculty on campus. If they were missing the building, then they were also missing many opportunities to get live help when they needed it. Virtual reference was seen as part of a broader struggle to offer the same level of service on our website that we offered in the building.

This struggle was articulated, officially, in "Critical Choices: Perkins Library System Plan: 2000-2005." Under the heading "Theme 2: The Library as Facilitator of Learning, Teaching and Instruction" our library committed itself to the following:

GOAL 2.3: Develop Innovative, Customized Reference Services for Users Regardless of Location

Since many of the library's resources are available on the Web, it is highly desirable to offer reference service instantly to users in their offices, homes or dorms. Users currently have access to telephone and e-mail reference, but both have limitations. We propose to offer remote reference service to users in computer clusters, the student center, or wherever students might be studying. With the increased emphasis on study abroad, the library will also ensure that participants in international programs enjoy the same level of access that on-campus students do.

Strategies

- *Live real-time reference. Initiate the use of one of the new web-based services, such as LivePerson (see www.liveperson.com) or the Virtual Reference Desk (www.lssi.com), which use call center chat software to deliver reference service to users regardless of location or time. A reference librarian would be available to answer questions about library and free web resources throughout the hours the service is available. This is often more convenient than e-mail or telephone, especially when the user needs help with databases or web searching. The main audience would be on-campus remote users, but the service would also be especially helpful for distance users, such as study-abroad students. Beginning with limited hours, with an e-mail default after-hours, the goal would be to expand to a 24/7 service, probably in collaboration with other area universities.*

- *Remote reference stations. Establish "remote reference" locations around campus using web-based videoconferencing. Installing webcams in locations such as Lilly, the Levine Science Research Center, the Sanford Institute, the Bryan Center, and the computer clusters would make this possible, when broad-band communications are sufficiently advanced to make this feasible.*
- *Other possibilities include a web telephone system and remote applications sharing or remote control software.*

DETERMINING NEED AND EVALUATION: WINTER 2000-SPRING 2001

To pursue our strategic plan, the Executive Group established a Virtual Reference Planning committee. The charge was, "in consultation with students, faculty and professional schools, determine potential need for and interest in real-time digital reference service using call center software at Duke." Our first step was to design a survey to test the validity of our assumptions. The survey was posted on the home page and (since the service itself would be available to anyone who used the library or home page) was open to everyone. Our assumption that the home page is more dominant than the building was partially supported by the results.

How many times a week do you visit the . . .	Building	Website
More than Three	31.3%	50.4%
Three times	11.9%	11.3%

Twice	15.8%	14.9%
Once	34%	13.1%
Less than once a week	6.6%	9.6%

335 respondents

Other questions determined the users' familiarity with chat software (two-thirds had never used it) and their experience with reference (over half had asked more than three questions).

We also interviewed undergraduate and graduate student representatives about the service. Undergrads liked the idea of expanded hours of service, which they perceived as being part of the project. While it was a long-term goal, it was not an immediate plan and it led to an important insight: people assume virtual reference is 24/7. Even in our strategic plan, virtual reference was linked to 24/7 service. When they were pressed, the undergraduates admitted the real need was for reference help from 10 p.m. to midnight (our reference desk closes at 10 p.m. Monday through Thursday). Further evidence that 24/7 was not an immediate need was provided by our web statistics, which showed a remarkable decrease of activity on our home page after 2 a.m.

Graduate students too generally seemed to like the idea of the service. Some of them worried that their dial-up service from their home offices would be too slow. Others worried that the service's costs or staff time would come at the expense of traditional services. In interviews with both the graduate and the undergraduate representatives it became obvious that "virtual reference" or "real-time help" were not intuitive terms. Often the only way to clarify how it differed from traditional chatting (AOL Instant Messenger was the dominant model at the time) was to demonstrate it. Based on the interviews and the survey results, it was determined that Duke did have a need for this service. In retrospect, one issue we never addressed was how many people would use it. I'm still not sure I would know how to reliably determine that without actually trying it.

SELECTION: SPRING 2001

Distinguishing between chat services in spring of 2001 was dreadful. Terms like "cobrowsing" and "escorting" meant different things to different vendors (and indeed to different librarians as well). Some of the vendors with competitive products seemed to arise out of a void and at times, looked like they might go back at any time. The Internet bubble had officially bust by then and companies who never designed themselves to deal with the academic market began cold calling. In addition, the different functionalities between systems made it clear that there were different ways to do virtual reference. It wasn't enough to simply pick the best one; Duke realized we had to determine our overall philosophy of service as well as evaluate the vendors' products. Almost in desperation, I decided to make a table that would demonstrate how the products met with our informal and formal criteria (http://www.lib.duke.edu/reference/liveonlineref.htm#Evaluation). The table is shockingly simplistic compared to formal analysis done recently but was our first step in evaluation.

In the end, our decision to have one product that was compatible with most browsers and almost all platforms weeded out most of the competition. Also, the promise of collaboration with the nearby University of North Carolina at Chapel Hill and North Carolina State University, both of whom adopted LSSI, affected our decision more seriously than the bells and whistles of each individual product.

TRAINING: SUMMER 2001

LSSI's Virtual Reference Desk required more training than any other system. Librarians from three different departments and two different independent libraries (about 25 librarians in all) spent two days learning how to use the software. Due to the extensive time commitment for training, some adjunct reference librarians did not receive training and to this day, opt out of participating in virtual reference. The training was done in person and the morale of librarians who went through it could be described as "anxious." Several of them asked if I would be available on their first day. In retrospect, the training was too exhaustive and some of the functionality of LSSI's Virtual Reference Desk we have never used. For instance, I instantly decided to encourage librarians to never use the "escort" function but to send pages selectively and deliberately by using the push page button. The ability to host meetings and share files are also used very little, if at all, at Duke. By the end of summer in 2001, we had a virtual reference service and a group of librarians ready to help.

IMPLEMENTATION: FALL 2001

To determine policies and hours, an implementation committee was established. It was Phil Blank, reference librarian along with Ann Miller, head of Public Documents and Kelley Lawton, head of Lilly library, a branch on the undergraduate residential campus. Collaboration to provide a single service among the three departments was rare but has since happened more often. In some ways, asking and trusting the librarians from all three departments to provide reference service to any patron helped us all refine our "generalist" skills. We predicted lots of referrals.

The first year was seen as a pilot program designed to test both the technical service as well as its actual usefulness. The hours were originally Monday through Friday 1 p.m.-5 p.m. Hours were divided according to the staffing levels of the three departments and departments were then responsible for staffing those hours (and covering them in the case of sickness or absence). Shifts were based on our desk model, with librarians responsible for two hours at a time. All shifts assumed the librarian responsible would be in their office. To facilitate communication between librarians, we established an internal listserv and encouraged librarians to join the profession-wide digital reference or virtual reference listservs.

By the end of the year we had changed three crucial aspects of this model: (1) we changed the shifts to one hour, (2) we expanded coverage to 10 p.m. and (3) we shifted responsibilities for shifts from the department to the individual librarians.

Being chained to your desk for two hours was too much. Meetings became harder to arrange and since shifts were overly burdensome, substitutes were occasionally hard to find. Also, hourly shifts encouraged more librarians to become involved and kept people's skills sharp.

Expanding hours into the evening involved making the controversial decision to staff virtual reference on the desk. At the same time, we merged our public documents service point with the general reference service point in the evenings. This allowed both librarians to handle all incoming phone, email, virtual and in-person questions. A student, who was heavily encouraged to refer users to the main desk, staffed the documents desk in the evening. While this is still being tested, librarians here generally do not have difficulties with this arrangement.

I've recently heard staffing virtual reference at the desk referred to as a "disaster" at the most recent Virtual Reference Desk conference. In fact, we have had few problems with it. Before trying it, we were concerned that in-person patrons would not be able to be helped due to our attention being focused on our virtual patron. In fact, that situation has been easily overcome by simply explaining what we are doing to the in-person patron. The most serious problem, which happens infrequently, is the opposite: it is awkward to pick up a call when already engaged in a "flesh and blood" patron. In theory, this issue is covered in the same way as our phone policy, which states that the phone should be ignored if you are already helping a patron at the reference desk. In practice, the desire to pick up the rare virtual question is more pressing than the desire to answer a phone call. Also, while most callers instinctively know to leave a message, it is unclear if virtual reference patrons leave their queries through email or not.

We also discovered that it made more sense to behave as one big committee rather than three different departments. As long as we could determine a reliable way to cover shifts due to sickness or absence, and the workload was equitably distributed, the librarian's departmental allegiance was irrelevant. At the beginning of a semester, I put out a call directly to the virtual reference listserv asking librarians to voluntarily sign up for an hourly shift. Usually we are able to fill the hours within a week. This has led to a flatter organization. Not only scheduling, but policy issues are also more broadly discussed. The implementation committee now meets very rarely and usually only to confirm that the system is working satisfactorily.

UNDERWHELMED BUT AMUSED: WINTER 2001-SPRING 2002

Duke is not alone in finding the number of questions disappointingly low. Many libraries offering virtual reference are seeing low statistics. During our first year we managed to register an average of about 1-2 questions per day. During a recent busy statistics week, we managed to field 51 queries out of 998 total reference interactions (5%-7% when adjusted for actual reference questions). It is still consistently less than email and phone interactions.

Staff morale is surprisingly high yet predictably skeptical about the future of virtual reference. Although they are asked to participate, the opportunities to engage patrons are few. And yet, many librarians here enjoy virtual reference. At Duke, librarians have noticed that reference in virtual mode, though similar in content to reference interviews conducted through email, phone and in-person, feels very different.

First, virtual interactions, surprisingly, are often highly rewarding for both the librarian and the patron. Based on anecdotal interactions with patrons and other librarians, I think patrons are still pleasantly surprised to find a helpful person on the other end of the call. These days, it is easy to see that anyone who uses any sort of virtual communication to accomplish something in the marketplace is happy when an actual person responds. Users also tend to be impressed at the convenience and the added functionality of the library web site. Certainly the novelty aspect of chatting and "pushing pages" adds to the satisfaction as well. The same things do not apply to email or phone interactions. Similarly, most librarians seem happy to get and answer virtual reference questions. This may be due to their infrequency and would certainly change if they were stuck in a "virtual reference bunker" with no other tasks to perform.

Amazingly, the virtual format, I believe, is more conducive to open and honest communication than any of the other formats. It has a strange, "confessional" like nature where students are free to admit any level of ignorance or academic delinquency without fear of shame. The lack of visual cues that so many librarians mourn may be what attracts some users to the virtual environment. In practice, callers whose first question is ably met by the librarian tend to then deluge the librarian with more questions. Again, this phenomenon is less common among phone, email or in-person interactions. During one interaction, I advised the patron to leave the chat window open during their entire research phase and ask questions periodically when they arose. This became a one hour and a half long question with long pauses in between. This option represents an entirely new way for librarians to do reference and students to do research.

Sadly, one thing we all miss is the sharing of reference questions. Since virtual reference tends to be both silent and done in the privacy of one's office, there are few opportunities to overhear good questions or even know if we've had a busy day.

The anxiety that accompanied most of the librarians on their first few days is now replaced with eager anticipation of the next call.

EXPERIMENTATION: SPRING AND FALL 2002

We were also able to use Virtual Reference in experimental ways, especially (1) in fun ways during library promotional events and (2) evening library classes. After being asked to be part of a spring celebration with the entire university, we decided to use virtual reference as a way for students to ask the "answer person," a legendary witty and honest librarian with a secret identity who would respond to any query. We set up wireless access outside in the quad where our tent would be. In the beginning, attendance trickled in, but soon there was a line. Five hours later, our exhausted answer person had finished the last call and had been chatting continuously for close to four hours. At another outdoor festival, we hosted a jeopardy game using the virtual reference software. Beastie Boys Trivia certainly was the most popular category. While I was in my office firing away questions, students in their dorms, at the computer set up at the festival and in one instance, their classroom(!) competed for prizes. Again, people seemed to be entertained not only by the competition but by the novelty of using the virtual reference software to play.

In a less successful effort, I began to offer classes online during evening hours. I offered classes on basic research skills for new students, help with a specific assignment for a writing class and an introduction to history resources. The classes were advertised either on the home page or on the class website. To prepare for the class, I set up a "meeting" using LSSI's software. Attendance at these classes was similar to attendance during our in-building voluntary classes, which is to say, one or two people.

There are other directions we can imagine virtual reference heading towards. Many students, who chat constantly with popular messenging software are confused about our software. Why not use something more familiar, like Windows or AOL Instant Messenger? Currently these don't satisfy our platform and browser compatibility issues, but chat software is developing and becoming more sophisticated and pervasive. Right now, I can request to hear a song from my local university radio station through AOL Instant Messenger. Also, will vendors start to offer live help? Ideally, virtual reference can funnel questions to experts distributed far and wide. Why not become an expert in a particular database, like PsycInfo, and provide help for worldwide users at their common point of need? This could be done in elaborate consortia relationships with libraries and vendors or straight from the vendor and built into the cost of the product.

PLANNING CONSORTIA: 2002-2003

In the last year, Duke has been involved with planning for two consortiums. The State Library of North Carolina has been developing a pilot project to provide virtual reference to the state of North Carolina using academic, public and school libraries. At the same time, the University of North Carolina and North Carolina State University have been informally examining how a consortia arrangement among academic libraries could improve our hours and service. If virtual reference questions remain at their current low level, it is feasible that one librarian could cover all three institutions' demand for reference during currently uncovered hours. During a recent reference meeting, I asked our reference staff if anyone would be willing to staff virtual reference from 10 p.m. to midnight at home. Out of a staff of thirteen, three people said they would be willing. Of course, there are many other issues that still need to be settled before we can begin working from home (books and reference collections being among them) but it is an indication that some librarians are willing to explore the non-traditional opportunities that virtual reference provides. Also, it is entirely possible that reference librarians working at Duke could provide part time virtual reference for LSSI's private call center or work with a variety of private companies to provide virtual reference outside of their work at Duke.

As the anxiety of the early years subsides, we are again reminded of our earlier anxiety: declining reference statistics. Over the water cooler, we are starting to question whether virtual reference is the right tool for this problem. Maybe the problem was not declining building attendance after all, maybe the students are not expected to research as much as they used to, maybe the faculty (who might find it hard to tell from the list of works cited if the student used Google or America: History and Life) are de-emphasizing research. Do they need us less? I'm not convinced. And still, every day, the students gather in the remote corner of the computer cluster with their eyes glued to the monitor, permanent smiles on their faces and their hands poised on the keyboard.

Evaluating Online Real-Time Reference in an Academic Library: Obstacles and Recommendations

Jana Ronan
Patrick Reakes
Gary Cornwell

SUMMARY. Online real-time or "chat" reference, while still in its infancy when compared to traditional reference services is beginning to come of age. The time has come to move beyond the earlier challenges and issues debated at length in the library profession and begin to consider how to evaluate real-time reference. This article will consider obstacles to evaluating chat reference and present practical recommendations. These obstacles are presented in four basic areas including; organizational structure, scarcity of resources, newness of the service, and difficulty developing techniques of assessment or applying existing methodology. *[Article copies available for a fee from The Haworth Document Delivery Service: 1-800-HAWORTH. E-mail address: <docdelivery@haworthpress.com> Website: <http://www.HaworthPress.com> © 2002/2003 by The Haworth Press, Inc. All rights reserved.]*

Jana Ronan is Reference Librarian and Interactive Reference Coordinator, Patrick Reakes is Journalism and Mass Communications Librarian, and Gary Cornwell is Head of Humanities and Social Sciences Services, all at the University of Florida.

Address correspondence to: Jana Ronan, George A. Smathers Libraries, Humanities and Social Science Services Department, University of Florida, P.O. Box 117001, Gainesville, FL 32611-7001.

[Haworth co-indexing entry note]: "Evaluating Online Real-Time Reference in an Academic Library: Obstacles and Recommendations." Ronan, Jana, Patrick Reakes, and Gary Cornwell. Co-published simultaneously in *The Reference Librarian* (The Haworth Information Press, an imprint of The Haworth Press, Inc.) No. 79/80, 2002/2003, pp. 225-240; and: *Digital Reference Services* (ed: Bill Katz) The Haworth Information Press, an imprint of The Haworth Press, Inc., 2002/2003, pp. 225-240. Single or multiple copies of this article are available for a fee from The Haworth Document Delivery Service [1-800-HAWORTH, 9:00 a.m. - 5:00 p.m. (EST). E-mail address: docdelivery@haworthpress.com].

10.1300/J120v38n79_15

KEYWORDS. Real-time, synchronous, chat, reference, evaluation, obstacles

INTRODUCTION

Online real-time reference, while still in its infancy compared to many traditional library services, is beginning to come of age. While there are many academic libraries that have not yet established a synchronous online reference service, at this writing there are a significant number who have paved the way. In a recent survey of Association of Research Library (ARL) member libraries, 54% of those institutions that responded offered some type of "chat" reference service, 31% had been offering the service for over a year, and several libraries had been offering it for over two years (Ronan and Turner, 2002). Among the institutions that initiated real-time reference are Cornell University, SUNY at Morrisville, University of Florida (UF), and the Alliance Library System, Illinois. By April 2001 it was reported that 272 libraries had chat reference services in place (Francoeur, 2001). These early adopters, who made up the "first wave" of libraries offering chat reference, dealt with a plethora of challenges and issues related to the establishment and implementation of these new services. Librarians investigated choices of software and vendors; debated effective models for the administration, staffing, hours and management of the services; dealt with technical infrastructure issues; and with questions about costs and funding. Online forums, such as DIG_REF and Livereference, as well as professional conferences such as Virtual Reference Desk, became popular forums for librarians struggling with these new services.

Until recently, most of the library literature that discusses online synchronous reference service focused on three general areas: surveys examining what libraries are currently doing (Francoeur, 2001; Janes and Hill, 2002; Ronan and Turner, 2002), articles and books describing the implementation of the service (Fagan, 2001; Foley, 2002; Kalikow, 2002; Kibbee, Ward and Ma, 2002; Meola and Stormont, 2002; Ronan, 2003), and articles forecasting the possibilities that chat technology will offer for the future (Sears, 2001). The argument can now be made that chat reference services have reached the second wave of development and investigation. Services have matured to the point where librarians can look beyond the nuances of learning to chat or exotic software features such as "push page." Now is the time to consider the quality of service that is being provided to library patrons. Libraries need to look at ways of measuring and evaluating the provision of chat reference and ensure users are receiving the same level of service online as they are in the more traditional reference models. Centering on online real-time reference, as opposed to other digital reference services such as e-mail or web-based forms, this article will explore obstacles to evaluating chat reference and present practical recommendations for assessment.

Libraries at the front edge of the second wave of chat reference are faced with a number of difficulties, especially as it relates to a true evaluation of service quality. As mentioned earlier, the literature dealing with evaluation is scarce, and most of that discussion is anecdotal (Lankes, McClure, Gross and Pomerantz, 2003). However, that is not to say the issue of reference performance as it relates to online users has not been investigated (see Kasowitz, Bennett, Lankes, 2000; Sloan, 1998; and Strom, 2002). Arguably, the most in-depth treatments of the topic have come about in the venue of recent Virtual Reference Desk conferences (http://www.vrd.org/conf-train.shtml). The Information Institutes at Florida State University and Syracuse University have collaborated on a manual titled *Statistics, Measures and Quality Standards for Assessing Digital Reference Library Services: Guidelines and Procedures* (McClure, Lankes, Gross and Choltco-Devlin, 2002). Additionally, the published proceedings from the 2001 Virtual Reference Desk Conference titled *Implementing Digital Reference Services: Setting Standards and Making it Real* (Lankes, McClure, Gross, and Pomerantz, 2003) include chapters on assessing quality in digital reference services.

STANDARDS AND GUIDELINES

Currently, the standards and guidelines for the reference profession are, understandably, lagging behind the rapidly evolving world of online synchronous reference. These guidelines were initially developed for more traditional forms of reference service and are generally inadequate when applied to the challenges associated with measuring and evaluating librarian effectiveness in the virtual environment. On the positive side, new and revised guidelines are beginning to emerge that should assist libraries as they attempt to deal with the complex issues associated with measures of quality in their real-time reference services. For example, the American Library Association's Reference and User Services Association (RUSA) *Guidelines for Behavioral Performance of Reference and Information Services Professionals* (http://

www.ala.org/rusa/stnd_behavior.html), issued in 1996, are being revised to include virtual reference. Draft copies of the new guidelines distributed prior to ALA Midwinter 2003 do clarify how to be approachable and effective when working with an online user. Similarly, the RUSA guidelines addressing *Professional Competencies for Reference and User Services Librarians,* updated in January of 2003, include a section on evaluation and assessment of services and acknowledge a "large and growing set of delivery channels" for the provision of information, including those delivered via "web-based virtual sessions." Other points discussed include the need to "develop service standards for new and existing information services," creating "an organizational climate in which all existing and proposed services are measured consistently against a standard," and the evaluation of "changes in services to users." Despite the generic nature of these competencies, they are nevertheless a step in the right direction. One of the most promising documents relevant to the evaluation of virtual reference is currently being drafted by an ad hoc committee within RUSA/MARS and is titled *Guidelines for Implementing and Maintaining Virtual Reference Services.* This document emphasizes that libraries should facilitate regular assessment and analysis of the service, evaluate effectiveness and efficiency using input from staff and patrons, and apply other standard guidelines of reference where applicable. However, it is still not at a level of specificity that results in any direct application to evaluating real-time reference.

Difficulty in measuring and evaluating reference service is not limited to new reference provision models. Assessment of traditional reference has always been problematic. Underscoring this fact is a section of the RUSA *Competencies for Reference and User Services Librarians* that states:

> Using evaluation measures for performance of the staff is a challenge. Many aspects of the information service interaction are intangible and difficult to measure objectively. However, the goal of assessing and evaluating performance remains valid, if elusive.

Add to this equation the rapid evolution taking place in the provision of reference in the online synchronous environment, and the element of elusiveness described above increases accordingly. Ironically, despite the lack of guidelines assessing online real-time reference the profession seems split on the best way to approach the problem. One school of thought is that chat reference services can be evaluated by simply modifying models previously developed for traditional reference services. Another is that an entirely new approach is required that will account for the sometimes drastic differences between the two types of reference provision (McClure et al., 2002). While an interesting debate, a discussion of the strengths and weaknesses associated with each approach will not be addressed in this article. Instead, it will concentrate on major obstacles to the evaluation of online real-time reference and practical recommendations for dealing with those obstacles.

OBSTACLES

For discussion purposes, the authors have divided the obstacles to evaluating online real-time reference into four major areas. These major obstacles are: organizational structure; scarcity of resources; challenges inherent in working within such a new area of communication; and difficulty in developing or adapting assessment methodologies.

Organizational Structure

- Volunteerism
- Position descriptions that do not include real-time reference duties and obligations
- Real-time reference operates as an entirely separate service or entity from other reference and public services
- Comfort level of the coordinator/supervisor doing evaluations
- Complex reporting lines and division of responsibilities in collaborative, consortial, or other settings

Organizational structure, or the way in which a service is staffed and managed, can hinder efforts to evaluate reference performance online. At some institutions, real-time reference is part of normal reference duties, and chat reference responsibilities are included in position descriptions. Clearly, when real-time reference is considered part of reference services as a whole and included in job assignments, assessment of staff performance online is easier to initiate. However, many libraries experimenting with virtual reference operate synchronous online reference separately from traditional reference services, or work in cooperative ventures. This can complicate the task of assessment. For example, in many Association of Research Libraries member institutions, a special coordinator manages real-time reference who is not the head of reference services or necessarily in the same department as all of the service providers (Ronan and Turner, 2002). Cross-departmental evaluation and skewed reporting lines can complicate any attempts to assess quality of services.

At the University of Florida, for example, more than thirty librarians and library professionals across six units provide chat reference assistance. A chat coordinator manages the day-to-day operations, including scheduling and training, troubleshooting, backup support and gathering of user feedback. While working across unit lines enhances communication and improves service to users in many ways, this arrangement also makes developing and implementing consistent evaluative measures problematic. Other than addressing glaring problems, the coordinator lacks the supervisory mandate and perhaps even more importantly, the time to examine hundreds of reference transcripts, then forward reports to a variety of supervisors to be included in regularly scheduled evaluations. Setting up a mechanism for supervisors to directly evaluate performance is difficult because many lack familiarity with real-time reference, and also because professional standards for performance are still in the making. This problem is magnified when several libraries are working together in a real-time reference cooperative headed by a central project manager. It is easy to see how evaluation of a librarian's performance by an individual in a completely different library is less than ideal.

The way in which a chat reference service is staffed can present obstacles as well. Many services debut with eager volunteers, rather than by immediately requiring library personnel to participate. A chat coordinator may not feel comfortable critiquing librarians' performance online with users when the service relies upon the goodwill of volunteers to operate. Another difficult scenario is when the person charged with the task of assessment lacks supervisory clout or is of a lower rank than some of the librarians being evaluated. For example, it could be ticklish politically for an entry-level librarian coordinating a chat service to tell a department chair that they flubbed a question. Consequently, when evaluating real-time reference it becomes much more comfortable to employ less controversial measures of success, such as numbers served or user feedback.

Scarcity of Resources

- Lack of time or human resources needed to develop and implement a program of assessment, including follow-up measures such as training

• Inability to easily collect and archive usage statistics and transcripts due to software functionality

Critics often cite scarcity of resources and "the drain on staff and finances that ongoing, systematic evaluation" of reference services entails (Gorman, 1987). Peter Hernon and Charles M. McClure (1987, 113-114) outline the evaluation process as follows:

Phase I: *Preparation:* the library makes certain that organizational goals and quantifiable objectives are established, staff are adequately trained to conduct evaluations, potential uses for evaluation are identified, and the library staff have a basic understanding of the issues, topics and techniques related to that evaluation.

Phase II: *Evaluation Research:* Here, the specific evaluation research questions, performance measures, research designs, and methodologies are developed and implemented to investigate the effectiveness/efficiency of the services and activities under consideration.

Phase III: *Organizational Development:* The final phase is one in which the library assesses the results of the evaluation process and makes value judgments concerning which services or activities to modify, how to modify them, and how to implement strategies to change those services or activities and improve organizational performance.

As can be seen from this outline, a real program of evaluation involves more than identification of problems. It involves a substantial amount of preparation, development of methodologies and follow-up with personnel to remedy any problems that are identified. Institutions with small numbers of staff or a dwindling budget may find it challenging to implement and sustain such a labor-intensive process. In addition, since most assessment measures must be developed locally, there is a good chance that they will not be developed at all. Until the *Assessing Quality in Digital Reference* project or other groups develop instruments that can readily be deployed in a variety of settings, libraries may find the process too labor intensive to delve into thoroughly.

Another obstacle in appraising performance can be a lack of transcripts or other information concerning sessions online. Unlike conversing with users in a traditional reference encounter, real-time reference often leaves a "trail" that can be used in evaluation. However, this is heavily dependent upon the software being used to provide synchronous reference assistance. Expensive call center software, such as divine Virtual Reference Desk, LSSI Virtual Reference ToolKit, 24/7 Reference, and QuestionPoint, archives transcripts and gathers a variety of information that can be used in evaluation such as length of time taken to greet a user upon log on. Other systems, such as instant messaging, often do not record transcripts. Some software archives transcripts, but does not facilitate easy manipulation of data to examine categories of questions, calculate duration of sessions, or even tally the number of sessions in a given period of time. If a library is using a hosted service, an additional obstacle may be arranging access to the data. For example, libraries that use LiveAssistance or QuestionPoint must access data via the vendor rather than pulling it off their local server.

Chat Reference Is a New Area of Communication and Service in Libraries

- Assumption that traditional reference skills migrate to the online environment
- Reluctance to discourage vulnerable staff learning a new technology
- Traditional evaluative guidelines don't translate directly
- Fear of failing

Chatting is a radically new way of communicating with users for many librarians. A recent survey of librarians in the field noted that 68.2% have never instant messaged and that 65% have never chatted in real-time (Janes 2002, 554). Based on experience at the University of Florida, it is safe to assume staff who are learning to chat typically feel very vulnerable with their computer and reference skills. In addition, the knowledge that the whole transaction may be recorded for posterity is an additional source of anxiety. Consequently, supervisors and staff may be reluctant to rush into an examination of reference effectiveness until librarians become more confident using the medium.

Because the most talented reference staff members are often the ones most excited about chat, there may be a misconception that evaluation can be delayed. The assumption being, if they perform well at the reference desk, won't they also provide effective assistance to users online? The answer is, no, not necessarily. When first beginning the University of Florida's chat reference service, *RefeXpress*, most librarians and library staff experienced difficulty translating traditional reference skills to online synchronous communication. Gifted reference librarians forgot to do simple things such as clarify ambiguous questions, greet users, or even communicate with users for extended periods, things they would never do at the reference desk. This, and a fear of short-circuiting the new service in a politically charged environment may be strong obstacles to implementing a program of assessment.

Difficulty in Developing Techniques of Assessment or in Applying Existing Methodology

- Absence of a "culture of assessment"
- Lack of a professional baseline or set of formalized standards for library reference assistance online in real-time
- Lack of institutional goals and objectives addressing user satisfaction and accuracy
- Over-reliance upon qualitative measures such as volume of use
- Over-reliance upon subjective measures such as user satisfaction surveys

The last obstacle identified here is a perception that evaluation is already being performed in an adequate fashion. At the University of Florida, the steadily growing volume of use over the past three years has been perceived as an indication of success. User exit surveys often praise the service; in 2002, eighty-five percent of *RefeXpress* users indicated that their questions were answered. Yet the literature of traditional reference service, as well as analysis of transcripts, indicate that this is subjective. Users often report that their questions were answered correctly or to their satisfaction, even though an outside examination of the process indicates that they were given a partial or even the wrong answer to a question. Conversely, there were several examples of exit surveys where the user indicated their question was not answered because the correct answer was not to their liking. For example, one student indicated their question was not answered because a particular journal that they needed was not available online. Incidentally, readers that are interested in viewing the *RefeXpress* exit survey can access it at: http://refexpress.uflib.ufl.edu/rxevalform.html.

Although transcripts are kept of every *RefeXpress* session at the University of Florida, they have never been used for evaluative purposes. User satisfaction has been gleaned from survey data as quoted above.

There has been no systematic examination of the transcripts to see if patron questions were answered correctly, if appropriate referrals were made, or if the patron would have been better served through a more traditional reference interaction.

In an attempt to deal with this shortcoming, a subsequent examination of *RefeXpress* transcripts was done in conjunction with this article. That examination revealed that while the overwhelming majority of questions were answered correctly, in those instances where the librarian was operating out of their field of expertise the reference interview process would suffer, and the patron was more likely to get incorrect or incomplete information. In addition, tasks routinely done at the Reference Desk, such as checking holdings at the public library or the local community college for materials not owned or available at the University of Florida, were not done with the same frequency online. The following provides a generalized summary of trends identified through an analysis of *RefeXpress* transcripts.

- Most reference questions received were of Ready Reference nature. Patrons were interested in whether the UF Libraries owned a particular book or had a specific journal article. The librarian on duty answered virtually all questions of this nature correctly. In instances where the material was not available at UF, referrals were frequently made to ILL, but checking the holdings of other local libraries appeared to be the exception rather than the norm.
- Advanced reference questions were much more problematic. While still answered correctly in the vast majority of cases, there were instances where librarians would rush to answer the question without conducting an appropriate reference interview. This seemed to be particular true when the librarian was working out of his or her field of expertise. In one example, because the librarian did not have a clear understanding of the user's need and available databases, the librarian was only able to find one article on the requested topic. With a deeper understanding of the question, a follow-up search of a more appropriate database resulted in over two hundred relevant articles. For research level queries, it is always a good idea to follow the session with an e-mail to the patron to determine if the answer was appropriate or if additional assistance is needed.
- While some librarians frequently called upon colleagues for assistance with questions where they lacked expertise, others appeared reluctant to tell patrons a question was beyond the scope of their

knowledge. This often resulted in a less than satisfactory answer to the question. Ironically, the user was often very complimentary of the librarian for all their help despite the fact they could have been better served if a referral had been made to the appropriate subject specialist.

- Some librarians appeared to be pressured to give the patron an immediate response to their question without first determining the timeframe in which the user was working. Others, after determining the user's needs and the exact nature of the question, offered to call or email the patron additional information at a later time. This approach seemed to work very well.

- Finally, there were a number of examples where the librarian would push pages to the patron without adequately explaining where the page came from. Leading the patron step-by-step to the anticipated result is sometimes much more time consuming and labor intensive, but at the same time it helps the patron learn how to find the information on their own the next time around.

RECOMMENDATIONS

- Administrative support for evaluation is essential
- Incorporate assessment of online real-time reference into existing evaluative programs whenever possible
- Approach evaluation in a positive manner
- Assimilate online real-time reference into the library organization and public services
- Incorporate responsibilities into job descriptions
- Investigate self-assessment and blind reviewing as evaluative strategies
- Adopt traditional instruments or measures of reference performance whenever possible
- Treat user feedback and usage statistics as just one measure of service effectiveness

It might be argued that the difficulties in assessing real-time reference services go beyond the service itself, and are just one part of the much larger issue of an absence of a "culture of assessment" within libraries as a whole. For a system of evaluation to be successful it is imperative that the implementation of an evaluative process be fully supported by the highest levels of library administration and reinforced at all lower levels of management. In these times of budgetary constraints, the argument can always be made that there is a lack of available resources for proper evaluation. Real-time reference often requires substantial investments of effort, time, staff, and money. It would be a costly oversight not to allocate at least a minimum of available resources to assessing the service. Cost effective ways to accomplish evaluation might include some form of librarian self-assessment or a blind review of session transcripts by colleagues. This would include reviewing only representative samples of transcripts, and raising awareness of the need for continual review of procedures among those librarians participating in the service. Another cost effective option would be to incorporate evaluation of the service into other evaluation efforts taking place, such as LIB-QUAL and other relevant surveys or measurement tools. Despite the fact that the initial cost of the software might be more expensive, another important consideration for providing cost effective evaluation of online real-time reference is to ensure that the functionality of the software will allow for collecting, storing and retrieving data in an efficient manner.

Those libraries that currently offer chat reference but lack an evaluation process, need to work toward its immediate implementation. In addition, they need to lobby for support among administrators for an evaluation program if that support does not currently exist. It should be emphasized that the evaluation process needs to be approached from a positive perspective. The purpose of the process should be clearly presented as a way for all staff members to get better at what they do and to provide reference via synchronous services in a more efficient and effective manner. Emphasis on what is being done right, and linking those behaviors to positive rewards, should be as important as pointing out what is being done incorrectly.

Although there is currently a lack of applicable baselines or professional guidelines on real-time reference, some promising advances are being made that should help libraries implement an assessment program. Monitoring or communicating with groups at the forefront of this effort, such as the Assessing Digital Quality project, the Virtual Reference Desk, the RUSA/MARS division of ALA, and the National Information Standards Organization (NISO), will be extremely helpful. Some consortia have instituted models that support member libraries in working on ways to evaluate their services, such as Q and A New Jersey where local project managers get support from central coordinators in finding ways to institute assessment. Handbooks describing these efforts are often available from consortia representatives.

The way in which the public services area is structured within the library can also impact the success of real-time reference evaluation. Real-time reference should be assimilated into the existing organization of the reference department and not treated as a separate entity. Evaluation should be infused into the structure either through the creation of a real-time reference coordinator position that includes supervisory responsibility and the time to address evaluation, or the requirement that other supervisors include real-time reference performance into current evaluation procedures. It is highly recommended that libraries move from volunteerism to assigning chat as part of regular reference responsibilities. In addition, real-time reference should be incorporated into position descriptions to integrate evaluation of online and traditional reference duties. Working expectations into position descriptions creates the opportunity to establish clear guidelines for performance in the areas of behavior, accuracy of responses and ability to refer.

For libraries just starting a real-time reference service, self-assessment is a gentle way to examine quality of service. This requires providing staff members with private access to their transcripts, so that they can look at the accuracy of their answers and the strategies employed when interacting with users. Consider supplying staff with evaluative checklists such as the *Reference Session Evaluation Checklist* of the Q and A NJ.org project (http://www.qandanj.org/manual/checklist.htm), to assist staff in assessing their performance. The *Evaluation Checklist* covers software, communication skills and accuracy of service. It should be remembered, that while self-assessment is an excellent tool for assessment, it is often hard to identify problems with one's own performance, and even harder to see a solution.

Another assessment strategy that can be less threatening for personnel, but is more time consuming to complete is that of a blind review. In the blind review, each staff member identifies one of their most problematic reference sessions, and the coordinator strips the transcript of all identifying information such as names or time stamps. The coordinator then distributes the sanitized transcript to another staff member who is asked to critique the session, identifying any problems and commenting on how they might have handled the user differently. This can be done in a group which will generate discussion, or privately if desired. If staff members are comfortable with blind reviewing, pool the "problem" transcripts (and suggestions for improvement) in a place that is available to all of the staff to consult.

While user exit surveys and volume of use are indicators of success, they are at best subjective measures of the experience between the librarian and the user. Positive exit surveys are great morale boosters and should be shared with the staff at large.

It is recommended that librarians adapt traditional techniques or assessment instruments (see *The Reference Assessment Manual,* 1995) whenever possible. While traditional reference tools do not fit all needs of online real-time reference, relevant portions could be adapted. These could include use of the "secret shopper," a common strategy to unobtrusively evaluate customer services in businesses and libraries alike. A similar mechanism is the Wisconsin-Ohio Reference Evaluation Program, also called the WOREP (Radcliff and Schloman, 2001). The WOREP examines a common reference transaction from the perspective of the librarian and the user. The online nature of real-time reference would make this relatively easily to administrate to both participants immediately. It should be emphasized that libraries may find it hard to establish an evaluation mechanism for a real-time reference service at a library if they do not perform regular assessment of other reference services. In other words, how can one justify evaluation of one medium of reference delivery without also addressing reference accuracy and effectiveness at the reference desk, via e-mail, or on the telephone?

CONCLUSIONS

Despite obstacles outlined earlier, the nature of online synchronous reference holds great promise for making valid assessment of real-time reference a more attainable goal than it has ever been at the traditional reference desk. Achieving that goal will require a commitment on the part of library administrators and librarians to establishing a program of assessment and to being responsive to the information gathered as a result of that assessment. It will also require going beyond a simple review of session transcripts to a comprehensive and continuous process of reviewing all facets of the service. As chat reference evolves, the associated measures and standards applied to the assessment of the service will need to evolve in response to new issues and challenges that arise. By incorporating the recommendations provided here, libraries providing online real-time reference services will have a raised awareness of how to more effectively measure and evaluate their performance.

REFERENCES

American Library Association, Evaluation of Reference and Adult Services Committee. (1995). *The Reference Assessment Manual.* Ann Arbor, MI: Pierian.

Fagan, Jody Condit and Michele Calloway. (2001). "Creating an Instant Messaging Reference System." *Information Technology and Libraries* 20.4 (December): 202-12.

Foley, Marianne. (2002). "Instant Messaging Reference in an Academic Library: A Case Study." *College & Research Libraries* 63.1 (January): 36-45.

Francoeur, Stephen. (2001). "An Analytical Survey of Chat Reference Services." *Reference Services Review* 29.3: 189-203.

Gorman, Kathleen. (1987). *Association of Research Libraries SPEC Kit #139, Performance Evaluation in Reference Services.* Washington, D.C.: Association of Research Libraries Office of Leadership and Management Services.

Hernon, Peter and Charles McClure. (1987). *Unobtrusive Testing and Library Reference Services.* Norwood, NJ: Ablex.

Janes, Joseph. (2002). "Digital Reference: Reference Librarians' Experiences and Attitudes." *Journal of the American Society for Information Science and Technology* 53 (March): 549-566.

Janes, Joseph and Chrystie Hill. (2002). "Finger on the Pulse: Librarians Describe Evolving Reference Practice in an Increasingly Digital World." *Reference & User Services Quarterly* 42.1 (Fall): 54-65.

Kasowitz, Abby S., Blythe Allison Bennett and R. David Lankes. (2000). "Quality Standards for Digital Reference Consortia." *Reference & User Services Quarterly* 39.4 (Summer): 355-63.

Kibbee, Josephine Z., David Henry Ward and Wei Ma. (2002). "Virtual Service, Real Data: Results of a Pilot Study. Real-Time Online Reference at the University of Illinois." *Reference Services Review* 30.1: 25-36.

Lankes, R. David, Charles R. McClure, Melissa Gross and Jeffrey Pomerantz, eds. (2003). *Implementing Digital Reference Services: Setting Standards and Making it Real.* New York: Neal-Schuman.

McClure, Charles R., R. David Lankes, Melissa Gross and Beverly Choltco-Devlin. (2002). *Statistics, Measures and Quality Standards for Assessing Digital Reference Library Services: Guidelines and Procedures.* Syracuse, NY: Information Institute of Syracuse, School of Information Studies, Syracuse University; Tallahassee, FL: School of Information Studies, Information Use, Management and Policy Institute, Florida State University.

Maxwell, Nancy Kalikow. (2002). "Establishing and Maintaining Live Online Reference Service." *Library Technology Reports* 38.4 (July/August): 1-78.

Meola, Marc and Sam Stormont. (2002). *Starting and Operating Live Virtual Reference Services: A How-To-Do-It Manual for Librarians.* New York: Neal-Schuman.

Radcliff, Carolyn J. and Barbara F. Schloman. (2001). "Case Study 3.1: Using the Wisconsin-Ohio Reference Evaluation Program (in the Reference Department of the Main Library, Kent State University)." *Library Evaluation.* Englewood, CO: Libraries Unlimited, 2001.

RASD Ad Hoc Committee on Behavioral Guidelines for Reference and Information Services. (1996). "RUSA Guidelines for Behavioral Performance of Reference and Information Services Professionals." *RQ* 36 (Winter): 200-203.

Ronan, Jana Smith. (2003). *Chat Reference: A Guide to Setting Up a Real-Time Reference Service*. Westport, CT: Libraries Unlimited.

Ronan, Jana and Carol Turner. (2002). *Association of Research Libraries SPEC Kit #273, Chat Reference* Washington, D.C.: Association of Research Libraries Office of Leadership and Management Services.

Sears, JoAnn. (2001). "Chat Reference Service: An Analysis of One Semester's Data." *Issues in Science and Technology Librarianship*. 32 (Fall). http://www.istl.org/istl/01-fall/article2.html (11 April 2002).

Sloan, Bernard G. (1998). "Electronic Reference Services: Some Suggested Guidelines." *Reference & User Services Quarterly* 38.1: 77-81.

Strom, Lorraine. (2002). "The Emerging Virtual Reference Desk." *Mississippi Libraries* 66.3 (Fall): 71-3.

Our Experience
with Two Virtual Reference Services
at IUPUI University Library

Polly D. Boruff-Jones

SUMMARY. Indiana University Purdue University Indianapolis (IUPUI) University Library first introduced virtual reference in May 2001 after four months of preparation. In the summer of 2002, University Library decided to reconsider the virtual reference software and provider and implemented a new service during the fall 2002 semester. A Reference Team Working Group was formed to review replacement options for the virtual reference software the library had been using for about a year. The decision to find a new virtual reference service was prompted by the connectivity and electronic resource compatibility problems experienced with the first virtual reference software the library chose. This article compares and contrasts the two virtual reference services used at IUPUI University Library and describes the two virtual reference proj-

Polly D. Boruff-Jones is Assistant Librarian and Reference Team Leader, IUPUI University Library, and Coordinator, Virtual Reference Working Group, 755 West Michigan Street, Indianapolis, IN 46202 (E-mail: pboruffj@iupui.edu).

The author would like to acknowledge Brenda L. Burk, Assistant Librarian, Special Collection Team and Virtual Reference Service Project Manager, May 2001-May 2002; and Charles E. Dye, Director of Technology and Operations Team Leader, both at IUPUI University Library, for the background information and insight they contributed to this article.

[Haworth co-indexing entry note]: "Our Experience with Two Virtual Reference Services at IUPUI University Library." Boruff-Jones, Polly D. Co-published simultaneously in *The Reference Librarian* (The Haworth Information Press, an imprint of The Haworth Press, Inc.) No. 79/80, 2002/2003, pp. 241-255; and: *Digital Reference Services* (ed: Bill Katz) The Haworth Information Press, an imprint of The Haworth Press, Inc., 2002/2003, pp. 241-255. Single or multiple copies of this article are available for a fee from The Haworth Document Delivery Service [1-800-HAWORTH, 9:00 a.m. - 5:00 p.m. (EST). E-mail address: docdelivery@haworthpress.com].

10.1300/J120v38n79_16 *241*

ects. Following the article is a checklist of "Seven Questions to Ask When Choosing a Virtual Reference Service." *[Article copies available for a fee from The Haworth Document Delivery Service: 1-800-HAWORTH. E-mail address: <docdelivery@haworthpress.com> Website: <http://www. HaworthPress.com> © 2002/2003 by The Haworth Press, Inc. All rights reserved.]*

KEYWORDS. Reference services, virtual reference, chat reference, academic libraries

Indiana University Purdue University Indianapolis (IUPUI) is an urban university, primarily a commuter campus with a very small portion of the student body living on-campus. For the majority of IUPUI students, school commitments compete with family and job responsibilities–more than 60% of IUPUI students work an average of 31 hours, or more, per week. Several of the professional programs at IUPUI offer courses, and even entire degree programs online, and University Library has been exploring ways to become more engaged in support of the online course and degree offerings. We looked to virtual reference as a way to extend and enhance our reference services in terms of distance and audience to better serve the University's commuter and distance education students. In addition to the IUPUI patron considerations, we were aware that, generally, academic libraries are reporting a decrease in the number of people using the physical library and in the number of reference desk transactions (Tenopir 2001), and we saw this trend in University Library, too; another compelling reason to reach out to our patrons.

IUPUI University Library first introduced virtual reference in May 2001 after four months of preparation. In the summer of 2002, University Library decided to reconsider our virtual reference software and provider and implemented a new service during the fall 2002 semester. A Reference Team Working Group was formed to review replacement options for the virtual reference software we had been using the previous year. The decision to find a new virtual reference service was prompted by the connectivity and electronic resource compatibility problems we experienced with the first virtual reference software we chose. We call our current virtual reference service InstantInfo@IUPUI (InstantInfo).

In this article, I will compare and contrast the virtual reference services we have used at IUPUI University Library and recount our experiences during the two virtual reference projects. I will refer to the two services as Vendor A and Vendor B, rather than identifying the vendors by name, because this article is not intended to be a software critique or review. My emphasis is on the selection, implementation and management of a virtual reference service and I am not recommending one vendor over another. I hope to provide some insight into problems and issues inherent in any virtual reference service and to highlight setbacks likely to be encountered with a new virtual reference service–regardless of the vendor or software chosen.

VENDOR A OVERVIEW

University Library's first virtual reference service, Vendor A, has an annual subscription rate of $6,000 for one "agent seat" plus an $8,000 fee for installation, customization and configuration, and two eight-hour days of onsite training. Technical support is included. Multiple agent seats may be purchased and additional training is available at an additional cost.

To fund this relatively expensive project, the library received grant funding to acquire and initiate the service. In part, the grant paid for a part-time librarian to fill in and allow release time to the librarian who managed the virtual reference project.

The software contract was signed in January 2001, but the service did not go live until May 2001. In February 2001, the Virtual Reference Desk Working Group began planning the implementation of the service. The Working Group received training and worked on customization of the software and interface during this period.

This vendor offers a technical support line, but often the person taking the calls was not the person with the technical expertise required to answer the question. This meant that we had to wait for calls to be returned or a follow-up call was necessary.

Vendor A was chosen to launch our virtual reference service in 2001 because, at the time, it offered many more features than its competitors. Vendor A offers the option to "push" Web pages to the patron or to co-browse. "Pushing" refers to the ability of the reference staff to bring up a Web page or do a database search on their screen and then send (push) the page or the results to the patron–all chat reference systems we researched offer at least this feature. Co-browsing allows the patron to follow along as the reference person initiates a search or navigates through the library's home page. This feature is especially important in an academic library whose mission is to educate our users to become self-sufficient using the library's resources. We found that using the co-browsing function as we narrate our movements over the telephone is especially effective.

Additionally, and uniquely, Vendor A offers a "meetings" mode that allows the librarian to conduct a session with as many as 20 simultaneous users. The meetings feature offers possibilities for library instruction and we had hoped to use the feature for that purpose, but the logistics of conducting a class this way was daunting and the 20-person limit was not sufficient for most of the undergraduate classes with which we work.

Vendor A's software also provides the ability to send documents in a variety of formats–Word, Excel, pdf, etc.–and we could create instructional slide shows to display to the patron. However, we seldom had reason to work with these various document formats in the chat environment and we did not develop the slide show potential due to the time that was required to create the slides. We felt the development of instructional Web pages, available to all patrons, was a more efficient approach.

The Vendor A software was created originally for commercial use as a customer service tool. Vendor A licensed the software from a third party and repackaged it for the virtual reference interface. We found that many of the special features, although attractive initially, were not particularly useful for our reference purposes.

VENDOR B OVERVIEW

After a year with Vendor A, we found there were more new, or improved, virtual reference systems on the market then in 2001 and, after comparison of several offerings, University Library chose to move to Vendor B for our chat reference service.

Vendor B offers five "seats" for $1,795 per year. The annual cost includes all upgrades. There is also a one-time set-up and customization fee of $1,995 (set-up fee is waived if the library uses the vendor's electronic reserve system–and our library does). We found this cost reasonable and no special funding is required.

With five seats to use (this means that five separate chat reference sessions can take place at once from five different locations) we decided to share the seats between general reference (two seats), philanthropic studies reference (one seat), and computer consultants who provide support in the library's public computer clusters (two seats). A user can select either reference assistance or a computer consultant from a list of available help. With the two general reference seats, we can conduct two chat sessions at the same time or easily pass a session to another librarian–as a referral to a subject specialist, for instance. However, the majority of the questions we field are ready-reference type questions and do not require referral.

No outside training has been necessary with Vendor B's software, an orientation to the new interface was sufficient for most librarians and other Reference Desk staff using the interface. This may, in part, be due to our previous experience with Vendor A–we were already familiar with a chat interface after a year working with the first service. Vendor B does advertise as requiring no special training.

The software was acquired in August 2002 and the service was activated in October 2002. During the two months between acquisition and activation, the new Virtual Reference Working Group learned the new software, made interface customization decisions, customized those options to which we have administrator rights, and sent the other requests to Vendor B's programmers.

Vendor B also offers the option of pushing Web pages or co-browsing. It is pertinent to note that, although Vendor B released their first virtual reference system in 2000, this vendor did not offer the co-browsing feature until the spring of 2002 and so, was not as competitive with some other systems, such as Vendor A, prior to the spring 2002 release.

The virtual reference software (chat and email) is produced and managed by the vendor. Vendor B allows the library to host the virtual reference software at no additional cost.

Vendor B technical support is good. We are welcome to contact the product creators and programmers via email or telephone and we have a personal contact. Response time is prompt and when requests cannot be addressed immediately we are notified that is the case. Most problems have been resolved in a reasonable period of time. The one outstanding exception is the email function of the service, which I will address under "Technical Issues."

This virtual reference software offers two unique features: an email function and an option to search a knowledge base, or list of frequently asked questions, within the same interface as the chat function. In the knowledge base, we include links to library services information, Web-based subject guides and research tools. Although Vendor B offers fewer special features, the features it does offer are sufficient for our needs and the developers continue to add and refine features with each new release.

TECHNICAL ISSUES

Customization. Vendor A and Vendor B have comparable flexibility in terms of interface and functionality customization. The primary difference is that all Vendor A customization requests were sent to the vendor, no self-customization was possible because the chat software is licensed from a third party. Every librarian using the system was entered into the system by the vendor. The library had no administrator privileges with Vendor A. Scripted replies and bookmarks can be added to expedite chat responses, but again, these must be sent to the vendor to enter into the interface.

Vendor B must do some of the interface customization too, but we have access to limited administrator functions and can do some of our own customization–such as adding our own scripted replies and bookmarks. We can add and remove librarians to the list of users at any time, or create generic screen names such as "Reference Desk" and "Computer Consultant," ourselves.

More do-it-yourself customization of the Vendor B interface would be a big plus. Even though we were working directly with the programmers, we could not know how a change would look until it was made and, more than once, we asked for adjustments to be made. The programmers were very patient and responsive to our requests, but I think it may become difficult for Vendor B to continue to provide this kind of personalized service when their customer list grows!

Compatibility with Electronic Resources. Our online catalog did not work well with the Vendor A software and we experienced intermittent problems with subscription electronic resources–some interfaces never worked correctly with this software. We struggled with Vendor A compatibility issues throughout the year because there was no single solution; it was necessary to work through the each problem case-by-case, application-by-application.

With Vendor A, certain Web pages (notably some government Web sites) tended to "blow up" the browser, meaning that the Web site would take over the screen and hide the chat session. The librarian, losing control of the session, would have to log out and back in, restart the session, and connect with the patron anew–if he was still there.

We do not experience the "blow up" phenomenon with Vendor B. Initially there was a problem accessing the library's home page and the online catalog through the Vendor B interface–both essential to providing reference service–and we encountered compatibility problems with some of our electronic resources, but the problems were almost completely resolved before going live. Now, all electronic resources work with this software except for occasional, and infrequent, glitches. The across-the-board resolution of Vendor B compatibility issues was possible due to the fact that we host the service on our own server.

Library Hosting. With Vendor A, hosting the software on our own library server was not an option. This was a significant factor contributing to resource incompatibility. Standard library database licenses restrict access to the library's resources by IP range and all transactions through the Vendor A interface were routed through Vendor A's server, which falls outside of the library's IP range. Between our Operations Team (responsible for supporting and developing University Library technology infrastructure) and Vendor A's technical staff, connectivity problems were resolved for some databases, but not all and, at best, it was never a seamless process.

Hosting is an option with Vendor B and we chose to do that. By hosting the software on the library's server, the library's Operations Team, working with Vendor B programmers, has been able to troubleshoot incompatibility issues as they arise so we have access to all of our Web-based resources through the chat interface.

Hosting does require technology expertise and an allocation of resources. Our library bought a server to dedicate to the virtual reference service (although the service does not require a dedicated server and could be hosted on a shared server) and an average of one to three hours per week is required of our Windows hardware and software administrator to upgrade, update, and maintain the server once the service was up and running. University Library is fortunate to have an outstanding Operations Team that worked closely with our Virtual Reference Working Group and Vendor B, from the beginning, to anticipate and address technical problems. This collaboration was essential to successful implementation.

Email. University Library has offered email reference for several years; adding chat reference gave us an additional access point and another login and password to remember–not a terrible imposition, but it did complicate reference services a bit. We were pleased to see that Vendor B offered email and chat in the same interface–this simplified the process and was more convenient for those of us monitoring the two services. When the chat service is off (we are not logged in to monitor) the patron is automatically sent to the email interface. We thought that was a real customer service plus–the patron did not have to leave the service, go back to the library's home page, and find the link to email reference as they had to do previously.

There are negatives to this arrangement, though. A few students appear to have confused the reference modes and thought they were in a chat session when they were in an email session. The most significant drawback is that Vendor B's email software does not allow for threaded conversations! This was not immediately clear. To send an email query, the patron must be in the Vendor B interface–a message cannot be sent directly from an outside email account. What that means is: the patron sends an email question and the librarian answers, the librarian's answer is sent into the patron's email account, but the patron cannot return a message back to the virtual reference email interface; if the patron does reply to the librarian's message it goes to the vendor's server and we never see it–but the patron does not know that. This makes it almost impossible to conduct the all-important reference interview. Vendor B's technical support assures us they will be altering the email software to allow threaded messaging very soon. Until then we have rerouted reference email to an outside account through a library-created Web interface and this works well.

SERVICE ISSUES

Reference Interview. We want to maintain the same quality of reference customer service in the virtual reference environment as we do in-person or over the telephone. Conducting a proper reference interview is just as important virtually and it is much more difficult. A reference interview via email may take hours or even days of back and forth messages, but the chat reference environment allows an immediate exchange between patron and reference staff and we can conduct a reference interview almost as efficiently as we can in person. Of course, we still lose the benefit of facial expressions, hand gestures, and body language–those non-verbal cues that are so important for conveying meaning in a face-to-face conversation.

Ease of Use. Although the chat experience is new to many of our librarians and staff, most of our students are very comfortable with this method of communication. Using chat is different from using email–it is much less formal, for instance, and less attention is paid to correct spelling and complete sentences. While we strive to send complete and correct messages to the patron, we may worry about that person becoming impatient, but that does not seem to be the case in actuality–our current generation of patrons tends to be accustomed to the inherent time lag of the chat interaction. Of course the speed with which we dispatch messages will increase as we become more comfortable with the interface and the chat environment.

To improve our response time, and facilitate the reference interview, we created pre-scripted phrases that we can select from a list. As previously mentioned, Vendor A required that we send the list to them and they added the phrases to the chat interface. Vendor B allows us to add these phrases ourselves. This is a plus because we found that some phrases were used much more often than others and some not at all. With Vendor A, it was not a simple task to make changes to the list, but the self-customization of Vendor B allows us to change, add and delete phrases at any time.

The scripted replies not only save typing time, but also *buy* us time to put together our next reply or question or to begin searching for sources to address the patron's query.

During our first virtual reference experience we created 34 different phrases to choose from in our list of scripted replies! This was too many. It was difficult to quickly find the appropriate phrase in the rather long list. We have now reduced the "scripted reply" list to 16 selections arranged in alphabetical order by "title":

SCRIPTED REPLIES

Electronic Resources: Are you only interested in electronic resources?

Enough?: Will the information I've provided be enough to get you started?

Good question: That's a good question. Let's see what we can find on that . . .

How may I help you?: How may I help you?

Internet warning: Please note: while we hope this list of web sites is helpful to you, the Internet is vast and uncontrolled. We therefore cannot guarantee the validity of the information found on these web sites.

Logging off: I am logging off now. Thank you.

Please elaborate: Can you elaborate on your question–provide more detail?

Pre-good bye: Have I answered your question to your satisfaction or do you need further assistance?

Sending results 1: I am sending you a search result.

Sending results 2: You will soon see a web page on your screen.

Still there?: I haven't heard from you in a while. Are you still online?

Too detailed: This could take a while. Would you like me to call or e-mail you when I find the information? If so, please provide me with a phone number or e-mail address where I can reach you.

Too many questions: Due to the high volume of questions we are receiving, we must limit the number of questions we answer for a single patron. Thank you for using our service.

Type of resources needed?: What type of information do you want (journal articles? books? web sites?)?

Waiting 1: Please hold while I search for information to respond to your request.

Waiting 2: Just a moment, please.

MANAGEMENT ISSUES

Eligible Users. Although we generally limit our online reference service to IUPUI-affiliated individuals, we make exceptions for people seeking information about, or from, our philanthropic studies and archive collections and for IUPUI specific inquiries. For this reason, we do not require authentication or restrict entry into the service, but reserve the right to politely decline assistance by noting in the introduction to InstantInfo that the service is intended for the "IUPUI community." With our first virtual reference service (Vendor A) we did require authentication at the login. Because an email address is required in the registration page of the current chat interface and is included in an email question, we can filter questions based on the email domain. It is not often that a question is turned away–our secondary mission, as a public university, is to the greater Indianapolis community–but as the service becomes busier, we may need to more strictly prioritize the questions we accept.

Explaining the Service. All links to the virtual reference service route through introductory Web pages rather than linking directly to the virtual reference service interface.

The current introductory pages briefly explain the purpose of the virtual reference service with examples of types of questions that can be answered; present the reference options–chat, email or telephone; list the hours of operation; and link to the privacy statement (see http://www.ulib.iupui.edu/vrs/home.html).

Privacy. Vendor A transcripts were automatically forwarded to an email account where they could be retained or deleted. Both the patron and librarian information is kept on the provider's server. There was some concern in terms of the security of this information and we made sure that a privacy statement addressing the library's use of patron information was clearly posted for users to see upon entering the system.

Vendor B allows the option of retaining transcripts of chat interactions. The library can save transcripts, but we do not save all transcripts, and patrons can choose to have a transcript emailed to them. The library and patron options are independent of each other.

Our current privacy statement reads:

A transcript record of your email question or chat session may be kept following your transaction on InstantInfo@IUPUI. The transcript will contain the text of the email or chat conversation between you and the librarian including all URLs visited or documents shared during the session. Along with the transcript the library will also have a copy of your name, email address and any other information you provide. The library will keep this information confidential–we will not share it with anyone. We may use the transcript content to develop Frequently Asked Questions (FAQs) for users of this service, or we may examine the content of our interaction with you to evaluate the service we are providing. This information will be used ANONYMOUSLY. All identifying information will be removed from the message before we use the content to create FAQs or evaluate our responses to your question.

Staffing. After offering the chat reference service for several months, we found that our in-library student users were major beneficiaries of the chat reference service. The ability to contact the Reference Desk without leaving the computer cluster in which they were working saved the students a good deal of time and aggravation–those students cannot pick up a telephone to call as can our at-home patrons. University Library has over 300 public computers with Internet access located on three levels of the library. If a student needs to ask a reference question, she must gather up her belongings and make her way to the second level Reference Desk where she may then have to wait to be helped and, during most times of the semester, will surely lose the computer she was using to another student. There are many students who come into the library to use our computers without ever visiting the Reference Desk and the chat reference service offers a way to begin a reference relationship with those students, too.

Based on the indication that in-library students were using the chat service at least as much as off-campus students, we decided that we did not need to strain our reference desk staff to cover additional virtual reference hours, rather we would schedule the chat reference for those busy times when we already staffed a third person at the Reference Desk. This person would be responsible for checking the email reference every two hours, handling telephone reference, and monitoring chat reference at a workstation at the back of the multi-workstation main Reference Desk while the other two people at the Desk handled in-person inquiries. The third person also served as back up for the front desk when not otherwise engaged with email, chat, or telephone reference questions.

We tested a variety of staffing configurations before deciding on this model. Originally, chat reference was monitored at the regular Reference Desk–just as we had been doing with email reference. When this became too hectic it was suggested that we take chat reference off the Desk and put it in librarian's offices–other academic libraries have found this to be the preferred staffing solution (West 2002). To monitor chat reference in our offices was decided upon after much discussion of whether we could provide proper reference without the benefit of reference materials close at hand. We considered outfitting a book truck of ready reference selections to push to our offices when on duty, but ultimately decided against that. I do not think anyone felt that was a bad decision. However, monitoring chat reference in our offices was a bit of a drag on our time. We were obliged to sit at our desks for one, two or three hour periods of time and, in addition to being responsible for chat duty, we were also the "on-call" librarian subject to summons to the physical Reference Desk to help out if things got busy.

Of the staffing options we have tried, I think the current model works well for the limited hours that we offer chat reference. Currently, we offer chat reference between the hours of 10:00 a.m. and 4:00 p.m., Monday through Thursday, and between 12:00 p.m. and 4:00 p.m. on Friday. We do not offer chat on the weekends or during semester breaks when we staff the desk with fewer people. We are looking at usage statistics to plan more effective staffing and, should we decide to extend the hours of service, we may need to rethink our staffing model. Last fall, the service became busier later in the semester. October and November were our busiest chat reference months during the fall semester with a total of 20 transactions in the last half of October (the service was officially launched on October 13) and 27 transactions in November. During any month, the heaviest usage occurs in the mid- to late afternoon. As the university continues to develop online education programs we may see more use of the service and an increased demand for evening and weekend hours.

Promotion. We are approaching promotion of the service cautiously and want to be sure we have most of the "bugs" worked out before we invite increased usage. We have not formally promoted the service yet, but we have placed links to the service prominently on the library's home page; librarians advertise virtual reference during bibliographic instruction sessions; our External Relations Team recently created a new poster campaign that encourages students to contact the Reference Desk for research help (those posters include the URL for virtual reference); and the Reference Team takes advantage of student services and information technology fairs on campus to demonstrate the chat reference service. So, people are finding us, and those who do respond positively.

Now that we have operated our new virtual reference service for a few months, have worked out the various (to be expected) technical glitches and established a level of comfort with the system, we will begin promoting the service more aggressively. Our users do not seem to notice the change of interface in the virtual reference system and, because we were already familiar with navigating in the chat environment, it was not difficult for librarians and other reference staff to make the adjustment from one system to another.

There are two features of the current system we would like to develop now that we have settled in with our new virtual reference service–the knowledge base ("Research Help and FAQs") for instructional purposes, and the capacity to transfer a session from one librarian to another. As mentioned above, we have not made much use of the ability to pass on sessions as referrals and our statistics offer some explanation for this. We find that the majority of our chat transactions, 76%, last for

10 minutes or less, 15% take 11-20 minutes to complete and only 9% last more than 20 minutes–we do not appear to be receiving many complex research questions. We hope this will change with increased promotion of the service. We think promotion directly to students during orientation and bibliographic instruction sessions will be especially effective.

Based on IUPUI University Library's experience with two virtual reference services, I created a checklist of questions to ask prior to selecting a virtual reference service:

Seven Questions to Ask When Choosing a Virtual Reference Service

1. For what purpose will the library use the service?
   - Purpose determines the special software features needed
   - Purpose will influence the staffing model and hours of operation
2. Does the vendor produce the software or license it through a third party?
   - Third party licensing may result in greater cost and a more cumbersome customization process
3. How many "seats" are included in the price?
   - Multiple seats allow much greater reference flexibility
4. Is hosting on a library server an option?
   - Library hosting is preferable in terms of electronic resource compatibility because the server is located within the library's IP range
   - Successful library hosting requires in-house technical support to troubleshoot, run and maintain the server
5. To what extent can the software and interface be customized locally?
   - More self-customization options allow more flexibility and control
6. How accessible and responsive are the software programmers and technical support?
   - During planning and implementation, the more direct the communication with the software programmers, the more efficient the process
   - Invariably you will encounter connectivity or compatibility issues once the service is running
7. How secure are the patron transactions?
   - Especially important if the vendor is hosting the service and retaining transcript records.

REFERENCES

Tenopir, Carol, "Virtual Reference Services in a Real World," *Library Journal*, July 2001, 38-40.

West, Kathy, "Managing and Staffing a Virtual Reference Services Pilot Project," *Feliciter*, Issue 2, 2002, 64-65.

KANanswer:
A Collaborative Statewide
Virtual Reference Pilot Project

Marcia Stockham
Elizabeth Turtle
Eric Hansen

SUMMARY. This paper relates the collaborative planning by a task force of public, academic, and special librarians to develop KANanswer, a statewide virtual reference pilot project. Major points include selecting software, developing policies and procedures, marketing, procuring partners, staffing and training, coordinating the project, and early impressions of the librarians who staff the service. *[Article copies available for a fee from The Haworth Document Delivery Service: 1-800-HAWORTH. E-mail address: <docdelivery@haworthpress.com> Website: <http://www.HaworthPress. com> © 2002/2003 by The Haworth Press, Inc. All rights reserved.]*

Marcia Stockham is Assistant Professor/Education Librarian, Kansas State University Libraries, 206 Hale Library, Manhattan, KS 66506 (E-mail: stockham@ksu.edu). Elizabeth Turtle is Assistant Professor/Science Librarian, Kansas State University Libraries, 127 Hale Library, Manhattan, KS 66506 (E-mail: bturtle@ksu.edu). Eric Hansen is Executive Director, Kansas Library Network Board and Project Coordinator of KANanswer, 300 SW 10th Avenue, Room 343N, Topeka, KS 66612-1593 (E-mail: eric@kslib.info).

The authors gratefully acknowledge the input provided by KANanswer Operators.

[Haworth co-indexing entry note]: "KANanswer: A Collaborative Statewide Virtual Reference Pilot Project." Stockham, Marcia, Elizabeth Turtle, and Eric Hansen. Co-published simultaneously in *The Reference Librarian* (The Haworth Information Press, an imprint of The Haworth Press, Inc.) No. 79/80, 2002/2003, pp. 257-266; and: *Digital Reference Services* (ed: Bill Katz) The Haworth Information Press, an imprint of The Haworth Press, Inc., 2002/2003, pp. 257-266. Single or multiple copies of this article are available for a fee from The Haworth Document Delivery Service [1-800-HAWORTH, 9:00 a.m. - 5:00 p.m. (EST). E-mail address: docdelivery@haworthpress.com].

KEYWORDS. Collaborative virtual reference, digital reference services, reference services/Kansas, multi-type libraries

INTRODUCTION

The Kansas Library Network Board (KLNB), a division of the Kansas State Library, represents regional library systems and academic, community college, public, school, and special libraries. KLNB develops and implements long-range plans and offers grants and support services to all types of libraries. With the proliferation of virtual reference services, and preliminary information from a pilot project conducted at Kansas State University, the Board expressed interest in researching a statewide collaborative service. The Executive Director of the Board was charged with forming a task force to gather information and prepare a proposal to present to the Board for possible funding. This paper will relate the collaborative planning done by the task force of public, academic, and special librarians and initial impressions of the implementation of KANAnswer, a statewide virtual reference pilot project.

PLANNING

In researching other collaborative virtual reference projects, it became clear that most consist of either all academic or all public libraries. Only a few other consortia consist of multi-type libraries making this project somewhat unique (Sloan 2002). Seventeen librarians representing multi-type libraries were asked to join the KLNB Executive Director on a task force to create a plan for a statewide virtual reference pilot project with the understanding that there was an opportunity to obtain funding through the KLNB. In order to request this funding, a proposal needed to be submitted by the next quarterly meeting of the Board, giving the task force only about six weeks to research and develop the plan.

The first meeting consisted of discussions concerning expectations and goals of the project and a brainstorming session to determine what issues needed to be researched prior to the next meeting. Each task force member volunteered to research one of the issues and report findings and recommendations at the next meeting. Having one person responsible for each area worked effectively to ensure a timely response and enable the coordinator to quickly develop a plan and proposed timeline to present to KLNB for funding. The research findings and recommendations were discussed and agreed upon by the task force at a second meeting and incorporated into the plan.

Once the plan was accepted and funded, preparations began for implementation of the pilot within six months. The major goals of the plan were to test whether a sustainable, statewide consortium for virtual reference service can be successfully created among Kansas libraries and other institutions, and to assess the effectiveness of such a service in meeting the informational needs of online patrons. The first five months of the project involved planning and decision-making in the areas of software selection, policy development, marketing/public relations, project partners, staffing, training, hours of operation, and assessment.

Software Selection

Due to limited funds, the major pre-qualifying criterion for software selection was price. However, ease of use for both operators and customers was also a primary consideration. After comparing the functions of several products (Information Services Management Committee 2002), the task force narrowed the choice to three software products using the following considerations as determining factors: price, ease of use, browser compatibility, hardware requirements, and training. Several librarians entered chat sessions at other libraries using these software products to view the user interface and to ask practical questions about the software. LivePerson (LivePerson 2003) was ultimately selected and the coordinator began negotiations with the vendor. Licenses for two simultaneous operators were purchased, and on-site training was arranged.

Policies and Procedures

Policies and procedures were developed to address the major issues identified by the task force. These issues included defining the nature of the service, quality of service, and privacy.

It was decided that the pilot project would provide ready-reference answers to users' questions. Sources to be used in order of priority would be free material available on the web, and statewide databases available via Blue Skyways or the Kansas Library Card. Additional resources or appropriate referral would be provided if necessary. The project would provide reference service to all residents of the state of Kansas and others needing information on state topics. This restriction is posted on the web page and all users are asked to confirm their state residency at the login screen.

Quality of service will be continuously evaluated during the pilot project. Issues to be considered include whether patrons and operators are pleased with the service and whether answers are thorough, accurate, and reliable. General reference practices should be observed such as using authoritative resources, citing sources or suggesting alternative sources of information. The Code of Ethics of the American Library Association (American Library Association 1995) will be followed.

Since transcripts are stored on the vendor's server, operators had strong ethical concerns about privacy issues. To inform users of the existence and purpose of transcripts, the following statement was created and placed on the KANAnswer home page: "Transcripts of KANAnswer chat sessions are stored on a remote file server, and are accessible only to the KANAnswer administrators for purposes of quality control and service assessment. Transcripts of chat sessions will be forwarded to KANAnswer visitors for their sessions only; transcripts are treated confidentially as outlined by law or American Library Association ethical standards" (Hansen 2003).

The coordinator compiled information from task force subcommittees to create the KANAnswer Operator's Manual. The topics covered in the manual include operator requirements, operator guidelines, website, service and referral procedures, and privacy issues. The manual was distributed in electronic format to all operators before the service went live.

Marketing/PR

It was determined that marketing and promotion of the project must begin early and must be ongoing–an initial advertising "blitz" would be less effective than a consistent campaign (Kawakami 2002). The State Library, specifically the KLNB, was the logical choice to assume responsibility for publicity and dissemination of materials for consistency. The task force selected the name KANAnswer, and a graphic designer was hired to create a logo early in the project to give it a recognizable identity. The logo was registered with the Kansas Secretary of State as a service mark. Members of the task force indicated that their institutions would reproduce, post and distribute promotional materials furnished to them. The name KANAnswer was registered as an Internet domain name with the extensions com, info, net and org.

A subcommittee of three persons provided the initial marketing plan. The plan included mailings to school districts across the state, posters at libraries, live demonstrations, flyers, bookmarks and websites. The KLNB prepared a press release that was forwarded to the office of the Governor of Kansas, who endorsed the project and had the release sent to all news media outlets in the state. An announcement concerning the service was also placed on the official Kansas web site. The KANAnswer web page was placed under control of the coordinator of the project for easy updates. Participating libraries then had the option of linking to this main page from whatever locations they felt were appropriate. It was determined that ongoing publicity should be provided through demonstrations at conferences, updated web pages (including "what's new" banners), periodic mailings, and testimonials. The coordinator arranged to attend and make presentations at an annual home school conference, and meetings of school librarians.

Project Partners

Efforts were made to include institutions in all geographical areas of the state. Institutions and areas that were not represented on the task force were approached about joining the core group. The project coordinator presented informational sessions at two statewide library meetings in an effort to recruit more partners. In addition, phone calls were made to specific libraries and presentations were made during regional training sessions. Awareness and recruiting sessions will continue at regional library systems and state meetings. At the time the pilot went live, partners consisted of the Kansas State Library, two regional library systems, eight academic, seven public, two community college, one technical college, and one special library. More than ninety librarians volunteered to staff the service from these various institutions.

Staffing

Because of the nature of the service, the task force recommended a consultation or tiered-reference model. The skill levels of operators were not defined for the project. It was assumed that capability to work a public reference desk at the home institution qualified a volunteer to be an operator. Each library provided staff time and expertise as in-kind contributions to the project. The coordinator developed a master schedule using the hours each institution was willing to provide. A statewide directory of volunteer librarians and their areas of expertise was developed. This directory served as a source for operators to use when referring questions. The directory was updated throughout the life of the project as more library staff became actively involved. Consortium guidelines state that KANAnswer operators must: be trained in the functions and use of LivePerson software; staff the service away from the public service desk; abide by the staff guidelines regarding referral policy and procedure; be affiliated with a Kansas library and adhere to the established policies and procedures of that institution; and subscribe to KANANSWER-L, the project e-mail discussion list.

Staff Training

The pilot project required that participating library staff be trained in the operation of LivePerson software, and that the training be ongoing throughout the life of the project. A representative from LivePerson offered the initial training in sessions scheduled at one of the participating institutions. All operators were divided into four groups with each group receiving an introductory session lasting an hour and a half. The trainer provided an overview of the software and its various features from both an operator and user perspective. Approximately 20-30 minutes were provided at the end of each session for chat practice. Most participants expressed concern that more time had not been allotted to this area of training. However, the coordinator made arrangements with the vendor to set up a 30-day practice account that allowed for fifty simultaneous operator logins using a statewide site ID. Operators could practice chatting and become familiar with the various features of the software on their own time and at their convenience. The assumption was that after the initial core group had been trained, specific persons might then advance to the level of in-state trainers.

Hours of Operation

The initial goal was to offer virtual reference service at all hours that participating libraries are open. However the goal was modified to accommodate hours of coverage that participating libraries could contribute. Hours of commitment by each library varied from one hour to nine hours per week for a weekly total of fifty-five hours. At the time of implementation, the service was offered 9:00 a.m. to 5:00 p.m. Monday-Friday and a few hours each on Saturday, Sunday and certain weeknights. The service does not operate on state and federal holidays.

Assessment

Assessment is a vital component of any pilot project. Assessment of this project will be done using information from the following sources: statistical data generated by the software, user exit surveys, session transcripts, information provided by patrons at login, post-session patron assessment recorded by operator, and any informal feedback.

PROJECT COORDINATION

The KLNB Executive Director also serves as the project coordinator. The coordinator has responsibility for administration of\the project, including communication with the vendor, operators, Kansas libraries, and the funding board. Other responsibilities include operator training, software management, scheduling and project assessment.

To facilitate project communication, the coordinator developed the KANANSWER-L e-mail discussion list to include all operators. Operators use the list to post their project questions and to make recommendations. The coordinator posts notices of project events and responds to suggestions. The list is unmoderated and archived.

The public entrance to the project is the home page found at http://www.kananswer.org. The chat log-in button appears at the bottom of the page to encourage users to read the policies before accessing the service. The coordinator created, maintains, and updates the site in response to the changing needs of the project.

Software administration includes communication with the vendor regarding technical questions or problems, managing operator accounts and passwords, and customizing canned responses and messages. Feedback was solicited from operators during the training period for recommended software modifications. Since the software was developed as a commercial tool and reflects a corporate interface, customization was done as much as possible to reflect KANAnswer's identity.

IMPLEMENTATION

The coordinator activated the account, sent out press releases and made the web page links available to the public. Operators were somewhat anxious about their first turn at answering questions, but most were eager to see the service go live. Three weeks into the project, operators were given the opportunity to respond to an informal survey about the service. Based on this information, some operator impressions can be reported.

Operator Impressions

Most operators who responded reported that staffing from their institution was adequate for the assigned hours, however, scheduling and time management were concerns for some. More time was involved with being an operator than working the assigned shift. Often, operators spent time following up a question with email responses. Several operators expressed surprise at the complexity of the requests and the question was raised as to whether patrons' expectations are too great for the scope of this service. The discussion list was valuable as a communication tool, but as with any listserv, messages were sometimes numerous, redundant, and overwhelming. Keeping up with the message traffic added to the time commitment for the operators.

Another operator concern was the perceived lack of knowledge or confidence on the part of operators to appropriately answer the different types of questions posed. This concern is understandable because the operators work in diverse libraries, and typical questions for one group may be completely foreign to another. Because some operators are not native Kansans or even U.S. citizens, it is not intuitive for them to find state information. Suggestions to provide better service include orientation to the Kansas State Government web pages and training on best referral practices for legal or medical questions. Operators from smaller libraries expressed concern about having the needed resources to answer questions. However, to this point, more than half the questions have been successfully answered using freely available online sources or statewide databases.

Software Issues

Most operators stated that the software was easy to use and somewhat intuitive. They appreciate the canned (prewritten) responses and the ability to push web pages. However, once operators started fully using the software, several asked for an additional or advanced training session. There were several issues with the software that presented problems. A technical problem the first week prevented some operators from logging in to the software at the appointed time. The coordinator worked with the vendor to identify and resolve the problem. Operators were not able to see the canned responses unless they were actually chatting. Some operators wanted the capability of viewing and familiarizing themselves with these responses at "down times" when not chatting. The project coordinator addressed this concern by collecting the canned responses in a Word file and distributing the file to KANANSWER-L. Another drawback was not being able to tell who the second operator was and when he or she was logged on unless that person was chatting. Two operator seats were purchased as a cost-saving measure, so that two operators would be on duty during each hour of operation. This did not allow the administrator to log on unless an operator seat was unoccupied. The project coordinator adapted to this by performing administrative tasks during off hours, or when only one operator was logged on. However, this arrangement has continued to be a source of frustration for operators. One feature of the software is an automatic message to the user after thirty seconds of inactivity. Operators commented that this pop-up message was annoying when they were searching for answers to questions. Even though privacy is carefully guarded, it is possible to view transcripts of the second operator's chat when online. This is a privacy issue that needs to be addressed.

Though the purpose of the project is to furnish real-time online answers to quick reference questions, the software was configured so that users have the opportunity to ask questions when the service is offline with the expectation of receiving an email response. There was much discussion on the listserv about the pros and cons of this option. Although there was mixed reaction among the operators, the current procedure is for the coordinator to forward email questions to volunteer operators.

Preliminary Findings

As of this writing, the project has been live for only three weeks. Preliminary figures show that the service averages seventeen chats a day, but this number includes practice and operator-to-operator chats. User exit surveys indicate that most users are accessing the service from a library, but home and school are close seconds. These surveys also indicate that roughly 85% of the users reported their questions were completely answered. Both users and operators have indicated positive interactions while using the service. While it is very early in the project, and these preliminary findings in no way represent true assessment, the response to the service is encouraging.

CONCLUSIONS

It is much too early to assess the pilot project as a whole. However, the planning process that was used worked efficiently and allowed KANAnswer to become a reality in a short amount of time. According to operators who responded to an informal survey, the greatest strength of the project is the collaborative commitment of multi-type libraries and librarians. The opportunity to work with colleagues across the state, to learn about the information needs of Kansas residents, and to offer them a unique service is rewarding. Whether this is a viable service that can be sustained will depend on assessment results, funding availability, and future commitment on the part of each partner.

REFERENCES

American Library Association, "The Code of Ethics of the American Library Association," 28 June 1995, <http://www.ala.org/alaorg/oif/ethics.html> (28 January 2003).

Hansen, Eric. "KANAnswer," 27 February 2003, <http://www.kananswer.org> (28 February 2003).

Information Services Management Committee, University of Waterloo. "Virtual Reference Feasibility Study Report, Appendix II, Software Evaluation Table," April 2002, <http://www.lib.uwaterloo.ca/staff/ismc/topics/virtualref/vrfinalreport.html> (29 June 2002).

Kawakami, Alice K. "Delivering Digital Reference." *Library Journal Net Connect* Spring 2002. *Library Literature and Information Science Full Text*. Online. H.W. Wilson. Available: <http://hwwilsonweb.com> 7 July 2002.

LivePerson, Inc., "LivePerson" 2003 <http://www.liveperson.com> (24 February 2003).

Sloan, Bernie. "Collaborative Live Reference Services," 21 June 2002, <http://www.lis.uiuc.edu/~b-sloan/collab.htm> (21 June 2002).

Virtual Reference Services:
The LSU Libraries Experience

Melanie E. Sims

SUMMARY. Traditional reference services are changing in response to the rapid growth of electronic resources available outside of the library. There are an increasing number of libraries that are providing digital reference services to meet the demands and expectations of remote users. This article provides an overview of virtual reference services at Louisiana State University (LSU) Libraries. It also examines the planning, implementation, marketing and user feedback of real time reference service after its first year. *[Article copies available for a fee from The Haworth Document Delivery Service: 1-800-HAWORTH. E-mail address: <docdelivery@ haworthpress.com> Website: <http://www.HaworthPress.com> © 2002/2003 by The Haworth Press, Inc. All rights reserved.]*

KEYWORDS. Electronic reference services, e-mail reference, chat reference, LSU Libraries, college and university reference services, reference surveys

Libraries often experience many changes in response to new emerging technologies in an effort to meet the demands of their customers. Therefore, it's no surprise that the rapid growth in access to the Internet is revolutionizing how libraries provide reference services.

Melanie E. Sims is Reference Assistant Coordinator, 141 Middleton Library, LSU Libraries, Baton Rouge, LA 70803 (E-mail: notmes@lsu.edu).

[Haworth co-indexing entry note]: "Virtual Reference Services: The LSU Libraries Experience." Sims, Melanie E. Co-published simultaneously in *The Reference Librarian* (The Haworth Information Press, an imprint of The Haworth Press, Inc.) No. 79/80, 2002/2003, pp. 267-279; and: *Digital Reference Services* (ed: Bill Katz) The Haworth Information Press, an imprint of The Haworth Press, Inc., 2002/2003, pp. 267-279. Single or multiple copies of this article are available for a fee from The Haworth Document Delivery Service [1-800-HAWORTH, 9:00 a.m. - 5:00 p.m. (EST). E-mail address: docdelivery@haworthpress.com].

10.1300/J120v38n79_18   267

In general, both public and academic libraries are witnessing a decline in the number of people actually visiting the library. The Association of Research Libraries indicated a 21% decrease in the number of reference transaction from 1991-2001.[1] In order to combat this decline, a growing number of libraries are offering a variety of services to remote users including searching online public access catalogs, interlibrary loan requests and electronic mail reference. However, the latest trend is to provide reference services to remote users through real time or chat reference services.

Digital reference, also known as electronic reference, e-reference, online reference and virtual reference is "a mechanism by which people can submit their questions and have them answered by a library staff member through some electronic means (e-mail, chat, Web forms, etc.) not in person or over the phone."[2] In 2001, Louisiana State University Libraries began investigating the establishment of a virtual reference service. Although electronic mail reference service has been provided to users since the mid-1990s, there was a perceived need to expand the service to include a live, online chat reference service.

There were several reasons that prompted the desire to provide online chat reference services. Fewer people are visiting the library because of the increased number of electronic resources being provided by the library for outside usage. According to the latest *ARL Supplementary Statistics*, libraries are spending more than 16% of their library materials budget on electronic resources.[3] Many of the electronic resources also provide full-text information that further negates the necessity of the user to come to the library. An article in the *Chronicle of Higher Education* indicated that more students prefer to work online and are finding new study spaces in dorm rooms, apartments, coffee shops and bookstores.[4] Many universities like LSU are increasing the number of distance education courses. The Department of Education statistics show that there was a 72% increase in the number of institutions offering distance education from 1995 to 1998.[5] Participation reports of distance education from 1999-2000 indicate that undergraduate students (7%) and graduate students (10%) with more family and employment responsibilities tend to participate in distance education classes.[6] The increase in electronic resources and DE courses facilitates the need to provide assistance to remote and DE students. Real time reference provides remote users and DE students with the same service that they would receive if they were to visit the library in person.

In an effort to provide reference services to remote users, Middleton Reference Services at LSU Libraries established a Virtual Reference

Committee in June 2001. The committee consisted of four librarians, one library paraprofessional and one graduate assistant. The committee conducted a literature review to examine the current practices in digital reference. Carol Tenopir concluded after surveying 70 Association of Research Libraries, "Although most do not yet offer real time virtual reference services, all offer some reference services to their remote users, and expanding virtual reference services is in the planning stages at many others."[7]

The Virtual Reference Committee developed several goals for the 2001/2002 fiscal year. The first goal was to create virtual reference services to aid remote users. The committee developed policies and procedures for virtual reference services. The policy states, "The primary goals of Middleton Virtual Reference Services are to support the curriculum and research needs of the faculty, students and staff of Louisiana State University and to educate remote users to retrieve and utilize information in an increasingly digital environment. The following services are available through the Middleton Virtual Reference Services:

1. Ask A Librarian: This service allows researchers to electronically ask questions they might ask at the reference desk. Replies are sent to users via e-mail within 24 hours, excluding weekends and holidays.
2. Middleton FAQ: This service provides quick answers to frequently asked questions.
3. Real Time Reference: This service is designed for users to ask questions and get answers in a real time online environment from library staff using chat room technology."

POLICY ON E-MAIL REFERENCE

Having written a policy to define the virtual reference services provided by the LSU Libraries, the committee began immediately to revise its Ask A Librarian service. Although LSU Libraries has been providing electronic mail reference for several years, this service was not heavily promoted because the link for the service existed in a second tier of Web pages. Thus the link for the Ask A Librarian service was quickly moved to the main LSU Libraries home page and a new Web form was designed for e-mail reference. The following guidelines were established for this revised Ask A Librarian service:

1. This electronic reference service is designed to promote brief answers to factual questions and/or suggestions for locations and sources that might help to answer questions.
2. Questions may be submitted 24 hours a day, 7 days a week via the library's website using the following URL address: http://www.lib.lsu.edu/lib/dear.html. Questions should be stated as clearly as possible to facilitate a prompt response.
3. Replies are normally sent via e-mail within 24 hours, excluding weekends and holidays.
4. When necessary, questions will be referred to the appropriate subject specialist.
5. Priority for this service is given to faculty, students and staff of Louisiana State University. Others will be assisted if their request concerns Louisiana State University or unique resources of Louisiana State University.
6. This service does not allow users to request services normally provided by Interlibrary Loan (i.e., requesting books or articles) or Circulation (i.e., renewals, recalls or holds). Users requesting such services will be referred to the appropriate department.
7. Patrons with extensive research needs should visit the library for further assistance.
8. Citations to the source of information should be given whenever possible.
9. If the volume of this service becomes too heavy, the service will be limited only to faculty, students, and staff of Louisiana State University.

The number of questions per day increased to an average of eight questions per day when the Ask A Librarian link was moved to the main library homepage. Organizations can control the amount of exposure of their Ask A service by the placement of service access on their Web site. The highest level of visibility of a service can be gained through a link at the "top" of the sponsoring Web site (i.e., the home page or one of the first Web pages accessed upon arrival to the site).

The Virtual Reference Committee also created an FAQ page for Middleton, the main campus library. The web page contains brief answers to commonly asked questions both at the reference desk and through the Ask A Librarian service. Answers are reflective of the most appropriate source(s) either in print or electronic format. The Middleton FAQ page also refers users to online tutorials and Internet subject guides.

PLANNING REAL TIME REFERENCE SERVICE

The second major goal of the Virtual Reference Committee was to evaluate and select a software package for real time reference services. The committee evaluated the following software packages for real time reference: Human Click Pro, LSSI, LiveAssistance, Live Helper and several freeware packages. In addition to reviewing the different packages, the committee sought feedback from other universities who were presently providing real time reference. In reviewing each package, the committee took into consideration the following criteria: system requirements, ease of use, cost, customer service support, and special features. One of the main goals of the committee was to find a product that would not require users to download any software in order to use the service. The committee also wanted a product that would be easy to use for both staff and users.

The committee selected LiveAssistance as the software package for real time reference. LiveAssistance was chosen for the following reasons:

- It was Web-based and it didn't require additional installation of hardware/software on staff computers.
- Users didn't have to download any software to use the service.
- It was easy for both staff and users to use.
- Special features such as push pages, transcripts of chat sessions, statistics and reports were available.
- Cost was relatively inexpensive.
- Customer service support was good.
- Positive responses from others who were using Live Assistance.

In planning the service, it was decided upfront that the new chat reference service would not be provided at the reference desk. Chat requires undivided attention, rarely possible at the public reference desk. Patrons are accustomed to seeing someone typing at a reference desk computer, but expect librarians to look up, drop what they're doing and invite dialog.[9] Therefore, the new chat reference service would be provided by all the reference staff persons in their cubicle. All of the reference staff computers were assessed to determine if they were equipped to handle the provision of real time reference. All of the computers had sound cards, however, speakers had to be purchased for each reference staff member. The library only purchased one "seat" for chat reference service. (Cost is based partially on the number of seats purchased.) In addition to writing procedures to govern the chat service, the committee also wrote a Virtual Reference Etiquette Policy. Both policies are linked to the initial chat service Web page, http://www.lib.lsu.edu/virtual/liveassistance.html.

In December 2001, the committee launched a contest to name the real time reference service. A service with a memorable name that can be readily promoted provides a non-threatening entrance point to the library for users.[10] The contest was advertised on the library home page and on flyers. The committee received over 40 entries in the contest that lasted a week. Ultimately, the committee decided to use the company name, Live Assistance because it wouldn't infringe on any trademarks and it was indicative of what the service provided. The committee selected five entries as runner-ups in the contest. The runner-ups each received a $10 Tiger Express Card that could be used on campus for printing, copying and/or purchasing other items.

A training session was conducted for reference staff on how to use the new chat service. During the training session, the committee discussed the policy for Middleton Virtual Reference Services. Staff were shown how to log into the system and how to respond to questions. A demonstration of an actual chat session was given. The training session also included information on how to conduct a reference interview. Tips were also given on the different skills and habits associated with virtual vs. face-to-face reference service.[11] The staff members were paired together and were required to practice using the service as both the librarian and user in order to become familiar with the new service.

PUBLICITY

During the Spring 2002 semester, the newly implemented chat service was publicized through a variety of venues. Successful marketing being a key component to any new service. A link was placed on the library home page. Library liaisons were encouraged to announce the new service during their instructional sessions. Flyers were distributed around campus, sent to departments and displayed in the library to advertise the new real time reference service. The campus newspaper, The Reveille, featured an article on the new service and the library ran a total of 10 advertisements in the paper during 2002. There were also a series of 8 ads that ran on the campus KLSU radio station in March 2002. An article on virtual reference services was included in the Fall 2002 issue of the library newsletter distributed to faculty, students and staff. Information on the chat service was also included in the library outreach kits that are distributed to faculty and students during various library presentations. Bookmarks have been designed to market the virtual reference service as well.

IMPLEMENTATION

On January 28, 2002, LSU Libraries began offering real time reference service. Live Assistance is open to the general public, requiring no authentication to prove university affiliation of any kind and requests about users' affiliation to the university are not made. Chat users are asked to enter their name, telephone number and e-mail address before they log on to the chat session. The initial hours of operation for the real time reference service were Monday-Friday from 10:00 a.m.-12 noon and 1:00 p.m.-4:00 p.m. The service was staffed a total of 25 hours per week by a combination of librarians, library paraprofessionals and graduate assistants from Reference. During the initial planning stages of this project, it was decided that all reference staff would participate in providing real time reference, and this service would not be staffed on a voluntary basis. Staff was given a virtual reference schedule to follow in addition to their regular reference desk schedule. Therefore, everyone staffed the virtual reference desk for at least one hour per week. Despite the publicity for the new real time reference service, there was not an overwhelming response to the service. During the spring semester, there were a total of 178 successful chat sessions. However, there were a total of 519 unfiltered chat sessions. This number includes answered chats as well as unanswered chats, abandoned chats, disconnected chats, quit chats, and no operators available. The system records all transactions in its statistics regardless of whether or not an actual chat session really took place.

One of the major problems that staff encountered during the first semester of providing real time reference was being disconnected in the middle of a chat session or while waiting for someone to log on to the service. After keeping a log of how many times staff were being disconnected, the Committee immediately contacted Live Assistance to determine the problem. Live Assistance staff checked into the problem, and it was not a problem with their system. Live Assistance staff began to work with the computing services staff at LSU to determine the problem. It was determined that LSU did not have enough bandwidth to support the service. Therefore, LSU Computing Services increased the bandwidth for the service to resolve the problem. The only other problem incurred was having staff remember to log on to the service. In order to remedy this problem, at the end of each shift, the person on duty would phone the next person to make sure that they had logged on to the service.

USER FEEDBACK

At the end of the spring semester an e-mail survey was sent to all customers who had used Live Assistance. The survey was not sent to any staff that had used the service. A total of 121 surveys were sent out. However, six of the e-mail addresses were incorrect and the surveys were returned. Each respondent was asked to answer five questions. There was a 39% return response rate. Below are the results from the Live Assistance e-mail survey.

1. Besides Live Assistance, which other LSU Libraries reference services have you used? Check all that apply.

Telephone reference	8
E-mail reference	16
In-person at the reference desk	29
Web pages	26
No response	3

2. Overall, how do you rate the Live Assistance service?

Excellent	25	56%
Very Good	14	31%
Satisfactory	4	9%
Needs Improvement	2	4%
Unsatisfactory	0	0%

3. Do you agree with the following statement: I found Live Assistance easy to use.

Strongly Agree	23	51%
Agree	19	42%

Neutral	3	7%
Disagree	0	0%
Strongly Disagree	0	0%

4. Would you recommend this service to others?

Strongly Agree	28	62%
Agree	15	33%
Neutral	1	2%
Disagree	1	2%
Strongly Disagree	0	0%

5. How did you find out about the service? Mark all that apply.

Libraries' Web site	32
Radio (KLSU)	0
Reveille	1
Teacher	6
Word of Mouth	5
Other	3

Here are a few of the additional comments that were submitted by the survey respondents:

- Excellent idea.
- More hours of availability might be good. I don't know how much traffic you get, but the person I talked to was knowledgeable and helpful.
- I am a non-LSU student comparing various online reference chat services. Yours was quite nice.
- The only thing I'd suggest is to improve the visual interface.
- This service helped me out when I really needed it. Thanks and keep up the good work.
- This was great! Although, they did not give me the immediate answer to my question, they pointed me in the right direction to what I needed. And they did it within 5 minutes! I did not have to wait for days to get a response. Keep up the good work.

- Live Assistance should always provide some response to a request even if it is to indicate that no answer could be found. Live Assistance should seek to respond as quickly as possible, in the event that the request is needed immediately. Overall, it is a good library tool. I am glad that it is available.
- I think the service worked exactly how it should. It was prompt and useful information that helped me tremendously in locating information for my biology term paper. The only suggestion I have is perhaps to advertise the service more so that more people may take advantage of it.

The same hours of operation were provided for the summer semester as in the spring semester. An exit survey was created to pop up at the end of each chat session for the user to complete. The exit survey included the same questions that were used in the e-mail survey sent to users at the end of the first semester of providing real time reference service to users.

After reviewing the statistics for virtual reference, the hours of operation were expanded for the fall 2002 semester. The LSU Libraries currently provides 37 hours of real time reference. Virtual reference service is provided Monday-Thursday from 9:00 a.m.-5:00 p.m. and Friday from 12 noon-5:00 p.m. A "Help" tab linking directly to our virtual reference services was added to most of the library Web pages and to the library online catalog.

Although more people are beginning to use chat reference, the usage of real time reference was very low for the first year. There were a total of 485 successful chat sessions. However, there were a total of 1,246 unfiltered chat sessions recorded by the system which once again includes answered chats, unanswered chats, abandoned chats, disconnected chats, and no operators available. The service is not provided during intersession and holidays when the students are not in classes.

The majority of the questions fell into the catalog (27%) or database (27%) categories. The catalog category included questions on searching, specific holdings, electronic reserves and renewals. The database category required the librarian to suggest a database, to explain how to access a particular database, or to offer search tips. Twenty-two percent of the users required assistance with specific library information such as hours, location of materials, fines, interlibrary loan, printing, and etc. There were about sixteen percent of the users who asked short factual questions and/or in-depth questions. To a lesser extent, users requested assistance with university information (3%) and Web navigation (2%).

The average chat session lasted 3 minutes 5 seconds. The average time in queue was 18 seconds.

The library has not received an extremely high response rate to the pop up exit survey. Only 64 people have responded to the exit survey from June 2002 to January 2003. Despite the low response rate, many people continue to rate the service as excellent and very easy to use. All of the respondents would recommend the service to others except for one person. Most people have discovered the service through the Libraries' Web site.

E-mail reference has remained constant since the real time reference service was offered. It is also interesting to note that a number of e-mail questions are received during the same time that chat reference service is available. This is a definite indication that asynchronous reference service will not disappear quickly. Lankes and Shostack state, "real time systems and asynchronous systems will need to coexist (or rather digital reference systems will need to support both forms of interaction). It is posited that different questions and different users will require different forms of interactions."[12]

The LSU Libraries was the first academic library in the state to provide real time reference services. The staff at the LSU Libraries has responded extremely well to the new service. Most staff enjoy the ability to provide reference service to patrons outside of the library when it's most convenient to the patron or at their point of need. Virtual reference also allows more people to access the library for assistance. Staff also found patrons to be very courteous and appreciative of the service. Many users have expressed gratitude for the service which provides staff with a sense of satisfaction. While many staff like the ability to work in their offices on virtual reference, others find it somewhat confining because they would like to easily access ready reference materials that are available at the reference desk. A few staff has experienced anxiety because they sensed an obligation to provide an exact answer in a short amount of time. They were further frustrated if the answer was not readily available on their desktop or it required an extensive amount of typing when they were not a good or fast typist. The lack of visual clues sometimes makes virtual reference difficult. Staff also find it frustrating when there is a lag in communication or network congestion or when they are disconnected in the middle of a session.

At the beginning of the spring 2003 semester, staff were given another training session on chat reference service. The training session was a refresher on how to access the predefined quotes and how to push pages. Committee members also discussed the virtual reference interview and netiquette as well as user statistics. The primary focus of virtual reference services at LSU Libraries in the future will be to increase usage of chat reference services while continuing to improve the quality of service being provided to the users. Statistics will also continue to be monitored to determine the need to change and/or expand the current hours of operations to include nights and weekends. LSU Libraries will also explore the idea of possibly joining a statewide or regional virtual reference consortia. The idea of participating in a virtual reference consortium has many advantages as well as disadvantages. However, it is evident that virtual reference services will continue to grow as staff strive to reach more users in an increasingly digital world.

NOTES

1. Kryillidou, Martha and Mark Young, "Service Trends in ARL Libraries, 1991-2001," Association of Research Libraries, 2002. Online, <http://www.arl.org/stats/arlstat/graphs/2001/2001t1.html> Accessed: January 13, 2003.

2. Janes, Joseph, David Carter and Patricia Memmott, "Digital Reference Services in Academic Libraries," *Reference & User Services Quarterly*, v.39, no. 2 (Winter 1999): 146.

3. Kryillidou, Martha and Mark Young, "Research Library Trends," Association of Research Libraries, 2002. Online, <http://www.arl.org/stats/arlstat/01pub/intro.html> Accessed: January 13, 2003.

4. Carlson, Scott, "As Students Work Online, Reading Rooms Empty Out–Leading Some Campuses to Add Starbucks," *Chronicle of Higher Education*, November 16, 2001: 35.

5. Wood, Patricia A., "The U.S. Department of Education and Student Financial Aid for Distance Education: An Update," ERIC Clearinghouse on Higher Education, 2001, ED 457762, ERIC Abstracts, Ovid Technologies, Louisiana State University.

6. Sirkora, Anna and C. Dennis Carroll, "A Profile of Participation in Distance Education: 1999-2000 Postsecondary Education Descriptive Analysis Reports," U.S. Department of Education, 2002, NCES 2003-154. Online, <http://nces.ed.gov>.

7. Tenopir, Carol, "Virtual Reference Services in a Real World," *Library Journal*, v. 126, no. 12 (July 2001): 38.

8. Lankes, R. David and Abby S. Kasowiz (1998), *The AskA Starter Kit: How to Build and Maintain Digital Reference Services*, Syracuse, New York: ERIC Clearinghouse on Information & Technology: 154.

9. Curtis, Donnelyn (2002) *Attracting, Educating, and Serving Remote Users Through the Web: A How-To-Do-It Manual for Librarians*, New York: Neal-Schuman Publishers, Inc.: 99.

10. Gray, Suzanne M., "Virtual Reference Services," *Reference & User Services Quarterly*, v. 39, no. 4 (Summer 2000): 370.

11. Lipow, Anne Grodzins and Steve Coffman (2001) *Establishing A Virtual Reference Service: VRD Training Manual, LSSI's VRD (Virtual Reference Desk) software, service policies and guidelines, design and content of screens*, Berkeley, CA: Library Solutions Press: Module 1-2.2-2.5.

12. Lankes, R. David and Pauline Shostack, "The Necessity of Real-Time Fact and Fiction in Digital Reference Systems," *Reference & User Services Quarterly*, v. 41, no. 4 (Summer 2002): 354.

Ask a Penn State Librarian, Live: Virtual Reference Service at Penn State

Susan A. Ware
Joseph Fennewald
Lesley M. Moyo
Laura K. Probst

SUMMARY. After a 22-week pilot study, Penn State launched a university-wide real-time virtual reference service in Fall 2002. The Penn State Virtual Reference Service (VRS) features chat, co-browsing, and authentication into licensed databases. VRS serves students, faculty, and staff at 21 residential and commuter campuses statewide, as well as students enrolled in World Campus distance learning courses. This paper

Susan A. Ware is Reference & Instruction Librarian, Penn State, Delaware County Campus, Media, PA 19063 (E-mail: saw4@psu.edu). Joseph Fennewald is Head Librarian, Penn State, Hazleton Campus, Hazleton, PA 18201 (E-mail: jaf23@psu.edu). Lesley M. Moyo (E-mail: lmm26@psu) is Head, Gateway Library, and Laura K. Probst (E-mail: lkp5@psu.edu) is Head of Public Services, Penn State, both at University Park Campus, University Park, PA 16802.

The authors wish to thank the Penn State Virtual Reference Service librarians for their insightful comments and their dedication to the success of this service. Special thanks also go to Mary Frances McLaughlin, Reference Librarian, Delaware County Campus, for her essential statistical support and William Moyer, English Instructor, Delaware County Campus, for his helpful comments on the preparation of this manuscript.

[Haworth co-indexing entry note]: "Ask a Penn State Librarian, Live: Virtual Reference Service at Penn State." Ware, Susan A. et al. Co-published simultaneously in *The Reference Librarian* (The Haworth Information Press, an imprint of The Haworth Press, Inc.) No. 79/80, 2002/2003, pp. 281-295; and: *Digital Reference Services* (ed: Bill Katz) The Haworth Information Press, an imprint of The Haworth Press, Inc., 2002/2003, pp. 281-295. Single or multiple copies of this article are available for a fee from The Haworth Document Delivery Service [1-800-HAWORTH, 9:00 a.m. - 5:00 p.m. (EST). E-mail address: docdelivery@haworthpress.com].

http://www.haworthpress.com/store/product.asp?sku=J120

10.1300/J120v38n79_19

presents an analysis of the users, questions, exit surveys, and a VRS librarian survey. *[Article copies available for a fee from The Haworth Document Delivery Service: 1-800-HAWORTH. E-mail address: <docdelivery@ haworthpress.com> Website: <http://www.HaworthPress.com> © 2002/2003 by The Haworth Press, Inc. All rights reserved.]*

KEYWORDS. Virtual Reference Service, digital reference, real-time reference, statistics, survey, Penn State, LSSI

Penn State is a multi-campus university, often described as "one university, geographically dispersed." In addition to the main campus at University Park, there are 20 campus/college locations statewide[1] and three Penn State affiliated institutions.[2] The Penn State University Libraries strive to be "one library geographically dispersed" through a dynamic, integrated information system called LIAS (Library Information Access System). LIAS provides electronic access to a wide range of library resources including more than 4.6 million volumes, 56,000 serial subscriptions, 350 databases, and 8,000 electronic full text journals. Remote authentication offers authorized users off-site access to an array of licensed databases, as well as automated circulation services such as renewing materials, placing recalls and holds, accessing course reserves, and requesting materials via intra-campus loan, electronic desktop delivery, and interlibrary loan from a host of consortium partner institutions. In Fall 2002, the University Libraries launched a real-time virtual reference service to support the use of LIAS resources by a growing community of remote users. This service joined the suite of University Libraries reference services now accessible through the ASK! button[3] found on the top two levels of the Libraries' web site and on all pages of the library catalog.

PENN STATE VIRTUAL REFERENCE SERVICE: PILOT

The Penn State Virtual Reference Service (VRS) started on October 23, 2001 as a pilot project to test the feasibility of offering multi-campus, online reference service through real-time chat and browser sharing. Funding for software installation, annual service subscription, local advertising, and assessment came from the University Libraries, the World Campus (distance education), and teaching and research support grants awarded by the Penn State Center for Excellence in Teaching and Learning (CELT) and the Penn State Commonwealth College.

The invitation to "Ask a Penn State Librarian, Live" appeared on library home pages at three campus locations and on two World Campus courses with home pages in the WebCT course management system. The library pilot locations included: the Delaware County Campus, a commuter campus; the Hazleton Campus, a residential campus; and the University Park Gateway Library, an undergraduate and 24-hour laptop library. In January 2002, seven additional campus libraries and one additional World Campus course added a link to VRS. The VRS pilot project was a night-owl service, open from 9 p.m. to 12 a.m., Sunday-Thursday. Eight librarians[4] from the three pilot campuses staffed the service from library offices and from their homes through cable modem or DSL phone line. The Penn State VRS home page was modeled on the layout of the University of Florida's Ref eXpress home page, with links to information about the scope of the service, hours, staffing, the University Policy on Computer and Network Use and Security, chat netiquette, general rules of conduct, and privacy.[5] Prominent warnings about system compatibility (the AOL browser and the Macintosh operating system were not supported) also appeared on the service home page.

After in-house testing, demonstrations, and discussions with sales representatives of the leading software products at that time,[6] LSSI's hosted Virtual Reference Desk 2.0 (VRD 2.0) software was chosen for the pilot. Both LSSI and Metropolitan Cooperative Library System (MCLS) 24/7 Project are based on eGain software that supports co-browsing without requiring the user to download an applet or plug-in. In addition to chat and co-browsing, VRD 2.0 featured materials sharing, scripted messages and bookmarked URLs, session transcripts emailed to the user and the librarian, a transcript archive, a session exit survey, and custom reports. The most critical feature for Penn State's service was the software's ability to support remote authentication into licensed databases. While the public is free to use licensed databases on-site at any campus location, remote access is limited to users with a valid Penn State user id and password. In keeping with this policy, VRS is open to non-University researchers, but only users who are able to log in with a valid user id and password are permitted to co-browse licensed databases.

EARLY TECHNICAL CHALLENGES

Opting for a vendor-hosted virtual reference service does not supplant the need for dedicated local technical support. Troubleshooting the compatibility of LSSI's software and the Penn State Libraries' local area network proved a major challenge during the pilot. Server downtime and periodic software changes at both LSSI and Penn State resulted in numerous service failures that were difficult to diagnose. Problems ranged from chat failures and database disconnects to screen freezes and system failures. Sometimes a service shutdown and restart solved the problem; other times, a complete system reboot was required. On a number of occasions, a shift ended without resolution of the problem. In response, the University Libraries' Department for Information Technologies and LSSI assigned dedicated technicians to review the vendor's and the University's system specifications and security settings. After their collaborative analysis, a number of basic incompatibilities were resolved.

VRS PILOT STATISTICS

The VRS question login page collected demographic data (name, email address, and campus affiliation), and an exit survey at the end of each session asked users if they were satisfied with the service. After 22 weeks of service (October 26-May 9, 2002), VRS had answered 48 questions from 38 users. Sixteen percent of the users asked questions on two or more occasions. Users affiliated with the campus/colleges initiated 75% of the questions, 23% came from World Campus students and faculty, and the remaining 2% were from students at University Park. Fifty-five percent of the users completed the exit survey at the end of a session. Eight percent completed the survey at the end of two or more sessions. In total, 26 exit surveys were completed. Eleven write-in comments were submitted. Eighty-four percent of the exit survey respondents were satisfied with the answer provided and would use the service again. Additional service and survey information is available at a Penn State VRS web site.[7] Exit comments like these confirmed that VRS was meeting a significant student need:

> *Even though I was aware of Penn State online library resources, I was spending too much time trying to figure out how to get to journals and how to search for information. This evening was my first experience with the service and the librarian was very helpful and I was very please with this service. Please continue to offer it in the future. I think it will be a great asset to us Adult DE learners. Thanks again!*

The librarian was simply great. [name deleted] assisted me when I thought I was lost completely.

In May 2002, it was recommended that VRS continue with additional afternoon hours, additional staff, and greater visibility through higher placement of the service link on the University Libraries web site. In addition, a Virtual Reference Service Task Force was appointed to coordinate the development, implementation, training, and assessment of VRS across the University Libraries system.

PENN STATE VIRTUAL REFERENCE SERVICE– UNIVERSITY-WIDE

Fall 2002 marked the addition of VRS to the ASK! menu of University Libraries reference services. Anyone visiting the University Libraries' web site may now use ASK! to submit a question online by real-time chat or by email. In addition, the VRS link was added to the WebCT template of all World Campus courses and to all campus/college library home pages. Eleven librarians[8] from University Park, the campus/colleges, and the Hershey Medical College volunteered to staff the university-wide VRS for thirty-nine hours per week: Sunday from 6 p.m.-9 p.m. and Monday-Thursday from 3 p.m.-12 a.m. Ten VRS librarians used at least one campus workstation for service, while six also adjusted their home computers to serve as VRS workstations. Each librarian covered a weekly three-hour shift and one or two Sundays in rotation.

Fall 2002 service began with several enhancements to the user entry procedure. Bolder warnings about browser and operating system compatibility now appear on the VRS home page. In addition, users are forced to click through a "tips and guidelines" page before submitting a question. On the question login page, the user status entry was changed from a write-in text box to a drop-down menu with the following choices: undergraduate, graduate students, faculty, staff, non-PSU. The menu added consistency to the statistical analysis of user status. After two months of service, LSSI upgraded VRS software from VRD 2.0 to Virtual Reference Toolkit 2.5 (VRT 2.5). With the upgrade, patron load time and service reliability improved greatly.

VIRTUAL REFERENCE TOOLKIT (VRT) COMPATIBILITY

Through LIAS, Penn State offers more than 350 electronic databases, and the number is growing. Maintaining VRT 2.5 compatibility with these databases requires periodic tests and checks as databases adopt new features and as VRT 2.5 is tweaked and upgraded. Microsoft Internet Explorer versions 5.0 and higher appear to be compatible with all VRT 2.5 service features. Recent technical notes from LSSI report that compatibility with Netscape varies. Netscape 4.7x must have java enabled and Netscape 7.0 must have java disabled. Since most users are not aware of their browser's java settings, VRT 2.5 has been modified to detect when a Netscape user's java setting is not compatible and displays a pop-up message with instructions for changing the setting. Co-browsing cannot be conducted with Netscape 7.0 users or Macintosh users. During Fall 2002, the most frequently used browser and operating systems were Microsoft Internet Explorer (89%) and Windows (96%).

Some users who require assistive technologies to access the Internet and LIAS resources cannot be served through VRS. Accessibility tests using JAWS, a popular screen reader, discovered that the VRT 2.5 user interface consists of twelve frames. A lack of descriptive labels on these frames made it difficult for JAWS to find the two frames that support chat and co-browsing.[9] Much more attention must be given to labeling VRT 2.5 frames for screen readers and testing all design features for compatibility with assistive technologies.

POPULAR SERVICE FEATURES

At Penn State, the most frequently used service features are chat and Interact (co-browse). During co-browse, the user and the librarian have equal control of the shared browser. However, ultimate control of an interactive session is in the hands of the librarian, who can change co-browse to "escort" (librarian-side page push only) and back with the click of a button. Using chat and co-browse, VRS librarians are able to guide students directly to databases and demonstrate or coach them through searches. Chat and co-browsing are also valuable tools in meeting the high demand for assistance with electronic course reserves, which are accessed through the CAT, Penn State's online catalog.

The Multiple Inbox is another feature that is used routinely. The Multiple Inbox allows a librarian to toggle among multiple users and to interact with each one in a separate full-featured console. While the Multiple Inbox will hold 16 users at one time, Penn State's configuration limits the number of simultaneous users to three. The next user to arrive receives the option to hold until the librarian is available or to submit a question by email. The limit on simultaneous users is an individual librarian setting. A librarian can have a personal limit of two or only one, if desired.

The Librarian Monitor feature is the key to sharing and transferring sessions between librarians. Through the Librarian Monitor, a second librarian can join a session in progress and participate fully. The librarians can also send private chat messages to each other during a joint session. This feature was used occasionally to transfer a session between librarians for a question referral or to simply pass on a user during a shift change.

VRS FALL 2002 STATISTICS

Fall 2002 was the only full semester of service completed at the time of this report. In 17 weeks, VRS had answered 418 questions from 355 users. Eleven percent of the users asked questions on two or more occasions. The majority of questions came from undergraduates (82%), with 51% of them located at University Park and 43% at the campus/colleges. No peak day, time, or week of the semester occurred. Ninety-five percent of the questions were equally distributed Monday through Thursday. However, 80% of the questions arrived during the fifth through final week of the semester.

Forty-five percent of the users completed the exit survey at the end of a session. Six percent completed the survey at the end of two or more sessions. In total, 169 exit surveys were completed. Eighty-two write-in comments were submitted. Only seven were complaints, and most complaints related to system failures. In summary, the exit survey reported that:

- 93% of respondents felt that the VRS met their needs
- 96% would use the service again
- 98% found the service easy to use
- 81% do their research most often between 5 p.m. and 12 a.m.
- 75% were undergraduates; 15% were graduate students
- 67% discovered the service through a web link; 11% from workshops and teachers; 16% through "other" unidentified means.

VRS QUESTION ANALYSIS

The 418 VRS questions asked during Fall 2002 were similar to those typically asked of librarians at the reference desk, by phone, or by email. The majority of the questions were specific to class assignments. Students needed help getting started on their research paper, finding a specific database, locating electronic reserves, identifying a scholarly publication or valid web site, completing a library assignment, or citing their sources correctly. At the same time, the library, through VRS, continued to be seen as a campus information center. Sixteen percent of the VRS questions dealt with non-library issues, such as exam schedules, class cancellations, and campus events.

Knowing the types of questions asked in VRS can provide practical insight into the development of user and service support resources such as FAQs, pathfinders, and VRS training exercises. Question analysis can also be used to inform collection development and to improve web page design. The 418 VRS questions received in Fall 2002 and the 48 questions received during the pilot service were analyzed in accordance with the field-tested Lankes/McClure Reference Question Typology outlined in *Statistics, Measures and Quality Standards for Assessing Digital Reference Library Services: Guidelines and Procedures*. The greatest appeal of a standardized typology is the potential it presents for longitudinal comparisons of data across libraries and the identification of national and international norms.

Fall 2002 VRS reference questions fell into five categories: Instructional, Research or Subject Request, Ready Reference, Technical, and Out of Scope. Thirty-nine percent of the questions were Instructional. Most of them asked for the location of a specific database or item. More than half of the Instructional questions asked how to find ProQuest, Lexis Nexis, ERIC, PsycInfo, or another recommended database. Almost one-third asked for assistance in locating a book, yearbook, dissertation, or journal in the collection. Questions that were specific to locating electronic course reserves ranked third in this category. Sixteen questions came from a library workbook assignment given by one of the campus libraries.

Of the questions, 32.5% were Research or Subject Requests. Frequently, students identified the type of material needed, and most often, they asked for scholarly, peer-reviewed, or refereed publications. They also asked for resources that were good, reliable, valuable, legitimate, reputable, recommended, or analytical. Professional or trade journals, case studies, or technical reports were also in high demand. However, approximately 60% of the questions in the Research or Subject Request category were more general. Students often presented their research topic at the onset, but few indicated whether they had conducted any database searches before coming to VRS. Twelve questions asked for help getting started in finding materials. One student presented different approaches to an assignment and asked the VRS librarian to help narrow the search topic.

Ready Reference was the classification assigned to 22% of the total questions. VRS librarians answered most Ready Reference questions directly or by pushing a page or co-browsing to a suggested web site. Seventy-five percent of the Ready Reference questions involved issues related to the University or to the libraries. These included questions on class or exam schedules, campus events, or academic programs. Library-related questions included a person's eligibility to use the library, borrowing privileges, library hours, the availability of equipment, or the location of materials (i.e., storage, audio-books, archives, children's section, or textbooks). Because librarians at so many different campus locations cover VRS, those who were new to Penn State or who had not visited the campus from where the question was directed were unable to answer some of these questions. The location of the printer in Paterno Library or whether the typewriters were currently in use could not be answered without knowledge of the library or without being physically present. Thirteen percent of the Ready Reference questions asked for information on citing articles, books, or web sites. Five percent asked for information on how to evaluate a web site or to distinguish between scholarly and popular publications. For both topics, students were pushed or co-browsed to a suggested web site that was listed among the URLs stored in the librarian's service console.

Technical questions accounted for 24%, and they were fairly sophisticated. Users often described the difficulties they were having connecting to the network. Most of them were trying to access a specific electronic resource when they encountered technical difficulties. Some were trying to connect to a licensed database. Others encountered error messages when they were trying to use the library's online catalog or access electronic course reserves. The remaining questions involved general problems using a password or downloading materials found in a database. Only two questions were classified as Out of Scope. Those questions asked for clarification on a class assignment, and only the instructor could answer those questions definitively.

Looking back at the pilot service questions, the type and frequency of questions asked were consistent with those asked when the service was expanded university-wide. Of the 48 pilot questions, 42% were Instructional. Students were seeking articles or books on a given topic. Of these, four students wanted a specific item and asked for assistance in locating a book, an article, or a reserve item. Thirty-one percent of the questions fell into the Research or Subject Request category. Students requested assistance in locating information for a research paper or class presentation. Many of these questions included phrases such as, "desperately trying not to panic," or my searches, "came up with nothing." Ready Reference queries made up 16%. Most often, they asked for help with citing sources or had questions about the exam schedule.

VRS STAFF SUPPORT RESOURCES

To support a geographically dispersed work team, VRS utilizes ANGEL, Penn State's web-based course management system. In ANGEL, a private virtual team space was reserved and labeled Penn State Virtual Reference Librarians. The team space in ANGEL includes an array of features that support collaboration and personal interaction among members. Staffing schedules and message boards for coverage exchange, problem reports, and assignment alerts are posted there. Members can also share documents, files, web pages, internal messages, and email. ANGEL is web-based, but only those librarians enrolled in the VRS team can login. Recently, a new message board called Tech Talk was added for those who would like to discuss questions and share insights about the technical side of VRS. In addition to ANGEL, a "VRS Toolbox" web page provides links to training manuals and a transcript archive that is updated daily. The transcripts that appear in the Toolbox archive have been extracted manually from the LSSI archive and reformatted to remove personal identities. Copies of follow-up emails are also appended to related transcripts in this local archive.

VRS LIBRARIAN FEEDBACK

To learn more about the views and experiences of Penn State VRS Librarians, the authors asked them to compare their VRS experience to traditional reference service and to describe the rewards and challenges of VRS after four to nine months of practical experience. In addition, they were asked about motivation, workload, training, and recruitment.

The comments of the Penn State VRS librarians echo those reported in other informal surveys by Janes, Hill, and Boyer.[10]

Professional Reference Experience and Motivation

The length of time a librarian has been in the profession was not a factor in who chose to join the VRS team. Three of the present VRS librarians have 1 to 3 years of professional reference experience, three have 7 to 10 years experience, and five have more than 10 years experience. Despite these differences, all of them volunteered with a similar high level of enthusiasm. They expressed a variety of motivating factors ranging from a general love for reference work to interest in reaching remote students who might not have been helped through traditional means. A common motivating factor was the librarian's interest in working with cutting-edge technologies. Other factors included an opportunity to collaborate with other librarians across Penn State campuses, staying relevant to students and faculty, and offering point-of-need assistance to students who work predominantly online.

VRS Staffing and Workload

At least five librarians alternate VRS coverage between campus locations and home. When asked to identify all service locations that apply, eight librarians reported coverage from their offices, six from their homes, and three from a public service desk. The use of public service desks for VRS coverage is not ideal, and it occurs because of insufficient local staffing. In reply to a question about how VRS has added to their overall workload, eight librarians reported no reduction in other responsibilities, and three reported a partial reduction. Willingness to take on additional responsibilities with partial or no reduction in overall workload is more evidence of the level of interest in and commitment to this service. However, working with no reduction in other responsibilities is not an optimal staffing model for VRS. One librarian recommended payment of extra compensation or compensatory time whenever VRS is an overload. Workload will be a major issue in our efforts to maintain and expand VRS staffing.

VRS vs. Traditional Reference Service

When asked to compare the way they answer reference questions in VRS and in traditional reference settings, the VRS librarians' replies were mixed. Some librarians indicated that their practice was the same; just the mode of communication was different. Others felt pressure to speed up the transaction in VRS or experienced anxiety because of the potential for technological glitches. Five of the librarians stated that they offer less in-depth reference interviews during VRS than face-to-face; three stated that the interviews were the same. Three other librarians stated that they actually perform more in-depth interviews during VRS because more probing is needed to substitute for lack of physical cues. Most of the librarians reported that they offer instruction and use databases and other online resources to answer questions as often in VRS as face-to-face. Finally, one-third of the librarians reported making more referrals and follow-ups in VRS sessions than in local face-to face reference. In Fall 2002, 16% of the VRS sessions were followed-up by personal email messages containing additional information. Generally, referrals and follow-ups were necessary when a librarian encountered complex questions outside of his or her subject specialty or questions related to the policies of non-library departments. The diversity of the university-wide population served by VRS presents more opportunities to encounter such questions.

VRS Training and Staff Development

Pilot service librarians received one day of training from vendor trainers, and librarians new to the service in Fall 2002 received one day of formal training from a veteran VRS librarian. As follow-up, they all worked independently to refine their skills through self-study of system manuals and practice sessions with colleagues and friends. When asked about training, the majority of the VRS librarians felt that mastering the service software was the most important factor in building their virtual reference skills. Others ranked cross training in subject and other information sources as most important. Keyboard skills were also noted as a significant factor in achieving a level of comfort with chat communication.

In open comments, a minimum schedule of three hours per week was recommended in order to maintain VRS skills. Continuing staff development was also highlighted. To improve service quality, one or two virtual team meetings (by electronic or telephone conferencing) per semester were requested. These meetings were seen as an opportunity for VRS librarians to share war stories, review interesting questions, and discuss answering strategies.

VRS Rewards, Challenges, Wish Lists

By far, the most common reward articulated by VRS librarians was the students' excitement and appreciation of help they got online. Reaching patrons who might not be reached through traditional services, involvement with innovations, and working with students and colleagues across the Penn State system were all perceived as significant rewards. Technical difficulties challenged everyone. Coping with system malfunctions and conducting a reference interview with technology that is "not quite there," were the most often cited challenges. Those who worked in particularly understaffed locations cited staffing the reference desk and VRS at the same time as a major challenge.

Technological enhancements topped the list of improvements recommended by VRS librarians. They would like to see more server stability, wider browser and operating system compatibility, ADA accessibility, and voice recognition. They also recommended better organization of the Libraries' web resources to make navigation and information retrieval more efficient, more VRS access points on library web pages and in online course environments like ANGEL, and more marketing throughout the University.

VRS Recruitment

When asked if they planned to continue with VRS next year, one VRS librarian expressed a definite no, and one was undecided due to the increased workload. The remaining librarians planned to continue for another year. A number of suggestions were offered for recruiting new VRS librarians. It was strongly felt that virtual service should remain voluntary. In general, the present staff felt that the factors that first motivated them to volunteer would also motivate others. They recommended a recruitment campaign that emphasizes how VRS can bridge the gap between the library and users who cannot be reached by traditional services, how rewarding it is to get positive feedback from users, how VRS is the wave of the future, and how VRS fosters collaboration across the University. Finally, it was suggested that we emphasize how much fun it is (when it works).

VRS FUTURE DEVELOPMENTS

The Penn State Virtual Reference Service is envisioned as an integral component of the University Libraries' suite of on-site and remote user services provided through the LIAS network to all Penn State locations. A VRS Task Force, charged to coordinate its future development and integration, is working to refine service policies and training procedures, develop a University-wide marketing campaign, and design evaluation tools to assess program effectiveness, user satisfaction, and user needs. In addition, Task Force members are planning the integration of VRS follow-up with the web-based ASK! email service as one step toward developing and managing a shared reference knowledge base.

VRS at Penn State faces the same challenges as multi-institutional consortia with staff and user populations who are highly diverse and geographically dispersed. However, the University and the University Libraries have a long history of meeting such challenges. Telephone and video conferencing, as well as the ANGEL course management software, are available system-wide to support VRS team communication. The comprehensive and integrated LIAS network serves as a system-wide platform for the full range of Penn State library services. Remote access to LIAS resources and services through the World Wide Web and proxy server authentication opens wide the range of reference service that can be offered virtually.

With the recent placement of the ASK! button on the top levels of the Libraries' web site, reference services have taken a prominent place in the LIAS network. ASK! offers users choices: real-time chat, email, telephone, or reference desk assistance. Users can also choose to contact specific librarians by location or subject specialty, to request technical assistance, or to simply submit a comment or suggestion. VRS, with real-time chat and browser sharing, is an exciting and collaborative new service that enriches the goal of the University Libraries to offer comprehensive, user-centered reference services throughout the Penn State system.

NOTES

1. Penn State's statewide campus/college system is comprised of the twelve-campus Commonwealth College (Beaver, Delaware County, DuBois, Fayette. Hazleton, McKeesport, Mont Alto, New Kensington, Shenango, Wilkes-Barre, Worthington Scranton, and York), Abington College, Altoona College, Berks-Lehigh Valley College, Behrend College, Capital College, and Great Valley School of Graduate Professional Studies (http://www.psu.edu/ur/cmpcoll.html).

2. The libraries at three Penn State affiliated institutions: Milton S. Hershey College of Medicine, Dickinson School of Law, and the Pennsylvania College of Technology did not post a link to the Virtual Reference Service. The Pennsylvania College of

Technology library independently offers real-time service through Docutek Virtual Reference Librarian software.

3. See ASK! home page at: http://apps.libraries.psu.edu/questions/comments.cfm.

4. The Penn State pioneers in Virtual Reference Service were: Joseph Fennewald (Hazleton Campus), Janet Hughes (Life Sciences Library, University Park), Lesley Moyo (Gateway Library, University Park), Shannon Richie (Hazleton Campus), Susan Ware (Delaware County Campus), Sara Whildin (Delaware County Campus), Gary White (Business Library, University Park), and Carol Wright (Education and Behavioral Sciences Library, University Park).

5. See About VRS at: http://www.de2.psu.edu/faculty/saw4/vrs/about.html.

6. The products reviewed included: LSSI, Metropolitan Cooperative Library System (MCLS) 24/7 Project, Webline, LivePerson, FaceTime, Hipbone, iServe, eShare, Instant Service, Quintus Web Center, and AOL Instant Messenger.

7. Additional VRS pilot and full service data are available at: http://www.de2.psu.edu/faculty/saw4/vrs/data.

8. The Penn State Virtual Reference Service began university-wide service staffed by: Paula Contreras (Paterno Library, University Park), Joseph Fennewald (Hazleton Campus), Russell Hall (New Kensington Campus), Janet Hughes (Life Sciences Library, University Park), Ellen Kempf (Paterno Library, University Park), Deborah Lovett (Hershey Medical Center and College of Medicine), Tierney Lyons (Wilkes-Barre Campus), Lesley Moyo (Gateway Library, University Park), Shannon Richie (Hazleton Campus), Susan Ware (Delaware County Campus), Sara Whildin (Delaware County Campus).

9. Linda Klimczyk, University Libraries Department for Information Technologies, performs regular tests of the compatibility of the Libraries' web pages with assistive technologies. Her findings from tests of VRS are available at http://www.personal.psu.edu/staff/l/g/lgk1/accessidentity_files/frame.htm.

10. Joseph Janes and Chrystie Hill. "Finger on the Pulse," *Reference and User Services Quarterly* 42, no.1 (2002): 54-65; Joshua Boyer. "Virtual Reference at North Carolina State University: The First Hundred Days," *Information Technology and Libraries* 20, no. 3 (2002): 122-128.

REFERENCE

McClure, Charles R., R. David Lankes, Melissa Gross, and Beverly Choltco-Devlin. *Statistics, Measures, and Quality Standards for Assessing Digital Reference Library Services*. Syracuse, NY; Tallahassee, FL: Information Institute of Syracuse, School of Information Studies, Syracuse University; School of Information Studies, Information Use Management and Policy Institute, Florida State University, 2002.

Chat Reference:
One University's Experience

Kathy A. Campbell
Marie F. Jones
Jerry Shuttle

SUMMARY. Chat reference is becoming prevalent in academic libraries across the country. This paper details the experience of East Tennessee State University's Sherrod Library when initiating such a service at their institution during the 2001-2002 academic year, which began as a response to the addition of a new online degree program in the state. Software selection, staff training, management issues, and statistical data are presented. Data analyzed includes use patterns, types of questions, and categories of users. The paper details librarians' reactions to providing reference services in this format, including the problems encountered. It also offers suggestions for a more successful implementation. *[Article copies available for a fee from The Haworth Document Delivery Service: 1-800-HAWORTH. E-mail address: <docdelivery@haworthpress.com> Website: <http://www.HaworthPress.com> © 2002/2003 by The Haworth Press, Inc. All rights reserved.]*

KEYWORDS. Digital reference, real-time reference, chat reference, reference statistics, case studies

Kathy A. Campbell (E-mail: campbeka@mail.etsu.edu) is Reference Librarian, Marie F. Jones (E-mail: jonesmf@mail.etsu.edu) is Extended Campus Services Librarian, and Jerry Shuttle (E-mail: shuttle@mail.etsu.edu) is Reference/Instruction Librarian, all at East Tennessee State University, Box 70665, Johnson City, TN 37614.

[Haworth co-indexing entry note]: "Chat Reference: One University's Experience." Campbell, Kathy A., Marie F. Jones, and Jerry Shuttle. Co-published simultaneously in *The Reference Librarian* (The Haworth Information Press, an imprint of The Haworth Press, Inc.) No. 79/80, 2002/2003, pp. 297-309; and: *Digital Reference Services* (ed: Bill Katz) The Haworth Information Press, an imprint of The Haworth Press, Inc., 2002/2003, pp. 297-309. Single or multiple copies of this article are available for a fee from The Haworth Document Delivery Service [1-800-HAWORTH, 9:00 a.m. - 5:00 p.m. (EST). E-mail address: docdelivery@haworthpress.com].

10.1300/J120v38n79_20

BACKGROUND AND HISTORY

East Tennessee State University's (ETSU) journey into chat reference began as a response to a new online degree program in the state of Tennessee. The Regents Online Degree Program (RODP) accepted its first students in the Fall of 2001. Students who take RODP courses select a "home school" from among the Tennessee Board of Regents' (TBR) 27 technology centers, 13 two-year community colleges, and 6 universities. All courses are taught in an asynchronous online format, using WebCT. Courses are developed by faculty at individual institutions within the system but may be taught by faculty at other institutions. Support services for RODP students are distributed among the cooperating institutions.

This kind of distributed and cooperative system poses unique challenges to library services, as no central library with staff or collection has been established as part of the system. The Tennessee Virtual Library provides access to state-wide databases available through the Tennessee Electronic Library and has e-mail reference services staffed by a librarian at one of the member institutions. Although the Virtual Library Reference Services Task Force recommended that chat services be implemented, funding and coordination of services among member libraries postponed the unified delivery of such services for the near future.

Over 2,000 of ETSU's 11,300 total students take courses via Internet, interactive television, or "live" at off-campus sites. With the addition of RODP, it became clear that we needed additional means of providing real-time reference services to all of these students. We also recognized that on-campus students would benefit from the addition of chat reference. The library faculty decided, during the planning stage, that chat services should be available to both on and off-campus students. Since younger students routinely use chat services to communicate with friends, it seemed a good idea to reach out to them in a venue that had become familiar to them, if not to us.

CHOOSING A SERVICE

ETSU's Extended Campus Services Librarian served on the Virtual Library Reference Services Task Force for RODP, and as part of that committee, identified and evaluated six of the live reference packages available at that time: Groopz (www.groopz.com), Liveperson (www.

liveperson.com), LiveAssistance (www.liveassistance.com), Livehelper (www.livehelper.com), LSSI (www.lssi.com) and 24/7 Reference (www. 247ref.org). All packages that required end-user downloads were discarded without evaluation. Each package was examined for the following criteria: set-up cost, monthly per seat cost, customizable interface, text chat, voice chat, view site traffic in real-time, transfer calls, keep notes on users, push pages, canned messages, usage statistics, customizable event sounds, support, send transcript, server down time, co-browsing, designed for libraries, ease of use, up-front information form, log file size, server, training, and other comments and drawbacks. After evaluation of these features, ETSU chose LiveAssistance as its software provider, since it fit all of the criteria that we were looking for except co-browsing. While we would have preferred a co-browsing package, cost limitations made that choice impractical.

TRAINING

We purchased a subscription to LiveAssistance in Fall 2001. During the trial period, the Extended Campus Services Librarian conducted a training session with the reference staff. The Extended Campus Services (ECS) Librarian conducted a hands-on training session for the reference staff that included handouts with screen shots and detailed directions. After the training, the project was piloted by placing a single button on the Extended Campus Services Librarian's personal web pages. Faculty members were encouraged to practice using the service, but few actually did (see Problems, below). Also, because we waited to post an entirely revamped library website before making links to the service available, a considerable delay occurred between the training and actual implementation of the service. Since the creation of the new website took more time than originally anticipated, there was a five month time-lag between training and implementation. Add to the time delay the fact that the ECS Librarian, who had acted as lead implementer and trainer on the project, was working at a distant branch library, covering for a staff turnover when the new web pages appeared and chat reference questions started rolling in. One librarian described the experience:

Our Live Assistance chat reference service went live during Spring Semester 2002. The librarians at the reference desk anxiously awaited the first reference question, hoping the honor would fall on somebody else. Even though Marie [our Extended Campus Librarian] had trained us on using Live Assistance, it had been several months since we had been shown how to use the chat service. Some of us spent time the first morning that it was up and running taking a "refresher course" offered by our very competent graduate assistant. It had been decided that our service would be open to anyone with an Internet connection, and one of our first questions, "What kind of noise did the hadrosaurus make?" was from an elementary school student writing from the West Orange Public Library, West Orange, New Jersey. After the question was successfully answered, we all felt more confident in our ability to handle chat reference.

DAY-TO-DAY OPERATION OF ETSU's LIVE ASSISTANCE

Planning for Staffing

The faculty that provides reference service met early in Fall 2001 to discuss the implications of implementing the Live Reference service. In order to avoid increasing staffing levels, we decided to run our chat service, which we ultimately named "Ask A Librarian," from the reference desk during regular desk hours.

As a result of our discussions, it was decided that the reference desk would be the logical place to set up our chat reference service for two reasons. First, the desk is staffed for most of the time the library is open. Librarians staff the desk from 10 a.m. until 7 p.m.; graduate students work from 8 a.m. until 10 a.m. and from 7 p.m. until 10 p.m.; there is no staffing from 10 p.m. until the Sherrod Library closes at 11 p.m. Not only would the service be available for most of the time the library is open, but it would be operated by the people most able to handle any type of question. Second, the close proximity of the print reference collection was deemed essential to answering those questions which could not be resolved using online sources.

Sherrod Library's Reference Department is located to the right directly inside the main entrance of the library. The desk is designed so that four reference librarians could work at the desk at one time; however, we only staff with one person at a time. The librarian at the reference desk is responsible for answering questions by telephone, by e-mail, and from patrons using the reference room. Other responsibilities include checking computers and straightening the reference room.

While the librarians agreed that chat reference was a natural outgrowth of reference and a service which we should offer, many were worried about whether it would put a strain on the reference librarian, especially if it proved to be a popular service. How could we give good service to people in the library while conducting a reference chat? What about the person at the other end of the chat? Could chat take the place of the reference interview–that give-and-take session between librarian and patron that involves body language and what is not said, as well as what is actually being said?

Other Decisions

We had other decisions to make before our chat service could be unveiled to the public. For starters, the service would need a name. After discussing the relative merits of different names, the faculty settled on Ask a Librarian. We also had to decide whether to limit access to ETSU students, faculty, and staff or to leave it open to all. To make it consistent with our other reference services, we decided to leave access open to all users with the provision that our policy could change if demand became excessive.

How It Works: The Student Side

Live Assistance is an easy program to use. Students enter a chat session by clicking on a button labeled "Ask a Librarian" on the Sherrod Library home page. This will open a page titled, "For help with your research, chat with a librarian" (see Figure 1). This page has a clean, uncluttered appearance, which facilitates ease of use. The patron provides basic information, including name, e-mail address, status (ETSU student, faculty, staff, Regent's Online Degree Program or non-ETSU), and location. After typing a question, the patron enters the chat session by clicking on the button labeled "Enter Chat." The sidebar on the left contains a brief statement on the type of help which the student can expect to receive. A window then opens in the upper left hand side of the screen, which the student uses to continue the chat session (see Figure 2).

How It Works: The Librarian Side

A low, pleasant, male voice, or as one librarian dubbed it "Euromale," informs us of a question with the statement, "Incoming chat request."

FIGURE 1

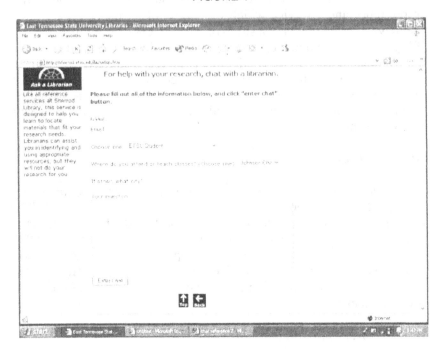

This voice is not distracting to people near the desk and works very well if the librarian is not busy, but it is hard to hear if an individual is away from the desk or working with a patron. Once the librarian enters the chat, a screen on the right side gives the person's name, e-mail address, and question. On the left side, there is a box for the librarian's replies and a larger box that can be used to follow the transaction (see Figure 3).

Ask a Librarian has required librarians to conduct the reference interview in a different manner. Interpretation of the patron's question can be challenging. Sometimes the librarian needs to type several questions in order to understand what the patron is really asking. Impatience on the part of both the student and librarian can also lead to misunderstandings. Some patrons expect instant replies, and there have been instances where the patron has dropped transmission while the librarian was in the process of answering their question. In that case, it is possible to use the address from the screen to e-mail information. On the flip side, there are times when the librarian is left waiting for a response. Did the person decide to do laundry, make a cup of coffee, or go to the store? Some-

FIGURE 2

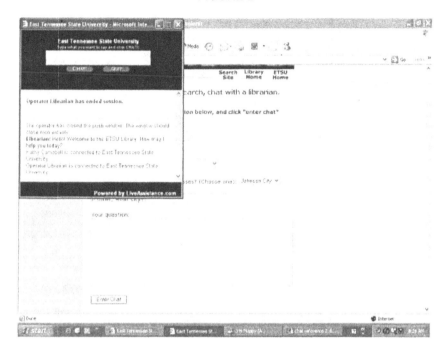

times the librarian has no choice but to discontinue the chat if the wait is too long.

MARKETING ASK A LIBRARIAN

The Sherrod Library has not marketed Live Assistance broadly because faculty and graduate students who work the reference desk are still in the process of becoming comfortable with live chat. Despite this, the service is marketed in several ways. Each web page on the Sherrod Library site has a toolbar that includes a button labeled "Ask a Librarian." Librarians who teach library instruction mention the service in their classes. However, since these classes are arranged at the discretion of the professor, we reach only a limited number of students this way. Since off-campus and RODP students were the groups we felt would benefit the most from a chat service, our Extended Campus Librarian has done the lion's share of publicity for Ask A Librarian, including dis-

FIGURE 3

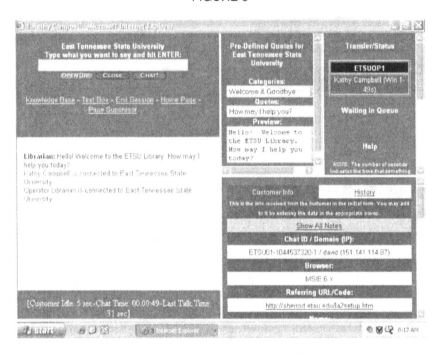

tributing handouts at all off-campus sites, sending mailings to extended campus faculty, and writing articles in site newsletters.

ANALYSIS OF SERVICES

Chat Narrative

When the chat reference service began, librarians had no information as to who would use it, when the highest demand would be, or what types of questions would be asked. We thought many of the questions might come from people who were not associated with the university and that the highest use of the service would probably come during the evening hours after classes were finished. We also wondered if the majority might be academically related reference requests or would many of the questions pertain to mundane items such as hours or how to print a file? Several of those who work the reference desk were also concerned there would be a problem with a chat call interrupting service to people already at the reference desk or on the phone. An analysis of the data indicated that most of our early assumptions about the service were erroneous and that there might indeed be a problem responding to chat requests when other types of requests were being addressed.

Though the service went online in late January 2002, it was not fully operational until February. Chat request data was examined for the months of February through the end of the fall semester in December of the same year. A total of 656 attempts to access the service were made, but only 300 were answered (see Table 1). Of the 356 failed attempts, 92 made connection, but were simply not answered by the reference librarian. This indicates a problem exists with reference staff not being able to respond to chat requests due to other demands in the library. Another 115 attempts were disconnected before any communication was initiated. This was due either to the patron discontinuing the attempt or the software failing to maintain the connection. We have no way of knowing which, though it seems obvious that some of both occurred. During 149 attempts, no operator was online, meaning that the Live Assistance software was not operational. A closer analysis indicated that in 75 instances, the library was closed and the service was not available. In the other 74 instances, the library was open. The software tended to crash and disconnect the service. Many times the reference worker would not notice the software had crashed, so there were periods when the service was not available.

The types of chat requests indicated the service was used most often for questions related to academic endeavor (see Table 2). Of the 300 completed requests, 155 were for help in locating information on a specific topic or for a specific item. General library information such as hours or where in the library to locate an item accounted for 45 requests.

TABLE 1. Chat Requests by Month

	Feb	Mar	Apr	May	Jun	Jul	Aug	Sept	Oct	Nov	Dec	Total
Calls Answered	37	32	34	4	19	15	17	36	58	39	9	300
Not Answered	12	8	8	0	1	5	2	24	19	12	1	92
Caller Disconnect	18	8	10	3	9	6	3	21	22	14	1	115
No Operator	13	19	19	7	4	8	12	21	22	21	3	149
Totals	80	67	71	14	33	34	34	102	121	86	14	656

Statistics reported 32 questions concerning how to access databases from off campus or to report that access was denied, while 30 questions were asked on how to navigate the library's website. Connection was lost during 11 requests. There were 10 requests to renew library materials, 10 that were classified as other, and 7 genealogy requests. We conclude the service is being used for the purposes we hoped.

Our speculation that the service might be highly used by patrons outside the university community was not borne out (see Table 3). ETSU students accounted for 234 requests, faculty and staff made 40 requests, and only 26 came from community patrons. Of course, some of the callers who said they were students probably were not, but an analysis of the questions made it clear that most requests seemed related to academic work. We also found that most of the requests came from the immediate geographic area: 239 were from Johnson City, where our main campus is located, 26 more were from the immediate region, and only 35 were from outside the region.

Times of the requests were indeed surprising. Our thought that the

TABLE 2. Chat Requests by Type

Specific topic or item request	155
General library information	45
Access questions	32
Help navigating website	30
Connection lost	11
Renew materials request	10
Other	10
Geneaology	7
Total	300

TABLE 3. Chat Requests by Patron Type

ETSU Students	234
ETSU Faculty	32
ETSU Staff	8
Non ETSU	26
Total	300

evening hours would be heavily used was wrong (see Table 4). The majority of chats occurred from noon until 6:00 p.m., which is also the period of highest use for our reference room.

Librarians' Opinions About Chat Reference

Conversations with those who work the reference desk and have engaged in chat reference yielded several areas of concern and shared opinion. Most were not happy with the software we chose. They viewed it as slow and clunky and prone to crash. There was also dissatisfaction with the inability to have a real interactive session with callers. The system allows us to push a webpage to a caller, but the caller cannot see a search being done by a librarian, nor can the librarian see a search done by the caller. Several thought that the time it takes to communicate even simple information is too long and that a short phone call would be better than chat sessions that can run several minutes. A consensus evolved that the "Ask a Librarian" opening screen should also have options for calling via an 800 number and for e-mailing requests. This would allow users to communicate with our reference service in the way they feel most comfortable.

Everyone who used the chat service complained about the effectiveness of conducting a chat session while simultaneously serving patrons at the reference desk or while taking phone requests. This complaint seems justified given the high number of incoming chat requests that went unanswered. Our library can only afford one person at the reference desk, so the obvious solution of more staffing is not feasible. We discussed having the service staffed by one person all the time, or by ev-

TABLE 4. Chat Requests by Time

8:00 a.m.-10:00 a.m.	36
10:00 a.m.-12:00 p.m.	44
12:00 p.m.-2:00 p.m.	55
2:00 p.m.-4:00 p.m.	60
4:00 p.m.-6:00 p.m.	40
6:00 p.m.-8:00 p.m.	33
8:00 p.m.-10:00 p.m.	32
Total	300

eryone taking a scheduled time throughout the day, but agreed that neither of these solutions was feasible, either.

The general opinion seemed to be that chat reference was disliked, but that it must be offered because "everyone else is doing it." Most felt users were not being served as comprehensively as they could be in person or by phone and laid the responsibility on the chat software and the slow rate of data exchange. Suggestions for improvement included better software, adding a "Please wait" message to the initial greeting page, and offering an 800 number. Given the large number of requests that went unanswered during our initial year, it was felt that if the number of chat requests increases, we should develop alternative means of meeting the demand.

RECOMMENDATIONS

Our experience with instituting a chat reference service has not been a particularly positive one, and if we had it to do all over again, and we had all the money and staff in the world, we would do it very differently. As we reviewed the history of implementation, analyzed our chat transcripts and statistics, and talked to our colleagues in the reference department, we learned a number of things that might help others in their own implementation of such a service:

Some people will resist: Although we talked about implementing our chat service with the reference librarians before bringing it up and they seemed amenable to the idea, many felt from the outset that we were doing it because "everyone else is." They didn't–and still don't–see a real need for services to be delivered in this medium. Without that kind of acceptance, librarians will resent the additional work that chat reference entails.

Training must be timely: Librarians know this from library instruction. If you don't train at the time of need, you might as well be talking to an empty room. Even knowing that we were going to have to answer questions on the desk wasn't enough motivation for us to practice using the system between training and implementation times. Ongoing training and support at the actual implementation time is also important, so that no one feels stranded and panicked at the moment when they receive their first reference question.

Start with a real pilot project: While we tried to practice with the LiveAssistance software during the months between training and implementation, we didn't really plan and coordinate a true pilot project.

Doing so would have answered many of our questions and brought to light many problems that we might have been able to address earlier. It also might have helped us to be more comfortable adapting our face-to-face reference interview skills to this new medium.

Software problems: This technology is relatively new, so the software has a way to go to work efficiently. Some of our staff find the software we chose to be awkward. Those who chose the software will attest to the fact that much more awkward packages were eliminated in our initial evaluation. We have problems with network congestion causing the program to log off, which has lost some calls for us. We also recently moved to Windows XP, which has caused additional difficulties because of the way that minimized windows stack up in the taskbar. We also think the co-browsing feature, which only came with products we cannot afford, would make the chat reference interview more like a face-to-face session.

Don't try to do four things at once: If we could find another way to do it, we would choose to separate chat reference from the main desk. At busy moments, it becomes impossible to give everyone attention at once.

CONCLUSION

Our experience with chat reference has been a mixed bag. Some of us still feel very committed to the idea that we need to reach students online, while they're doing their research at home, and that chat is an everyday medium for some students who might not be willing to pick up the phone to ask a question. Yet, we feel that trying to answer questions from four directions at once is impossible to do well. If we had implemented it differently, perhaps attitudes would generally be more positive. As the reference staff gains more experience with the service and the technology improves, we hope that chat reference will become a more viable method of serving the information needs of our users.

Going It Alone:
Can a Small/Medium-Sized Library
Manage Live Online Reference?

Joyce Ward
Dana Mervar
Matthew Loving
Steve Kronen

SUMMARY. The Winter Park Public Library began Chat Live/Ask a Librarian (Chat Live), a live online reference service, on February 1, 2002. We first chose *LiveAssistance* as our library's service provider but later switched to *QuestionPoint*, sponsored by OCLC. This paper outlines our experiences with both chat services and includes the following:

Joyce Ward (E-mail: jward@wppl.org) is Head of Reference, Dana Mervar (E-mail: dmervar@wppl.org) is Reference Librarian, Matthew Loving (E-mail: mloving@wppl.org) is Reference Librarian, and Steve Kronen (E-mail: skronen@wppl.org) is Reference Librarian, all at Winter Park Public Library, 460 East New England Avenue, Winter Park, FL 32789.

[Haworth co-indexing entry note]: "Going It Alone: Can a Small/Medium-Sized Library Manage Live Online Reference?" Ward, Joyce et al. Co-published simultaneously in *The Reference Librarian* (The Haworth Information Press, an imprint of The Haworth Press, Inc.) No. 79/80, 2002/2003, pp. 311-322; and: *Digital Reference Services* (ed: Bill Katz) The Haworth Information Press, an imprint of The Haworth Press, Inc., 2002/2003, pp. 311-322. Single or multiple copies of this article are available for a fee from The Haworth Document Delivery Service [1-800-HAWORTH, 9:00 a.m. - 5:00 p.m. (EST). E-mail address: docdelivery@haworthpress.com].

http://www.haworthpress.com/store/product.asp?sku=J120
© 2002/2003 by The Haworth Press, Inc. All rights reserved.
10.1300/J120v38n79_21

our reasoning behind initiating a chat reference service; the selection process; how we trained and implemented the service into our daily routine; marketing the service to patrons; our day-to-day experiences (including a chat session transcript); the importance of script writing; some brief statistics on usage; and our overall thoughts on the process. *[Article copies available for a fee from The Haworth Document Delivery Service: 1-800-HAWORTH. E-mail address: <docdelivery@haworthpress.com> Website: <http://www.HaworthPress.com> © 2002/2003 by The Haworth Press, Inc. All rights reserved.]*

KEYWORDS. Interactive chat service, *LiveAssistance*, live online reference, QuestionPoint/Ask a Librarian

INTRODUCTION

Winter Park Public Library is a small to medium-sized city library serving a population of 27,000 people. Located in Orange County, Florida, on the outskirts of Orlando, the Library has no branches and is not affiliated with the larger, county library system. Despite its size, it is a well-used community resource and is currently first in the state in per capita reference questions answered. After several months of needs assessment, the Director and Library Board approved a five-year, long-range plan on September 17, 2001. One of the plan's objectives was the implementation of an interactive chat service with the overall goal of providing timely, accurate, and useful information electronically. The plan's specific needs assessments included:

1. Taking advantage of the community's high number of internet-active residents by delivering information directly to their desktops.
2. Responding to local history questions and promoting use of recently digitized photos, narratives, and other historical documents from the Library's Winter Park Historical Archives.
3. Creating an online reference chat on Monday evenings with the Young Adult Librarian.
4. Linking City departments with the library reference staff to facilitate The City of Winter Park's popular tourist industry.

With these goals in mind and a budget large enough to contract with a premium provider, the reference staff began to research available options for acquiring an online chat service in September of 2001.

FINDING A SERVICE PROVIDER

While the reference staff's more recent library school graduates were familiar with public and academic online chat services, others were excited but inexperienced. Staff began reading the literature and searching the Web. Two Internet sites proved useful in our initial decision-making. Duke University's "Live On Line Reference" (http://www.lib.duke. edu/reference/liveonlineref.htm) helped us understand chat terminology and outlined the various software providers according to the advantages and disadvantages of their services. It also provided information about several virtual reference software vendors including features of their services, installation requirements, ease of use, and cost. The other site, "Registry of Real-Time Digital Reference Services" (http://www. public.iastate.edu/~CYBERSTACKS/LiveRef.htm), gave hyperlinks to libraries presently offering online chat.

In addition to our research, we attended the Virtual Reference Desk (VRD) conference November 14, 2001 at the Orlando Rosen Plaza Hotel. This annual conference offers workshops on various aspects of digital reference technology. We attended a presentation entitled "Building a Real-Time Reference Service" that focused on fulfilling the information needs of remote users. After our initial preparation and basic exposure to the technology, we felt prepared to weigh our options.

CHOOSING A SOFTWARE

It was now time to examine chat software vendors first-hand. We evaluated three: *24/7 Reference*, *LiveAssistance*, and *LiveHelper* (the free version). We quickly discovered that trial periods were the best way to evaluate the various service providers. They allowed staff hands-on experience that reviews of the literature could not convey. We began to narrow down the important elements that would affect the Library's decision. The ease of operation for librarians was first and foremost on our minds. The second most important point was the ease of installation. We also agreed with Edana Cichanowicz's idea that the service one chooses should require "no special equipment, plug-ins, software, or downloads on the part of the patron" (Cichanowicz 2001, 50).

After experimenting with co-browsing, call transfer, and other bells and whistles, we realized not every feature would be necessary. However, we determined that capabilities beyond a basic chat service were needed. Pushing pages to the patron's computer screen or sending an active link seemed essential in delivering electronic sources to remote users. These features would also help librarians avoid errors in transcribing URLs. Not knowing how our patrons would react to the new technology or whether they would even utilize the new service, we began with a modest service.

LiveAssistance

In December of 2001, we selected *LiveAssistance* for a number of reasons:

1. The software is simple to use and resides on the *LiveAssistance* server. The operator screen can be accessed from any single computer by inputting username and password. No operator plug-ins are required.
2. There are no plug-ins for library patrons to download. The patron simply clicks on the Chat Live logo and fills out a brief form to begin chatting with a librarian.
3. The operator interface is easy to manipulate and can be learned quickly.
4. It features a clear audio alert, "Incoming Chat Request," freeing the librarian from the chat desk until necessary.
5. *LiveAssistance* allows for pushing pages, sending canned scripts, and providing voluntary evaluation forms and transcripts of the session. Various statistical reports concerning chat activity are also available.
6. The cost was reasonable. The initial setup was $500 plus $150 per month for one operator. We opted for a single operator until more could be justified. The Library signed up with *LiveAssistance* in January of 2002 for six months. The company designed an easy to use patron chat form that would pop up when patrons clicked a hyperlink located on the Library's Web site.
7. We received a URL from *LiveAssistance* that provided a link to their server. It could be embedded in the HTML code on the Library's Web page. The link had the capability of being either text or a button. A button seemed like the best choice.

WHAT TO CALL IT?

A great deal of discussion was generated as we narrowed down our choices for a name. We finally decided on the following two names:

"Chat Live" and "Ask a Librarian." The problem with using just "Chat Live" was that it did not imply a reference interview. The problem with using just "Ask a Librarian" was that it sounded too much like an email service and did not suggest the live chat aspect. In addition, the Library Director requested that the Winter Park Public Library logo and name be located on the button in the hopes it would eventually be placed on other community Web sites. We opted to combine the two to form the term "Chat Live/Ask a Librarian," confident it reflected what the service had to offer. Our digital imaging technician designed the button and placed it on an in-house Web page.

WRITING SCRIPTS

We next prepared canned scripts that would shorten patron wait times, cut down on typing errors, and safeguard against lapsing into informal lingo. In developing the first few scripts, we considered common scenarios then created pre-typed messages to address them. We revised these and created others as we became more familiar with chat and what our needs might be. We will give sample scripts and examples of their use later in our discussion of *QuestionPoint*.

PRACTICE, PRACTICE, AND MORE PRACTICE

Even for the most seasoned reference librarian, the first time using a live chat service is–well, scary. We placed the chat terminal in the workroom away from patron traffic then fed each other practice questions from within the Reference Department. We felt that chat users would probably be contacting the service because they were unable to locate information they needed on the Internet. Under these circumstances, quick online resources seemed appropriate. Even so, knowing Google would not answer every query, we added an almanac, a dictionary, and a general encyclopedia to ready reference. When we felt comfortable, we fielded questions from the other library departments. In February of 2002 the Library was ready to place the chat button on the home page and open the service to the public.

MARKETING

How do you market this service? As we were launching Chat Live, the Library was also involved in an extensive and time-consuming self-checkout project. Faced with implementing two new services, we began secretly hoping against a rapid Chat Live success. We were not disappointed and were soon questioning our marketing tactics.

To introduce the new chat service, the Community Relations Director issued a press release. The Reference staff made announcements on the Library home page and hung posters throughout the Library. A Board member made lapel buttons to advertise the new service and the Head of Youth Services Department sent brochures to the local schools. The results were underwhelming. Still, as time went along, patrons slowly began to try Chat Live and were pleased with the service.

A NEW SERVICE

Winter Park Public Library has been a member of the Collaborative Digital Reference Service (CDRS), with OCLC and the Library of Congress since March of 2001. In March of 2002 CDRS was adding a new online reference service, *QuestionPoint*. Being a small to medium-sized library, we decided this change would provide a good collaborative opportunity that could help to expand our chat service. Another benefit was that *QuestionPoint* allowed for more than one operator at no additional cost and included the ability to refer questions to a global reference network. So at the end of our six-month contract with *LiveAssistance*, we switched to *QuestionPoint*. In choosing a new service provider we did not change our marketing, daily procedures or policies. From a patron's point of view, the only noticeable difference was the initial login and chat interface. From a staff perspective, a lot of time and energy went into adapting the new electronic chat forms, creating new canned scripts and training. We wanted the change to be as seamless as possible for patrons. Like *LiveAssistance*, *QuestionPoint* is easy to use for both librarians and patrons.

DAY-TO-DAY

The following day-to-day descriptions apply to our *QuestionPoint* service:

Chat Live is available from 10 a.m.-12 p.m. and 2 p.m.-4 p.m., Monday-Thursday. Librarians are assigned to monitor sessions by the hour, typically not more than one hour per day. We do not have enough staff to oversee the service on Fridays, nights, or weekends. However, Monday nights from 6:30 p.m.-8:30 p.m. were recently added so that school-aged children could take advantage of the service. The Young Adult Librarian is responsible for these supplementary hours and another reference librarian is always logged on if extra assistance is needed.

With *QuestionPoint*, librarians can open the operator screen on computers throughout the Library simultaneously, allowing staff to intercept chat sessions if the assigned librarian is unable to respond. This function was successfully put to the test when one of our staff was confronted with seven simultaneous incoming chat requests.

Patrons enter Chat Live by clicking on the button located on the Library's home page. This button opens a page where patrons fill out a simple electronic form, entering their name and email address. However, because we did not want to limit access, the form does not ask for library card information. Once the session page appears, a message indicates if and how many other chat users are logged on. Meanwhile, on the librarian's screen, a "new chat user" box pops up from a previously minimized position indicating a new chat session. This, and a "BING" sound, alerts the librarian that a patron is attempting to ask a question.

SCRIPTS

As mentioned above, staff members use scripts rather than typing directly into the text box when responding to frequently asked questions. A variety of scripts ensure the quality of the reference session and the continuity of the interaction by giving quick and easy responses. To start a chat session the librarian sends the following script:

- Welcome to the Winter Park Public Library. How can we be of assistance?

This greeting quickly establishes the information needs of the patron. Once a question is posted, it is important to respond as quickly as possible so the patron knows the question has been received and an answer is en route. The following script is used during this step:

- One minute while I try to find the answer to your question.

If a Web site best answers the question, the librarian forwards the appropriate hyperlink. This is sent within the context of a script:

- Please click on the following active link to get the answer to your question. If this Web site does not answer your question, please contact us again. Click here:

If a new chat is initiated during an ongoing session, the librarian can inform the new patron that the question is in line to be answered using the following script:

- I am helping another patron at this time. I will be with you as soon as possible. If you cannot wait, please try back in a few minutes. Or, I can email or phone you (local calls only). If you would like us to phone you, please leave your phone number.

The Library's chat service is intended to respond to ready reference questions. If the patron needs more information or supplementary print material then librarians respond to these chat queries with the following chat script:

- The question that you asked requires further research. We can email or telephone you with the answer.

This lets the patron know their question requires further research and they will need to go a step beyond the chat format. Because the Library is currently using *QuestionPoint*, we are able to forward questions beyond the scope of the Library's collections to the Global Reference Network (a group of libraries and institutions worldwide working with the Library of Congress and OCLC to respond to digital reference questions).

Finally, an important step in the online transaction is concluding the chat session. Occasionally, patrons leave the session without officially logging off. When this occurs the session remains active and the patron appears still logged on. We try to avoid this confusion by sending the patron an "End Session" script:

- If you have no other questions at this time and you want to end the chat session, please click 'End Session' on the upper corner of this screen.

ANSWERING THE QUESTION

The majority of questions received so far have been from patrons seeking Internet assistance, which can usually be answered with a hyperlink. A few questions have required traditional print sources, or have concerned library related information such as late fees, holds, or driving directions.

If for any reason a session is lost or terminated we are able to follow up using the patron's email that is on-file from the initial login. This also applies to patrons contacting the chat service outside of the monitored chat hours. Regardless of whether a session is missed or answered live, a transcript is produced and remains in the *QuestionPoint* "Active Questions." This archive allows staff to analyze previous chats for quality control.

A SAMPLE TRANSCRIPT

The following example represents a typical chat interaction. Some of the responses are scripted, some actively typed:

Librarian: Welcome to the Winter Park Public Library. How can we be of assistance?

Patron: I need to get some information from the government.

Librarian: What kind of information do you need?

Patron: I need to get a copy of my mother's birth certificate.

Librarian: We can help you with that. What state was your mother born in? You will need to fill out a form and send in a fee.

Patron: Great! She was born in Georgia.

Librarian: One minute while I try to find the answer to your question.

Librarian: Please click on the following active link to get the answer to your question. If this Web site does not answer your question, please contact us again. Click here: http://vitalrec.com/ga.html

Patron: Great, thank you!

Librarian: If you want to use the Internet, try the site we sent. If you want an address to write to, let us know and we can give you one. If you have no other questions at this time and you want to end the chat session, please click "End Session" on the upper corner of this screen.

Librarian: Thank you using the Winter Park Public Library Ask-A-Librarian service. Please contact us again with your reference questions.

Patron: I just checked it on the Internet. This will work fine. Thanks again.

Librarian: Chat session ended by Librarian.

With our previous provider, *LiveAssistance*, a patron survey was available rating the quality of assistance received. Forty-three out of forty-nine participants rated the new service "excellent." The other six indicated the service was "good." One satisfied patron commented: "This is a wonderfully innovative service. Thank you so much for the excellent help!" Many other encouraging comments were also made. A few negative comments regarded our limited chat hours. Another complaint concerned how pushed pages obscured the chat box.

QuestionPoint has not historically provided surveys so we were not able to gauge patron satisfaction in the same way. But they do provide statistics. The average chat time, for example, is 9.7 minutes. Other figures show that most questions are from patrons looking for Internet sources rather than needing traditional print material. The statistics also determine that patrons favored no particular time of day when initiating a chat.

CONCLUSION

Electronic chat service has provided a new means of communication between the Library and the public. Already, we have responded to more chat requests than email requests, making the service an improvement over our other electronic initiatives. We have received a number of questions about our Winter Park History digitized collections, questions from city employees, and homework questions for our Young Adult Librarian. In all of these ways, we feel this new technology has addressed our initial needs assessment. In relation to other reference services Chat Live continues to respond to only a small number of weekly reference questions, justifying our initial choice of a more modest service.

We hope that new marketing ideas, combined with the maturation of chat technology, will help inform the public about this new possibility in reference. We agree with Anne Lipow's "in your face" reference technique. She states, "Library reference service will thrive only if it is as convenient to the remote user as a search engine; only if it is so impossible to ignore–so 'in your face'–that to not use the service is an active choice" (Lipow 1999, 52). Incorporating this idea, our department will place the Chat Live button on every page of the Library's Web site. In addition, we hope to expand the service by seeking out collaborative opportunities within our consortium and elsewhere. Partnering will create more possibilities to expand hours and reduce costs.

We plan to keep abreast of advances in interactive reference. Our staff continues to read the literature and evaluate other libraries' electronic chat services, paying close attention to new and advanced features. As new features become available, the department will allocate time for training and evaluation. Our staff does, however, remain hesitant in investing in features that we either do not need or that are not consistently reliable. We are aware that there remain unresolved issues concerning the stability of many newly developed features such as application sharing. While these new tools promise to open up the virtual collection to remote users, they also bring up questions about the proprietary nature of such collections and whether or not contractual agreements require libraries to limit access to patrons only. These questions and problems will perhaps be sorted out as the technology continues to improve and mature, but, for the current time, these are issues that we are looking at very closely.

We remain positive about interactive online reference though we hesitate to speculate on its longevity. The technology allows us to bring our expertise to the virtual community. However, we recognize that many patrons are still unaware that they have access to a live librarian in the abyss of cyberspace. Perhaps many more patrons will use Chat Live as they realize the superiority of an educated information specialist and a reference interview versus floundering with search engine results. People who dial 800 numbers say, "I wish I could talk to a live person." We say, "Here we are!"

BIBLIOGRAPHY

Boyer, Joshua. "Virtual Reference at the NCSU Libraries: The First One Hundred Days." *Information Technology & Libraries* (September 2001):122-128. http://www.lita.org/ital/2003_boyer.html (23 October 2002).

Broughton, Kelly. "Our Experiment in Online, Real-Time Reference." *Computers in*

Libraries (April 2001): 26-31. http://www.infotoday.com/cilmag/apr01/broughton. htm (23 October 2002).

Cichanowicz, Edana McCaffery. "Sunday Night Live!–An Experiment in Real Time Reference Chat–on a Shoestring Budget." *The Charleston Advisor* (April 15, 2001): 49-51. http://www.charlestonco.com/features.cfm?id=59&type=fr (21 October 2002).

Coffman, Steve. "So You Want to do Virtual Reference." *Public Libraries Supplement–E-Libraries Issue.* (September/October 2001): 14-20.

Colvin. Gloria. "Remote, Accessible, and On Call: Reference Librarians Go Live." *Florida Libraries* (Spring 2001): 10-12.

Duke University Libraries. "Live On-Line Reference Systems." http://www.lib.duke. edu/rference/liveonlineref.htm (15 October 2002).

Francoeur, Stephen. "Chat reference." *The Teaching Librarian.* http://pages.prodigy. net/tabo1/chat.htm (16 October 2002).

Kenny, Brian. "Live, Digital Reference." *Library Journal* (1 October 2002): 46-50.

Lipow, Anne. "In Your Face Reference." *Library Journal* (15 August 1999): 50-52.

LiveRef(sm): *A Registry of Real-Time Digital Reference Services.* http://www. public.iastate.edu/~CYBERSTACKS/LiveRef.htm (14 October 2002).

Marsteller, Matt, and Paul Neuhaus. "The Chat Reference Experience at Carnegie Mellon University." Presentation at American Library Association Annual Conference, 2001. http://www.contrib.andrew.cmu.edu/~matthewm/ALA_2001_chat.html (15 October 2002).

Ronan, Jana. "Chat Reference: An Exciting New Facet of Digital Reference Services." *ARL Monthly Report 219* (December 2001). http://www.arl.org/newsltr/219/chat. html (13 October 2002).

Sears, JoAnn. "Chat Reference Service: An Analysis of One Semester's Data." Issues in *Science and Technology Librarianship* (Fall 2001): 32. http://www.istl.org/istl/ 01-fall/article2.html (15 October 2002).

Stormont, Sam. "Interactive Reference Project: Assessment After Two Years." Paper presented at *Facets of Digital Reference Service: The Virtual Reference Desk Second Annual Digital Reference Conference*, October 16-17, 2000. http://www.vrd. org/conferences/VRD2000/proceedings/stormont.shtml.

Index

Abuzz, 12-13
Acacia Ridge Community Library,
    Brisbane, Australia, 172-173
Academic libraries. *See also* specific
    library or university
    chat reference services in, 226-227
    digital reference services for,
    175-177
AddALL, 75
Affinity groups, 31
AllExperts, 13-14
Alliance Library System, Illinois, 226
Aska commercial digital reference
    systems, 10-14. *See also*
    Commercial digital reference
    services
Ask a Librarian, 6
Ask-an-Expert (Ask-A) services, 21
AskERIC, 20,37,41
AskJeeves, 10,11-12
AskNow, 207-208,209,210,212
Asynchronous systems, synchronous
    systems and, 36-38. *See also*
    E-mail
Australia, digital reference services in,
    22
    for people with disabilities,
    173-175
    for senior citizens, 172-173

Bartleby.com, 75
Best practices, establishing, for digital
    reference, 30-31
Bibliographic Enrichment Advisory
    Team (BEAT), 29

Blacksburg Electronic Village (BEV),
    Virginia, 172
Bowling Green State University
    (BGSU), 185-186
Breeding, Marshall, 15
Brisbane City Council Library Service,
    22
Britannica, 79
Browsers, 114

California State Polytechnic University
    Ponoma, 203. *See also* Live/
    web reference services
Call center software, 24,232
Canada, digital reference services in,
    22
Chat reference services,
    21,23-25,48-49,122. *See also*
    Digital reference services;
    Instant messaging (IM); Live/
    web reference services;
    Reference services
    in academic libraries, 226-227
    art of prodding and, 117-118
    assessment obstacles of, 233-235
    challenges of being a new form of
    communication and, 232-233
    factors for answering questions for,
    159
    getting to know patrons and, 116
    language for, 115-116
    length of responses in, 118-119
    literature review of, 226-227
    organizational structure obstacles
    of, 229-230

pauses in conversations and,
  116-117
recommendations for, 235-238
reference interview in, 118
resource obstacles of, 230-232
setting up, 114-115
at Southern Illinois University,
  122-123
standards and guidelines for, 227-229
strengths of, 119-120,158-159
suggestions for librarians for,
  159-161
vs. telephone conversations, 7
text chat and, 158-161
tracking interactions, for usage
  data, 89
traffic volume of, 115
using other mediums in, 119
at Winter Park Public Library,
  312-320
Citizen information and participation
  services, 171-172
Cleveland Public Library, 2-3,21
Clientele. *See* Patrons
CMC (computer-mediated
  communication), 123-124
Co-browsing, 24
Collaborations, 31
Collaborative Digital Reference
  Service (CSRS), 21
Collaboratives, challenge of, for
  VRRCs, 82-85
Commercial digital reference services,
  6,10-16
  comparing, to library reference
    services, 14-15
  expert systems of, 12-14
  search engine types of, 11-12
Communication strategies, for online
  reference interviews
  human element in, 125-126
  personal space and, 136-140
Community, building, 27
Computer-mediated communication
  (CMC), 123-124

Consortia, 21,31
  Duke University and, 223-224
Contact center software, Web-based,
  202
Cornell University, 226
Corp Tech, 79

Databases
  licensed, for VRRC, 79-81
  proprietary, access problems of, 37
  top ten, 80
Digital divide, 124
Digital reference, 102,158,164-165,
  268. *See also* Digital
  reference services; Virtual
  Ready Reference Collection
  (VRRC); specific library or
  university
  beginning with a vision for, 28-29
  building community and, 27
  building trust for, 31
  defined, 22-23
  determining patrons for, 30
  early feedback on, 24
  establishing standards and best
    practices for, 30-31
  examples of, 167-168
  history of, 23-25
  innovation and, 31-32
  internationalization of, 32
  kiosks for, 169-170
  library considerations for
    purchasing packages for,
    42-44
  literature review of, 103,158
  marketing of, 25-27
  next level of, 27-28
  obtaining staff buy in, 29
  overstatement of, by librarians, 47
  perniciousnous of, 54
  personal experiences illustrating
    restrictions of, 50-53
  professional development for, 30

reasons for, 102-103
rethinking reference for, 29-30
Digital reference librarians, 69. *See also* Librarians
Digital reference services. *See also* Chat reference services; Marketing; Mediated online searching; Reference services
for academic libraries, 175-177
arguments against, 6-7
defined, 2
evaluating, 8
expert systems and, 12-14
extra burdens of, 49
getting staff on board for, 104-106
identifying staff for, 107
for librarians, 14-15
literature review of, 58-60
locating, on library's web page, 108
organizing for successful launch of, 104
paying for worldwide, 5
for people with disabilities, 173-175
placement of workstation for, 108
policies for, 71-72
pros and cons of, 9-10
for public libraries, 165-175
questions to ask prior to selecting, 254
requirements for successful, 7
for school library settings, 179
selecting software for, 106-107
for senior citizens, 172-173
setting hours of operation for, ʻ108-109
for special library settings, 177-179
vs. telephone conversations, 7
training for, 109-110
troubleshooting for, 110-111
use analysis of, 184-192
user surveys of, 192-199
worldwide, 5
Digital Reference Services, 16
Dig_Ref, 16,27,31

Disabilities, people with, digital reference services for, 173-175
"Disappearing patron" phenomenon, 24-25
Distance learning, digital reference services for, 175
D-Lib, 15
Drew, Bill, 21
Duke University, 215-224
determining needs at, 217-218
experimenting with digital reference services at, 222-223
implementation of policies and hours at, 220-221
planning for consortia at, 223-224
reaction to digital reference services at, 221-222
software selection at, 218-219
strategic planning for digital reference services at, 215-217
Durrance, Joan, 125

EARs (Electronic Access to Reference Service), 20
East Tennessee State University (ETSU)
analsysis of digital reference services at, 304-308
day-to-day operations at, 300-383
digtial reference at, 298
marketing of digital reference services at, 303-304
recommendations for digital reference services, 308
selecting live reference package at, 298-299
training at, 299-300
Electronic Access to Reference Service (EARs), 20
E-mail reference services, 20, 48
policy on, Louisiana State University Libraries, 269-270

ETSU. *See* East Tennessee State
    University (ETSU)
Expert systems, of digital reference
    services, 12-14

FAQs (frequently asked questions), 3-4
Francoeur, Stephen, 23
Frequently asked questions. *See* FAQs
    (frequently asked questions)

General Digital Reference Model,
    37,39-40
    lag time and, 40-42
Google, 13,72,79
    library profession and, 20
GPO Access, 75

Hadid, Peggy, 15
Hirko, Buff, 31

Indiana University Purdue University
    Indianapolis (IUPUI) Library
    digital reference services at,
        242-243
    management issues at, 250-254
    scripted replies used at, 249-250
    service issues at, 248-249
    technical issues at, 246-248
    vendor overview at, 243-246
Information, modeling task for, 61
Information Institute of Syracuse
    University, 22
Information services, 170-171
Instant messaging (IM),
        3,23,48-49,122. *See also*
        Chat reference services
    personal space and, 136-140
    reference interviews and, 143-153
    at Southern Illinois University,
        122-123
    spelling and, 141-143

strategies for increasing human
    element in, 125-136
typing and, 140-143
International Federation of Libraries
    Association (IFLA), 30
Internet, age and education of users of,
    124
Internet Public Library (IPL), 22
Invisible redirect screens, 89
Iowa State University Library, 14
IUPUI Library. *See* Indiana University
    Purdue University Indianapolis
    (IUPUI) Library

Janes, Joseph, 24,32
Joan of Art, 20
Johnson, Samuel, 54

Kansas Library Network Board
    (KLNB), 258
    assessment of digital reference
        services at, 263
    developing policies and procedures
        at, 259-260
    hours of operation for digital
        reference services at, 262
    implementing digital reference
        services at, 263-266
    including project parnets for digital
        reference services, 261
    marketing digital reference services
        at, 260-261
    planning for digital reference
        services at, 258-263
    project coordinator for digital
        reference services at, 263
    selecting software, 259
    staffing for digital reference
        services, 261-262
Katz, Bill, 125,143
Kavanaugh, Andrea, 172
Keystone Library Network, 84
Kiosks, 169-170

KnowItNow, 3,21
Knowledge, types of, 54

L. L. Bean, 50-51
Lag time, General Digital Reference
    Model and, 40-42
Lands End, 24
Lankes, R. David, 30
Librarians. *See also* Digital reference
    librarians
    digital reference services for, 14-15
    mediated online searching and,
      62-63
    strategies for, to increase human
      element in instant messaging,
      125-136
    suggestions for, for using text chat,
      159-161
Libraries. *See* Academic libraries;
    Public libraries; School
    libraries; Special library
    settings; specific library or
    university
Library cooperatives, 31
Library of Congress,
    5-6,21,25-26,29-30
Library profession
    digital services and, 20
    overvalue of technology and, 46
    self-image of, 53-55
    undervalue of librarian expertise
      and, 47
Library reference services, comparing,
    to commercial reference
    services, 14-15
Library System and Services (LSSI),
    6,49
Libref, 16
Linking Up Villages (LUV) initiatives,
    171-172
Link rot, 87
Lipow, Anne, 69,72
ListServs, 16
LiveAssistance, 232,314

LiveRef, 14-15
Live Reference eGroups, 16
Live/web reference services. *See also*
    Chat reference services;
    Reference services
    building knowledge and acceptance
      for, 203-204
    defined, 202
    hours and staffing for, 207-208
    marketing for, 208-212
    rationale for, 203
    software and support for, 204
    staff issues for, 206-207
    training for, 204-206
Louisiana State University (LSU)
    Libraries
    establishing digital reference
      services at, 268-269
    implementing digital reference
      services at, 273-275
    marketing of digital reference
      services at, 272-273
    planning for digital reference
      services at, 271-272
    policy on e-mail reference at,
      269-270
    user feedback at, 274-278
LSSI (Virtual Reference Desk),
    6,15,20-21,22,232,283
    at Duke University, 219
LSU Libraries. *See* Louisiana State
    University (LSU) Libraries

McClure, Charles, 30
McGlammery, Susan, 203
McKiernan, Gerry, 14
Marketing. *See also* Digital reference
    services
    digital reference, 25-27,111
    at East Tennessee State University,
      303-304
    at Kansas Libarary Network Board,
      260-261

for live/web reference services, 208-212
at Louisiana State University Libraries, 272-273
at Winter Park Public Library, 315-316
Mediated online searching. *See also* Digital reference services
information problem modeling task of, 61
interaction task of, 61-62
librarians and, 62-63
multitasking search task of, 61
search system task of, 61
social task of, 60
successive searching task of, 60
Meola, Marc, 21
Metropolitan Cooperative Library System, 21
Millennium Library, Cerritos, California, 170
MOOS, 20
Mozilla-based browsers, 114
MUDS, 20
Multitasking online searching, 61
Multnomah County Library, 15

National Library of Australia, 22
National Library of Canada, 22
National Library of Medicine (NLM), 26
The New York Times, 12

O'Neill, Nancy, 165
On-line digital reference services. *See* Digital reference services
Online real-time reference. *See* Chat reference services; Digital reference
Online reference interviews, 125
chat reference services and, 118
human element in, 125-136
instant messaging and, 143-153
personal space and, 136-140

Patrons
determining, for digital reference, 30
developing VRRC and, 71-72
disappearing, phenomenon of, 24-25
getting to know, and chat reference services, 116
Pauses in conversations, chat reference services and, 116-117
Penn State University Libraries, 282
analysis of VRS questions at, 288-290
early technical challenges of VRS at, 283-284
expanding VRS university-wide at, 285
popular features of VRS at, 286-287
Virtual Reference Service (VRS) at, 282-283
VRS and compatibility with databases at, 286
VRS Fall 2002 statistics at, 287
VRS future developments at, 293-294
VRS librarian feedback, 290-293
VRS pilot statistics at, 284-285
VRS staff support resources, 290
People with disabilities, digital reference services for, 173-175
Personal space, 125
online reference interviews and, 136-140
Plateville Public Library, Colorado, 169
Policies, for digital reference services, 71-72
Professional development, for digital reference, 30
Proprietary databases. *See* Databases
Public libraries. *See also* specific library

citizen information and
participation services of,
171-172
digital reference opportunities for,
165-175
information and referral services of,
170-171
kiosks for, 169-170
Pushed pages, 24, 165

Questia, 10
QuestionPoint, 5-6,21-22,31,232,316
Questions
analsysis of types of, 190-191,192
levels of reference, 3-4
reviewing types of, for developing
VRRC, 72-73

Ready Reference Collection, 68-69.
See also Digital reference;
Virtual Ready Reference
Collection (VRRC)
Ready reference questions, 3-4
Real-time digital reference services.
See Chat reference services;
Digital reference services
Real-time online chat. *See* Instant
messaging (IM)
Real-time systems. *See* Synchronous
reference systems
Reed, Donna, 15
RefeExpress, 233-234
Reference interviews. *See* Online
reference interviews
Reference librarians, 166. *See also*
Digital reference librarians
Reference questions, levels of, 3-4
Reference services. *See also* Chat
reference services; Digital
reference services; Live/web
reference services
e-mail, 20,48,269-270
library *vs.* commercial, 14-15

rethinking, for digital reference,
29-30
Referrals, in VRRC, 77-78
Referral services, 170-171
Remote research facilities, digital
reference services for,
175-176
Research questions, 3
Richland County Public Library, 22
Rutgers University Library, 78

Santa Monica Public Library, 21
School libraries, digital reference
services for, 179
Scripted replies, 249-250
Search engines, 11-12
Sears, JoAnn, 158
Senior citizens, digital reference
services for, 172-173
Shelf reading the Internet, 72
Sloan, Bernie, 21
Software, selecting, for digital
reference services, 106-107
SOS, 28
Southern Illinois University, 122-123
Special library settings, digital
reference services for,
177-179
Staff
getting, on board, for digital
reference services, 104-106
identifying, for digital reference
services, 107
live/web reference services and,
206-207
obtaining, for digital reference
services, 29
Standards
for chat reference services, 227-229
establishing, for digital reference,
30-31
State University of New York (SUNY)
at Morrisville, 226
Stormont, Sam, 21

Stumpers, 21
Successive searching, 60
Suffolok County New York Library
    System, 167-168
Swick, Floyd, 54-55
Synchronous reference systems, 122.
    See also Chat reference
    services; Instant messaging
    (IM)
  asynchronous systems and, 36-38
  General Digital Reference Model
    of, 39-40

Talbott, Stephen, 52
TalkBack Project, 21
The Teaching Librarian, 15-16
Technology
    librarians' enthusiasm for, 47-48
    library profession and, 46
    proper place for, 48-50
Telebase, 20
Telephone conversations, 49
    digital reference services and, 7
Tenopir, Carol, 2
Text chat, suggestions for librarians
    using, 159-161. *See also* Chat
    reference services
Thomas Register, 79
Training
    for digital reference services,
    109-110
    for VRRC, 85-86
Transcripts, archiving of, 232
24/7 Reference, 83,232
24/7 services, 4-6
    commercial, 6
    local libraries and, 4-5
    QuestionPoint and, 5-6

University of Florida, 226,230,232-233
Use analysis, for digital reference
    services, 184-192
User surveys, of digital reference
    services, 192-199

Virtual Information Desk (VID), 84-85
Virtual Ready Reference Collection
    (VRRC), 69-71. *See also*
    Digital reference
  challenge of collaboratives for,
    82-85
  core set of licensed databases for,
    79-81
  current awareness services for,
    97-99
  determining scope, audience, and
    purpose of, 71-72
  developing, as training tool, 72
  development process for, 72-74
  evaluation of, 74-75,89-90
  list of top, available to public,
    93-94
  local section of, 77-79
  maintenance of, 85
  monitoring links in, 87-89
  organizing, 81-82
  referrals in, 77-78
  reviewing sources for, 76-77
  selection aids for, 94-97
  training for, 85-86
Virtual reference. *See* Digital reference
Virtual Reference Canada, 22
Virtual Reference Desk (LSSI),
    6,15,20-21,22,232,283
  at Duke University, 219
Virtual reference services. *See* Digital
    reference services; Penn State
    University Libraries
Virtual Reference ToolKit, 232
Voice over IP, 3, 25, 171
VRRC. *See* Virtual Ready Reference
    Collection (VRRC)

Washington Statewide Virtual
    Reference Project, 168
Web-based contact center software,
    defined, 202
Web-based reference services. *See*
    Digital reference services

Web pages, library, locating digital
  reference services on, 108
Web push, 3,24
Winter Park Public Library, Florida,
  312
  day-to-day operation of chat service
    at, 316-317
  finding service provider at, 313
  marketing chat service at, 315-316
  naming of chat service at, 314-315
  practicing chat service at, 315
  sample transcript, 319-320

scripts used at, 317-318
selecting chat software at, 313-314
types of questions summitted at,
  318-319
writing scripts for chat service at,
  315
Workstations, placement of, for digital
  reference services, 108
Worldwide digital reference services, 5

Yahoo!, 11

Printed in the United States
by Baker & Taylor Publisher Services